SECOND LANGUAGE ACQUISITION 28
Series Editor: David Singleton, *Trinity College, Dublin, Ireland*

Foreign Language Input
Initial Processing

Rebekah Rast

MULTILINGUAL MATTERS LTD
Clevedon • Buffalo • Toronto

For Jim and Ella

Library of Congress Cataloging in Publication Data
Rast, Rebekah
Foreign Language Input: Initial Processing / Rebekah Rast.
Second Language Acquisition: 28
Includes bibliographical references and index.
1. Second language acquisition. 2. Polish language–Acquisition. I. Title.
P118.2.R37 2008
401'.93–dc22   2007040077

British Library Cataloguing in Publication Data
A catalogue entry for this book is available from the British Library.

ISBN-13: 978-1-84769-042-5 (hbk)
ISBN-13: 978-1-84769-041-8 (pbk)

Multilingual Matters Ltd
UK: Frankfurt Lodge, Clevedon Hall, Victoria Road, Clevedon BS21 7HH.
USA: UTP, 2250 Military Road, Tonawanda, NY 14150, USA.
Canada: UTP, 5201 Dufferin Street, North York, Ontario M3H 5T8, Canada.

The policy of Multilingual Matters/Channel View Publications is to use papers that are natural, renewable and recyclable products, made from wood grown in sustainable forests. In the manufacturing process of our books, and to further support our policy, preference is given to printers that have FSC and PEFC Chain of Custody certification. The FSC and/or PEFC logos will appear on those books where full certification has been granted to the printer concerned.

Typeset by Datapage International Ltd.
Printed and bound in Great Britain by the Cromwell Press Ltd.

Contents

Acknowledgements ix

Abbreviations xi

Introduction xiii

Part 1: Theoretical Preliminaries

1. Input and Intake Revisited 3
   Reflections on 'Input' and 'Intake' 3
   Connectionism 5
      Connectionist models 5
      The Competition Model 11
   Interactionist Approaches 14
      Research within a sociointeractionist framework 14
      Research related to the notion of
         'comprehensible input' 17
   Generativist Models 20
   Cognitivist Models 23
      The Autonomous Induction Theory 23
      The speech production model and bilingual
         production model 24
      Processability Theory 26
      Conclusion 27

2. First Exposure Studies 29
   Objectives of First Exposure Studies 29
      Knowledge brought to the acquisition task:
         The pre-existing system 29
      The role of other factors 34
   An Overview of First Exposure Studies 36
   Conclusion 43

Part 2: The Study

3. Polish–French Contrastive Analysis 47
   An Introduction to Polish and French 47
   Written and Spoken Forms 48

The Polish alphabet 49
Consonants. 50
Vowels 50
Prosody 51
Syntax: The Simple Declarative Sentence. 51
Basic constituent word order 51
The implicit subject in Polish 53
Negation. 54
Reflexive verbs (the Polish reflexive pronoun *się*) 56
Morphology. 58
The noun 58
The verb 60
Expressions Using *Po*. 62
Summary and Hypotheses. 63
Conclusion. 65
4. Research Methodology. 66
Participants 66
The L2 Input 69
Monitoring the input 69
The Polish instruction. 71
Transcription of the verbal input. 73
Data Collection Procedures 74
Data Analysis and Interpretation. 77
Speech perception. 78
Comprehension. 78
Grammatical analysis 80
Conclusion. 81
5. The Adult's Available Knowledge at First Exposure to an
Unknown Language. 83
Prior Linguistic Knowledge and Hypotheses. 84
Word Recognition 86
Incorrect Word Recognition 96
Processing Morphosyntactic Markers. 97
Discussion 103
Conclusion. 106
6. Case Studies: Two Learners with Similar Linguistic Profiles. . . . 108
Case Study 1: Gilles. 109
Case Study 2: Luc 123
Discussion 140
Conclusion. 142
7. Speech Perception 143
Sentence Repetition Test 143
Hypotheses. 146
Results 150

	Hours of instruction	150
	Word length	151
	Word stress	152
	Phonemic distance	152
	Transparency	153
	Word position	154
	Word frequency	155
	Interactions between independent variables	156
	Discussion	161
	Conclusion	163
8.	Speech Comprehension	166
	Oral Sentence Translation Task	166
	Speech comprehension at Period 1h30	169
	Speech comprehension at Period 3h30	182
	Speech comprehension at Period 7h00	186
	Discussion	188
	Conclusion	191
9.	Grammatical Analysis	192
	Basic Constituent Word Order	193
	Placing the Negative Particle *Nie*	203
	Placing the Reflexive Pronoun *Się*	214
	Verbal Morphology	220
	Discussion	223
	Conclusion	225
10.	Concluding Remarks	226
	Learners' Language Activities	227
	Speech perception	227
	Comprehension	228
	Grammatical analysis	229
	Towards a Characterisation of 'Intake'	232
	The Need for First Exposure Studies	234
	Conclusion	236
	Appendix 1	238
	Appendix 2	240
	Appendix 3	241
	Appendix 4	242
	Appendix 5	245
	References	246
	Index	258

Acknowledgements

First and foremost, my unconditional gratitude goes to Clive Perdue for your phenomenal support, critical eye, sense of humour and, above all, for the plethora of 'useful' knowledge you have given me. Thanks Clive. I am also grateful to Jean-Yves Dommergues, whose expertise in psycholinguistics proved invaluable to this work, and whose patience, determination and enthusiasm helped bring it to fruition. Merci Jean-Yves. I would also like to thank the members of my doctoral jury, Marianne Gullberg, Daniel Véronique and Robert Vivès, for their pertinent and valuable comments on work that preceded this book.

A profound thank you goes to Marzena Wątorek for her enormous contribution to the study's methodology and data analysis; Nikos Voutsina for the many fruitful discussions we had about what all of this means; Ania Kaglik for her crucial contribution to the analysis of the Polish data; Aneta Kopecka for her help with deciphering the Polish language; Monique Lambert for her pertinent remarks throughout the duration of the project; Danièle Boone for her keen eye and comments that enhanced the content of this work; and Kathleen Bardovi-Harlig for giving me that contagious second language acquisition bug.

I would also like to thank those involved in making recordings, collecting data, providing informants and transcribing Polish: Patrizia Giuliano, Jean Charconnet, Robert Vivès, Anita Kopystecka, Urszula Paprocka-Piotrowska, Henriette Hendriks, Aoju Chen, Greta Komur, Hubert Piekarz, Krystyna Bourneuf, Elfrida Wątorek and her students at the professional high school Zespól Szkoł Gastronomicznych w Nowej Hucie (Nowa Huta, Poland), Anita Higgie and her students in the English Department of the Faculté des Lettres de l'Institut Catholique de Paris, and Sandra Benazzo and her students in Lettres Modernes, FLE at the Université François Rabelais (Tours).

I thank the American University of Paris for its support, in particular Marc Monthéard for aid from the Dean's office, Clark Taylor for ensuring that Polish fonts were always alive and well on university computers, Mano Banduwardena for sharing his superb computer expertise, Isabelle Dupuy for her ability to efficiently manoeuvre her way through the interlibrary loan networks, Lauren Allen for editing assistance, and Paweł Olejarnik and Gośka Pisuła, Polish students, for help recording and transcribing Polish.

A special thanks to the 19 students who took our Polish course at the Université Paris VIII during the spring of 1999 (especially to the 8 who attended *all* the classes) and to the 108 informants who agreed to being subjected to our tasks in Polish.

I express my gratitude as well to David Singleton and my anonymous reviewer who provided insightful and useful comments on earlier versions of this work.

A sincere thanks goes to Robert Préfontaine for sharing 'La Savatterie' and his knowledge of languages, to Marie-Annick Biette for her constant encouragement and to John D'Agostino for giving me perspective.

Thanks to Susanna and Walter Rast for encouraging me to follow my cultural, linguistic, intellectual and professional passions, and for the memory of my father trying to decipher earlier French versions of this work on the beaches of Michigan; my grandmother Minna Droege for exposing me to bilingualism at an early age; and Cathy and James D. Startt for the many intriguing conversations about language learning and for being the best child care providers a person could ever hope for. And a special thanks to my supportive brothers and sisters, Peter Rast, Zoe Kircos, Tim Rast, Diane Miller, Joel Rast, Clíona Draper, Jennifer Startt and Don Sipe.

Finally, a thanks beyond measure goes to James N. and Ella Startt, to whom this book is dedicated. To Jim for your continual presence, support and unfailing confidence in me, and to Ella for being you and for saying to the genie in the lamp, 'I wish I could speak all the languages in the world'. I do too.

Abbreviations

1p	first person
2p	second person
3p	third person
Acc	accusative case
Adj	adjective
Adv	adverb
AP	adverbial phrase
B	bilingual
C	complement
Conj	conjunction
Cop	copula
Dat	dative case
f	feminine
FLA	first language acquisition (the field of)
FT/FA	Full Transfer/Full Access hypothesis
Freq	frequency count in the input
Gen	genitive case
Instr	instrumental case
IP	On-line Input Processing
L1	first language
L2	second language
L3	third language (or more)
Loc	locative case
m	masculine
M	monolingual
n	neuter
N	noun
Neg	negator *nie* 'pas' (not)
Nic	negator *nic* 'rien' (nothing)
NL	native language
Nom	nominative case
NNS	non-native speaker
NP	noun phrase
NS	native speaker

O	direct object
OP	operating principle
pl	plural
Prep	preposition
PP	prepositional phrase
PP/Adv	prepositional phrase/adverbial
Pron	pronoun
Refl	reflexive pronoun *się*
S	subject
sg	singular
SLA	second language acquisition (the field of)
TL	target language
UG	Universal Grammar
Vf	finite verb
Vi	non-finite verb
Voc	vocative case

Introduction

My interest in the role a learner's linguistic environment plays in the process of acquiring a foreign language came out of a decade of teaching English to adult speakers of an array of other languages, in particular those whose jobs often required them to perform extraordinary feats in the English language with minimal training. I prepared them as best I could for their respective presentations and meetings, sharing the responsibility for what would result in either success or failure. The stakes were often high. Beginning to wonder to what extent my interventions helped, I made an attempt at determining the types of interventions that seemed at once most beneficial and economical. Although I found some ephemeral solutions, I was far from satisfied. I sought to learn more about what my students actually *got* from what I provided. Little did I know at the time that this was the beginning of a long journey into the study of initial processing of foreign language input.[1]

Having expressed my interest in examining how learners work on second language (L2)[2] input, I was given the responsibility of a pilot study at the University of Paris VIII on French learners of Polish at the absolute beginning of the acquisition process (cf. Rast, 1998). Following the pilot study, with the help of many, I conducted a large-scale observational study on initial processing of L2 input in adult second language acquisition, the material from which provides the foundation of this book. My initial questions included the following: what knowledge does a learner bring to the acquisition process? How, when and under what conditions do learners rely on target language (TL) input, on their native language (NL) or on other known languages to acquire elements of the TL? What strategies do learners use to accomplish a task in the TL at the moment of first exposure to that language? What hypotheses do learners formulate with regard to their new language, and what do they do with these hypotheses? In essence, how is a second language born, and how can the first hours of its acquisition be described?

Before moving on to the details of this book, let us think first about language in general. Pinker (1994: 7), when speaking of the ability to use a first language (L1), observes that, 'The ability comes so naturally that we are apt to forget what a miracle it is'. Most adult learners would likely *not* say this about the ability to learn or use a second language. Second language acquisition is often seen as a laborious process, one for which hundreds of language teachers and methods developers from Gattegno (*The Silent Way,* cf. Gattegno, 1976) to Lozanov (*Suggestopedia,* cf. Lozanov, 1978) have sought to unearth the magic formula. But what if we try to think of L2 acquisition in a different light? Is it not quite phenomenal in fact that after having somehow completely learned one complex language already, we manage to begin learning another, and that some adults even gain native-speaker or almost native-speaker proficiency? Not only this, some 'acquire' a third, fourth, fifth (or more) language in addition to the second, and this with everything else that is going on in our lives. How do we do it? What processes are involved that make L2 acquisition a feasible endeavour for an individual who is beyond the so-called 'critical period', if this period in fact exists (cf. Singleton, 2003; Singleton & Ryan, 2004)?

Research on first exposure to L2 input and during the first seconds, minutes and hours that follow is necessary for further insight into these questions. This book presents a study conducted at the absolute beginning of L2 acquisition, from the moment of first exposure to the TL through the 8 hours that follow. In this book, you as the reader will become acquainted with a group of native French speakers who had had no contact with the Polish language at the onset of the study. All the Polish input they received was recorded and analysed. You will, therefore, have the opportunity to contemplate the TL input to which these learners were exposed, to discern what the learners *do* with this input and to observe their development (or lack thereof) over the first 8 hours of their acquisition of Polish. We will also examine data collected from other groups of native French speakers at the moment of first contact with Polish. In short, this book describes certain aspects of the initial stages of L2 acquisition to which minimal research has been devoted until now. The in-depth analysis of the TL input, the type of analysis performed in this study, not only sheds light on questions still unanswered in the second language acquisition literature, such as what knowledge is brought to the L2 acquisition process and how that knowledge is used by a learner to process new linguistic information, but it also brings clarity to the role of input and intake at this early stage. My hope is that the data and analyses presented in this book will provide insights into language processing that will be of service to both language acquisition researchers and language teachers alike.

Four principal objectives have guided this study:

(1) Identify the knowledge available to learners before exposure to the TL and identify the strategies used by the learners upon first exposure to the input.
(2) Completely control the TL input provided to the learners.

(3) Analyse various language activities (perception, comprehension and grammatical analysis) relative to the input provided at this early stage of acquisition.

(4) Identify what aspects of this input are taken in by the learner, and to what extent this intake is subsequently used for further processing.

It is important to mention here that the current study is of a heuristic nature. This approach allows us to evaluate the potential contributions of various theories, models and frameworks proposed in the field of second language acquisition (SLA) to the study of initial L2 processing and acquisition. This is the first comprehensive study of its kind to attempt to completely control, measure and describe natural TL input with a view to observing its effects on L2 processing and on L2 acquisition.

A point about terminology needs to be made before moving on. Terms will be defined throughout the book within the context in which they appear. The exception is the term 'processing'. It is important to signal the abundance of definitions that exist for the term 'processing' in SLA and psycholinguistic research. To illustrate, VanPatten (2004) uses 'input processing' to refer to how learners make a connection between form and meaning. His usage of 'processing' is *not* analogous with 'perception' or 'noticing'. Carroll (2004: 294–295), on the other hand, points out that, 'Among psycholinguists investigating speech perception and sentence comprehension, the term *processing* can refer to any dynamic operation in real time that converts a stimulus into a message or a message into a motor-articulatory plan'. In this book, the term 'processing' is used in its most general sense, encompassing all of the above definitions, for the simple reason that we do not yet thoroughly understand the systems involved in 'processing' foreign language input. As this is an observational study about what learners *do* with the input they receive, aspects of the actual 'processing' are under investigation. Here, 'processing' is defined as what the learners *do*. This includes perceiving, noticing, segmenting, converting a stimulus into a message, parsing, mapping form to meaning or meaning to form, and so forth. Such aspects of processing, in particular initial processing, are the essence of the current study.

As mentioned earlier, few studies in the field of SLA have investigated the processing of TL input at this early stage of acquisition. Although numerous researchers have formulated hypotheses about the processing of input at various stages, including initial stages, these are, for the most part, based on data collected from learners who already had an interlanguage in place. This said, such studies have contributed enormously to our understanding of the role of input in L2 acquisition. To investigate this contribution, our discussion begins in Chapter 1 with an overview of the research concerned with 'input' and 'intake'. Chapter

2 describes first exposure studies and research objectives shared by the few working with learners at this early stage of L2 acquisition. The specificities of this study will be introduced beginning in Chapter 3 with a contrastive analysis of French and Polish, the two principal languages of the study, and followed in Chapter 4 by a description of the study's methodology. Chapter 5 provides an investigation into the question of what knowledge is available to the adult learner upon first exposure to an unknown language. Chapter 6 presents two case studies in which the first 8 hours of the acquisition of Polish by two learners is described in detail. Group results are presented in Chapters 7–9: Chapter 7 is devoted to speech perception, Chapter 8 to speech comprehension and Chapter 9 to grammatical analysis. Chapter 10 concludes the book with a discussion of the theoretical and methodological questions raised in Chapters 1–4 in light of the new data presented in Chapters 5–9.

As discussions about methodology, data analyses, theoretical frameworks and results contained in this book involved numerous individuals, I will now abandon my current usage of the first person singular pronoun 'I' and replace it with its plural form 'we' for the remainder of the book. I take full responsibility, however, for all errors, misinterpretations and omissions. We now begin Chapter 1 with our discussion of 'input' and 'intake' in second language acquisition research.

Notes

1. The terms 'foreign language', 'non-native language', 'second language' (L2) and 'target language' (TL) are used interchangeably in this book, as are the terms 'first language' (L1), 'native language' (NL) and 'source language' (SL).
2. See the list of abbreviations at the beginning of the book.

Part 1
Theoretical Preliminaries

Chapter 1
Input and Intake Revisited

Reflections on 'Input' and 'Intake'

In the field of applied linguistics, and more specifically in the field of second language acquisition, the terms 'input' and 'intake' can be traced back several decades. Corder (1967: 165) was the first to use the term 'intake' as distinct from 'input' in his renowned quote:

> The simple fact of presenting a certain linguistic form to a learner in the classroom does not necessarily qualify it for the status of input, for the reason that input is 'what goes in' not what is *available* for going in, and we may reasonably suppose that it is the learner who controls this input, or more properly his intake.

In the 1950s, Skinner (1957) and Chomsky (1959) had already made reference to these same phenomena without proposing the specific terms 'input' and 'intake'. At that time, the debate focused on the degree to which external factors influenced language acquisition, or rather, whether an internal innate structure, known as Universal Grammar guided language acquisition (cf. Chomsky, 1959, 1965). In his criticism of Skinner's work in which Skinner reflects on the notion of 'stimulus' (the environment) and 'response' (individual behaviour), Chomsky remarks that, 'We cannot predict verbal behaviour in terms of stimuli in the speaker's environment, since we do not know what the current stimuli are until he responds' (Chomsky, 1959: 32). In other words, we cannot know what the individual has taken in until the moment of response, leaving an important gap in our ability to observe language processing.[1]

Decades later, Hatch (1983: 81) reflects on this distinction between input and intake:

> If we wish to keep both terms, we may say that input is what the learner hears and attempts to process. That part that learners process only partially is still input, though traces of it may remain and help in building the internal representation of the language. The part the learner actually successfully and completely processed is a subset called intake. That part, then, is the language that is *already* part of the internal representation.

Hatch extends Corder's definition of intake from that which is controlled by the learner and actually 'goes in' to that which the learner 'successfully and completely' processes. That which is only 'partially' processed remains input. The distinction, in fact, is found in the role that this processed information will play in building internal language representations. This is all fine and well, but we are still faced with the problem of identifying what information is 'taken in' or 'processed'. Hatch's explanation is quite representative of our understanding of input and intake in the 1980s and 90s. A distinction between the two having already been made, researchers then attempted to articulate this difference more clearly. The essence of the problem, however, remains in our inability to measure the phenomena involved in these processes. How can we know what elements of the linguistic environment are processed completely, partially or not at all? How can we know if learners even 'hear' a signal in the input and if they process what they heard? How can we know what part of the signal is processed and what part is not? These are questions that continue to challenge us in the field of language acquisition today.

Numerous researchers concerned with the study of input and intake in SLA express a shared concern. VanPatten (2000: 294) articulates this in his article entitled 'Thirty years of input': '...in spite of the significant advances made by SLA research and the diversification of theoretical and research frameworks in which to conduct this research, our knowledge of the role of input has remained relatively unchanged during the last 30 years'. Carroll (2001: 1) confirms VanPatten's concerns when describing input as '...one of the most under-researched and under-theorized aspects of second language acquisition'. This lack of research has become apparent in part because everyone, regardless of the theoretical framework, seems to agree on the importance of input in language acquisition. As VanPatten (2000: 295) points out, 'We seem to concur that input is somehow central to SLA, that without it successful SLA is not possible'. Carroll (2001: 2) makes a similar remark: '...one point on which there is consensus is that SLA requires exposure to the second language'.

The study of 'intake' evokes similar concerns. According to Carroll (2001: 2), 'There is no agreement on what kind or how much exposure a learner needs. Indeed, we know very little still about the kinds of linguistic exposure learners actually get'. Consequently, we know very little about what learners *do* with what they get. In order to move forward in our understanding of input and intake, we need to analyse the divergence that exists between the different research perspectives, revealing at the same time the complexity of these two terms. According to the current dominant definition, 'input' refers to the linguistic environment of the learner, that is, to that which is available to be taken in, or rather, to everything in the TL that the learner is exposed to and has the opportunity to either hear or read. The dominant definition of 'intake' is less clear. Researchers disagree on how input is processed and on when and how intake enters the picture. Thus, their definitions reflect their research agendas. Wong and Simard (2000) provide a comprehensive overview of research conducted on intake, showing how researchers differ in their views as to whether intake is a process, a product or a combination of both. In fact, we appear to be in a deadlock in that the true debate focuses on the distinction between product and process, a distinction for which we have not yet found appropriate terminology.

It is unlikely that one approach alone will be able to resolve all the aspects of this debate. It is rather through collaboration and exchange of methodology, results and knowledge that we will come to discover what is actually going on in the mind of an L2 learner when exposed to TL input. Diverse theoretical frameworks have already contributed and will continue to contribute in their own way to our understanding of input and intake. This study in no way intentionally eliminates research findings due to difference of approach. On the contrary, it attempts to incorporate what we already know about learners' processing, regardless of the source (theoretical framework) of this knowledge. We will now review four of these sources: connectionism (including the Competition Model), interactionist approaches, generativist models and cognitivist models.

Connectionism

Researchers working within a connectionist framework must consider the distinction between input and intake for the simple reason that their approach is all about providing stimulus (input) to a network in an attempt to observe what the network can or cannot do with this stimulus under certain conditions. The following section provides a general description of connectionist architecture and its usage in language acquisition research.

Connectionist models

Connectionism involves the use of computer processing to simulate the functions of the mind and to predict what humans will do under specific conditions. The first specificity designated to a model depends on research objectives and the cognitive processes under investigation. In our case, for example, we will examine models designed to simulate language processes as opposed to other cognitive processes such as face recognition or serial recall. A connectionist architecture comprises a network of a large number of interconnected elements called 'nodes'. The 'knowledge' of the network resides in the information given to these nodes (e.g. phonetic or orthographic) and the strength of the connections between the nodes.

Generally we can distinguish between two types of connectionist models: localist symbolic models and distributed subsymbolic models. In the localist tradition, representations are coded for distinct pieces of information, such as visual information for all letters in the alphabet or for entire words. These models are designed to explain the functional mechanics of skilled human *performance*, such as word recognition processes (cf. Grainger & Jacobs, 1998). In distributed subsymbolic models, such as the well-known pattern associator of 'Parallel Distributed Processing' (Rumelhart & McClelland, 1986), information or knowledge is coded as a pattern activation across many processing units, and these units contribute to many different representations. The focus of these models is on the emergence of skilled human performance through *learning*. Distributed models generally comprise one or more internal layers of nodes in addition to an input and an output layer. The internal or 'hidden' layer is where the input is processed before becoming output. This layer is therefore adjusted over time following the learning process. Localist models, on the other hand, are concerned more with performance and therefore refer to 'bottom' or 'lower' layers, where a pattern of resources is stored (e.g. orthographic information), and 'upper' layers, where this pattern is categorised (e.g. entire words).

We will focus here on distributed connectionist models and their contribution to the study of language acquisition and, in particular, to the study of input and intake. At the outset, a network has no set parameters. No connections between input and output nodes have been set, nor has the strength of the connections been set. The network represents a 'tabula rasa' (Pinker & Prince, 1988: 90). Before initiating a simulation, researchers must set the nodes in the network, set the parameters or variables, and set the connections between the nodes. The strength of the connections will be developed during training. This generally occurs over a series of training sets. In order to train the network, the researchers provide it with input (linguistic, in this case) by activating the input layer, which then produces activation throughout the entire network, first on the internal layer(s) followed by the output layer. When the network is completely trained, each connection receives a scalar value that serves as input to the next node. According to Taraban *et al.* (1989: 172), 'This value is the product of the current activation level of the node on the input side of the connection and the strength or "weight" associated with the connection'. The 'output' of the system refers to the state of the output layer once the network has stabilised. A comparison between the 'real' output of the system and the 'desired' output (i.e. the correct form in the language of the study) allows for training of the system. In other words, the network 'learns' by example and by recognition of similarities. 'Similarities' here refer to elements that the network considers as similar relative to the training it received. The strength of connections can be changed according to the process involved, modifying the input/output function as it satisfies the network. For certain tasks, it is possible to train the network to calculate the function of a given input-output (cf. Cummins & Schwarz, 1992; Dreyfus, 1992; Taraban *et al.*, 1989).

To better understand the problem of input in these models, we turn to a study of the acquisition of gender in L1 German (Taraban *et al.*, 1989) in which the authors developed a connectionist architecture as a model for the acquisition of the declensional paradigm of the German definite article. Two simulations of child acquisition of L1 German were performed with a view to predicting whether German-speaking children can assign word classes through inferences based on the declensional paradigm. In both cases, a certain number of German nouns were presented one by one to the network. 'The input to the network consists of the kind of input considered to be available to a learner and the desired output is the correct form of the German article' (Taraban *et al.*, 1989: 173). The input used for the study consisted of a selection of words taken from a German corpus of 80,000 words. As the nouns were presented to the network, the input nodes encoded the presence or absence of cues associated with a given noun. Each input node described a cue which contained, at minimum, phonological, morphological and semantic information. When a specific cue was present in a given noun, the input node was completely activated. On the contrary, if the cue was absent, the node remained inactivated. In short, this system provides a concrete example of what the authors use as input that 'enters'. If the network recognises a cue as a particular word, it can then use this 'representation' to process the input and produce the correct output; if it does not recognise the given cue, the 'representation' will not be activated, and consequently the output will not be a correct form of the TL. Words become a sort of representation of a series of cues. The activation of the input layer triggers the activation of internal layers, which in turn triggers the activation of the output layer. 'We think of these internal layers as forming a useful internal representation of the input. In our simulations we would expect these to correspond to the grammatical categories that describe German nouns presented to the network' (Taraban *et al.*, 1989: 172). In essence, this analysis proposes an internal representation of the input by which the learner accesses corresponding grammatical categories as soon as a lexical item is presented. In other words, the authors suggest that input processing leads to an internal representation that corresponds to grammatical categories in the series presented to the network. The results of their study show that their network made use of a series of cues in the input about noun stems and noun usage in sentences to correctly select the appropriate form from the six possible forms of the definite article. The authors conclude that, 'We show not only that such a network can learn to correctly assign definite articles to a set of training items, but also that it forms consistent internal representations of its knowledge and is able to generalize this knowledge to new instances' (p. 173).

It follows that connectionism may be the framework that most directly treats the question of first contact with the input of any given TL in that researchers working within this perspective must formulate hypotheses about the 'learner's' knowledge *before* setting the parameters of the network. The problem of characterising the input, however, continues to trouble us. In the study by Taraban *et al.* (1989: 173), for example, the kind of input provided to the network is described by the authors themselves as, '...*considered* to be available to a learner...' (our emphasis). A related problem lies as well in the fact that in order to test their hypotheses about input processing, studies must be designed to show that learners themselves process input in the manner proposed by connectionist models. To put it simply, when one asks a computer to 'take in', it will 'take in', but when the same is asked of human learners, there is no guarantee that they will 'take in', or are even capable of 'taking in'.

In essence, those working within the connectionist framework are faced with similar questions to those posed in this book: what is the nature of the input available to a learner, and is it possible that learners fail to perceive information that we consider to be generally available or perceivable? How can we know what information should be presented to the network for a valid ecological simulation of what German children receive from their linguistic environment? Taraban *et al.* (1989: 173) are well aware of the methodological problems posed by using a corpus based on the average frequency of items in the environment: '...the input to the simulation can only be viewed as an approximation to the actual input received by the German-speaking child'. They propose the CHILDES database as a solution for future studies.[2] With the help of CHILDES, they foresee designing simulations that more accurately represent real acquisitional situations. Establishing tools that provide more precision proves a positive step toward resolving the problem of what is 'available' for further processing.

Sokolik and Smith (1992) applied the distributed connectionist model *pattern associator* (cf. Rumelhart & McClelland, 1986) to the acquisition of gender in French as a second language. It is important to note that within connectionist models, cognitive transformations do not rely on explicit rule systems. The transformation is, rather, a mapping of activity, or even the influence of one processing layer on another. In order to guide the learning of a rule system, the procedure uses the difference between the desired activation and the obtained activation, a sort of feedback system, as mentioned earlier. In order to respond to the principal question of the study, '...could the model reliably classify a set of nouns it had never encountered before, based solely on the learning experience it had with another set of nouns?' (Sokolik & Smith, 1992: 42), the authors performed a variety of experiments under distinct conditions. Results show that the network was capable of learning the gender of an important series of French nouns by 'experience'. 'It accomplished this without relying on article or adjective agreement, without knowledge of noun meaning, and without being programmed with (or inferring) explicit morphological or phonological rules of gender formation' (p. 50).

As noted in our discussion of the Taraban *et al.* (1989) study, Sokolik and Smith are also confronted with the problem of what knowledge to attribute to the network, or rather, to the metaphoric individual who is faced with the acquisition task at hand. According to Sokolik and Smith (1992: 48), '. . . it is reasonable to assume that a person learning gender associations comes to the task with some pre-existing pattern of connectivity'. The authors cite previous studies supporting findings that second language acquisition progresses more rapidly in children than in adults. They suggest, therefore, that the difficulty observed by real adult learners could reflect the decrease in the activation of the connection due to age. Following this assumption, they reduced the learning-rate parameter. They found that when the network performed a learning task with a pre-existing series of connections and a lower learning rate (configured to model the adult learner), the results were clearly less precise than under other conditions. Only after several learning experiences did the performance of the adult learner begin to approach the expected results. As predicted, the system learned neither as fast nor as well with the reduction of the parameter. The question, however, is whether this modification in fact reflects the true state of the learner who is acquiring a second language.

Carroll (1995) and Matthews (1999) use Sokolik and Smith's study to argue several problems related to the application of connectionist models to the process of L2 acquisition. Matthews comments on Sokolik and Smith's assumption about the nature of the input. Firstly, he notes that although research on gender attribution in French assumes a system of association that depends on phonological representation, Sokolik and Smith use orthographic representations as input in their experiments. Matthews (1999: 417) poses the crucial question, '. . . *what* is to be encoded and *how*?'. Secondly, he points out that Sokolik and Smith chose a 50:50 distribution of masculine and feminine nouns, whereas the actual distribution in French is 60:40. Unfortunately Matthews fails to provide a reference for this information, but it serves as a reminder of how vague we are about the input our learners get. Thirdly, he notes the assumption by Sokolik and Smith that the network learned all the nouns provided to the system at the same time. Matthews proposes that in a more natural version of the network, the size of a training set would gradually increase over time.

The criticisms of Sokolik and Smith's study outlined by Carroll (1995) concern the global structure of the network. She points to the following problems: (1) the network never has to discover that French has a gender system – it does not allow the choice of 'no gender' for a noun, a category that we could expect English speaking learners, for example, to choose; (2) the network never has to discover the exact number of gender classes; (3) as the input is comprised of only nouns, the system is unable to learn that only nouns, and no other lexical categories, mark gender; (4) the input consists of words, not sentences, so the network, in principle, does not learn to designate the gender of nouns within the context of a sentence. As Carroll (1995: 201) puts it, 'The reader needs to keep in mind that "learning gender" cannot be reduced to learning gender attribution. This is only part of the learning problem'.

Carroll also comments on the nature of the input supplied to the network. In connectionist theory, the network 'learns' by means of a system of feedback comparing the expected output with the real output. This implies that the learner 'learns' in this manner, that is, by means of a system based on feedback. According to Carroll, this hypothesis is problematic for the following reasons: (1) there is no empirical evidence that a learner actually relies on feedback to learn the gender system; (2) feedback provided to learners in a guided setting is neither frequent nor systematic – this goes against the methodology used in Sokolik and Smith's study where learning relies completely on regular feedback to output nodes.

A certain prudence is necessary with regard to hypotheses concerning not only the input provided to learners, but also the input that 'enters'. Connectionists are faced with a genuine obstacle: how does one provide the network with reliable input that reflects the mental state of the learner and the knowledge available to the learner when faced with a given acquisitional task? Connectionist research must be complemented by language data collected from real L2 learners. With reliable input supplied to the networks, connectionist models will be a step closer to making accurate predictions about what learners do with the input they receive. The problem, however, still remains as to what knowledge should be attributed to the learner in order to properly set the network's parameters. Though researchers working with connectionist models have developed interesting systems for making certain predictions about language acquisition, they need to be able to provide reliable input that reflects input to human learners, and they must be able to determine patterns of connectivity and associated weights that truly reflect what a learner 'knows'.

The Competition Model

The Competition Model, which formulates predictions about cross-linguistic similarities and differences based on connectionist principles, derives from the concepts of form-function mapping in comprehension, production and acquisition. It posits a multiplicity of form-function mappings, and is therefore not limited to one-to-one mappings. A given form may express several functions (e.g. 'the girl' could be actor or patient); likewise, a given function can be conveyed by means of several forms. The premise in this approach is that languages differ with respect to their surface cues, such as word order, animacy and inflexional morphology, and that when these cues are put in competition with one another (e.g. word order versus agreement or animacy), language-specific differences in the cue strength and validity emerge. Cue *strength* refers to the probability with which informants will assign a specific function to a given piece of information. It is a psychological construct inferred from the responses of informants under certain conditions (Kail, 2000). Cue *validity* refers to the objective and quantifiable relation between the cue (e.g. pre-verbal or post-verbal position of a noun) and the function it marks (e.g. agent or patient). In order to determine the validity of the cue, the *availability* and *reliability* of the cue must be calculated. Availability reflects how often the cue is present, whereas reliability refers to the percentage of correct interpretations of the cue over the number of cases where it is available. In this way, validity is defined as the product of availability multiplied by reliability.

Another notion worth mentioning here is that of cue *cost*. Cue cost refers to the 'relative detectability and assignability of cues' (Heilenman & McDonald, 1993: 511). Cues that are more difficult to perceive, for example, may pressure the processing system and, as a result, be abandoned.

In terms of adult L2 acquisition, this model provides the advantage of being able to statistically measure differences in the acquisition process by adults of different native languages. For instance, research shows that when interpreting sentences in a non-native language, native English speakers tend to rely on word order, whereas Italian speakers rely more on inflexion (cf. Bates & MacWhinney, 1987). The framework, based on real-time processing of decontextualised and very often ungrammatical sentences, provides an ecological means to test hypotheses and to modify them accordingly. It also has the advantage of not requiring us to claim all or nothing. The disadvantage of many theoretical approaches in SLA is their polar perspective: TL rules are viewed as being 'acquired' or not; parameters are considered as being 'set' or not. The developing middle ground clearly merits investigation.

In an overview of research conducted on bilingual sentence processing,[3] Kilborn and Ito (1989: 262) delineate four hypotheses tested within the framework of the Competition Model:

(1) First language (L1) strategies may be applied to both languages.
(2) A second set of strategies is acquired and applied exclusively in the context of L2, so that the learner behaves essentially as a monolingual in each language.
(3) L2 strategies are not only applied to L2 but may even supplant L1 strategies.
(4) New strategies may be adopted in the course of L2 learning, and become assimilated into one amalgamated set that is applied to processing in both languages.

The first hypothesis is of particular interest to our observation of initial processing of L2 input. In their overview of research conducted within this framework, Kilborn and Ito (1989) examined studies that used variations of a sentence interpretation task in which sentences generally comprised two nouns and one verb. A variety of cues, such as word order, agreement marking and animacy, were put into competition. Informants listened to the sentences and in each case were asked to identify the actor ('Who did it?'). Taken together, the studies reported in Kilborn and Ito (1989) confirmed the first hypothesis that learners often relied on L1 strategies; however, evidence was not found for a complete or full transfer of the L1 to the L2. Other factors played a role, even at the beginner level. Miao (1981), for example, investigated the reliance on word order versus animacy in sentence processing in Chinese L1 and in Chinese L2 by native English speakers. The results showed that the native Chinese speakers used semantic cues more often than syntactic cues, and that word order was not an important source of information. For the native English speakers learning Chinese, word order seemed to be the dominating factor. Kilborn and Ito (1989: 267) conclude that, ' . . . while we can be fairly certain that at least some transfer such as this is likely to occur, the characteristic second noun strategy in English NNV sequences was not found in Chinese NNV sequences, which suggests that simple transfer cannot completely account for the L2 findings in Miao's experiment'.

Ito (cited in Kilborn & Ito, 1989 as 'in preparation') conducted a study with three groups: Japanese NSs with an advanced level of L2 English; Japanese NSs with a beginning level of L2 English; and the monolingual English NS control group. Whereas the English NS control group showed a preference for word order as a cue to sentence meaning, both learner groups depended heavily on animacy as a cue to sentence meaning in English. A second study with English NSs learning Japanese (a novice group and an advanced group) and a monolingual Japanese control group confirmed these findings. In their analysis of Ito's study, Kilborn and Ito (1989) suggest that the direct transfer of L1 strategies to L2 sentence processing, as predicted by the Competition Model, is not the only kind of transfer. 'In particular, what may account for this finding is not the intrusion of a *language-specific* strategy, but rather an awareness of the potential for word order as a cue to thematic roles in sentences' (Kilborn & Ito, 1989: 281–282). They conclude that, 'The L2 speakers in this study may have adopted a "meta-word-order" strategy in their approach to processing Japanese' (p. 282).

Harrington's (1987) study of Japanese learners of English, with English NS and Japanese NS control groups, confirmed Ito's finding. The Japanese L1 sentence interpretations depended heavily on animacy cues, whereas the English L1 interpretations showed a preference for word order as a cue. The responses of the Japanese learners of English fell somewhere in the middle, showing signs of both animacy biases and English L2 word order effects.

Finally, Heilenman and McDonald (1993) studied sentence interpretation strategies conducted on English learners of French at four different proficiency levels (the first to the fourth semester of university French) using stimuli containing word order and clitic pronoun cues (type and agreement) in French. Their study also included two control groups: French NSs and English NSs. Results showed that the French NSs exhibited clitic pronoun agreement strategies, whereas the English NSs depended on word order as a cue. Although the novice learners of French applied the English word order strategy to French at the very beginning, they abandoned it quickly (sometime before their second semester of French). These learners, however, appeared not to transfer clitic pronoun agreement information. It was not until the fourth semester of French that learners began to use information coded by clitic pronoun agreement, for example. It is worth pointing out here that this finding is not surprising in that morphological information is generally transferred late, if at all (Odlin, 1989). Heilenman and McDonald conclude that while their study provides evidence that L2 learners attempt to transfer L1 strategies, it also shows that a strategy of transfer is not always applicable, as in the case of morphological cues for English learners of French. In addition, results showed that the learners abandoned their native strategy (word order) relatively quickly, which led the authors to discuss the important role that differences between the L1 and the L2 input play in whether or not an L1 strategy will be transferred or abandoned.

In sum, the results presented in this section suggest that a strategy of complete L1 transfer to L2 sentence interpretation does not fully explain what learners do when faced with a task in their L2, even at the beginning level. L1 transfer certainly prevails, but learners apply other strategies as well. Research conducted within the framework of the Competition Model has contributed to our understanding of the processing of syntactic, morphological and semantic information in L2 sentence interpretation, an important contribution to research on input processing. As yet, no studies within this framework have been conducted on learners' processing of L2 input at first exposure and in the few hours that follow. In Chapter 8 we argue that research on initial processing of foreign language input can and should be conducted within this framework in that the data it generates would, without a doubt, offer much to the field of SLA.

Interactionist Approaches

Research within a sociointeractionist framework

The general consensus in sociointeractionist L2 acquisition studies is that input can be defined, in its most basic form, as the interaction between learners and their environment (cf. Pekarek Doehler, 2000 for an overview). Py (1989) claims that L2 development or acquisition relies on the L2 samples presented to the learner. He proposes that both the form of these samples and the manner in which the learner accesses them are of utmost importance. This claim implies that language events in which learners participate (as author or observer) must not be ignored in studies of L2 acquisition. Similarly, Pica (1991) defines input as data in the learning environment that are useful and pertinent. Learners can choose and control these data for the development of their L2.

To illustrate how learners make use of these data, we refer the reader to Vion and Mittner (1986), who examine learners' use of 'reprise', that is the manner in which learners appropriate certain aspects of their interlocutor's speech to ensure that their own speech is legitimate and coherent. Vion and Mittner propose a typology of 'reprise', breaking down the term into several levels of appropriation. These include, but are not limited to, a simple 'repetition' of an interlocutor's word or phrase and a 'recoding', which involves translating an interlocutor's word or phrase into their native language. The use of such processes not only constitutes an aid for learners when encoding TL utterances, but is also dependent on the type of interaction in which learners find themselves. More 'reprises' are used in conversational settings than in argumentative, role-play type situations, for example, suggesting that learners are more dependent on their interlocutor in unconstrained, free conversation. Their autonomy is shown to increase over time in all settings with the number of 'reprises' decreasing as their interlanguages evolve.

From a similar angle, the Vygotskian perspective claims a strong correlation between cognition and interaction. According to this framework, individual construction of language cannot exist without considering interactive aspects (Pujol-Berché, 1993). In a review of Vygotskian psycholinguistics, Schinke-Llano (1993: 123) highlights Vygotsky's claim for first language acquisition: '...language acquisition and concept formation occur as the result of interaction. In other words, their development is social, not individual...'. She views such a claim as relevant for L2 acquisition as well. Along the same lines, Py (1989) points out, also for L2 acquisition, that input can be viewed as both objects of discourse and objects of perception. As objects of discourse, input is controlled by the utterances themselves, that is, by formal structures and transmission modes. As objects of perception, input is selected and restructured by the learner, at which point it becomes what Py refers to in French as 'prise' (intake or a form of intake).

Matthey (1996) analyses interactions in terms of different configurations of what she calls 'donnée-prise' tokens. Her choice of terminology here is essential to understanding her claim. The term 'donnée' refers to the item or utterance produced by the interlocutor, whereas 'prise' is that which is taken up by the learner from the 'donnée'. A 'prise' could be, for example, a mere repetition of something said by one's interlocutor, and it may or may not involve factors such as comprehension or verbal solicitation. Matthey also uses the term 'saisie', which refers to a phenomenon linked to processing and storing information. Although both 'prise' and 'saisie' are traditionally translated as 'intake' in English SLA texts, the reader can hopefully see the distinction Matthey attempts to make by using these two terms. According to Matthey, a 'prise' will not necessarily be assimilated into a 'saisie'. She claims that tokens of 'donnée-prise' result in a potentially acquisitional event linked to the human capacity to solicit, transmit and construct knowledge within the context of interaction, and therefore assumes that certain 'prises' constitute a part of the cognitive intake process. This leads Matthey to propose a typology of 'prises', suggesting that the different types of 'prises' can serve as an indication of the different stages of mental functions alluded to by Vygotsky (1962).

In an overview of research conducted within an interactionist framework, Pekarek Doehler (2000) warns of viewing interaction as a simple trigger for the process of acquisition. Interaction should *not* be understood as one factor that simply provides language data to learners, triggering and accelerating certain developmental processes, but rather as *the* factor that structures the developmental process. Pekarek Doehler points out that studies conducted within this framework show that L2 acquisition is not limited to the internal linguistic system, but that it presupposes a reconceptualisation of discourse objects and of world knowledge in general.

This assumption is confirmed by numerous studies conducted within the context of the European Science Foundation project, *Second Language Acquisition by Adult Immigrants* (henceforth ESF).[4] These studies, which attempted to reconstruct the activities of speech perception and production by adults in untutored learning situations (Perdue, 1993, 1995), investigated the cognitive and interactional activity of the learner who is faced with a particular problem: input. Their central question is: how do learners deal with aspects of the TL input when they do not yet have the tools necessary to do so? According to Giacomi and de Hérédia (1986), who view speech as dialogic, all linguistic learning occurs in and through dialogue, whether it be a case of first language acquisition or second language acquisition. The study of input, therefore, cannot be separated from the study of interaction.

Bremer *et al.* (1996) and de Hérédia (1986) also used ESF data to examine comprehension in adult learners, again in an untutored setting. According to these authors, comprehension, like production, depends on interaction. Hérédia points out that comprehension is not reserved exclusively for the receiver, just as production is not totally controlled by the transmitter. Comprehension solicits the active participation of the learner. Hérédia uses, as an example, the hearing-impaired who, within this perspective, become dynamic players in the evolution of dialogue. It is important to note here that in this perspective the notions of input and intake are tightly intertwined with interaction and dialogue, regardless of the specific language activity being studied. One final area of interest in SLA that often falls within the domain of interactionist studies is the effect of feedback on learners' acquisitional processes. Allwood (1993: 196) used ESF data as well to examine feedback, which he defines as '... linguistic mechanisms which ensure that a set of basic requirements for communication, such as continued contact, mutual perception and mutual understanding, can be met'. His data analysis concerns both native speakers (control group) and L2 learners engaged in interactive activities. He found that both native speaker controls and L2 learners consistently relied on feedback, but that this reliance was more noticeable in the first stages of adult SLA. He also concluded that different types of activities require more or less feedback.

Havranek and Cesnik (2001) pursue this line of questioning by measuring the success of 'corrective feedback' in an instructional setting. The results of a vast study reveal that the role of feedback depends on the following factors: (1) the type of feedback (e.g. recast, repetition, elicited self-correction); (2) the type of error corrected (e.g. pronunciation – stress, phonemes; grammar-verb tense, prepositions); and (3) the type of learner (e.g. proficiency level in TL, verbal intelligence, ambition, anxiety).

Carroll's (2001) work on feedback and correction responds to interactionist research in that she is concerned with what makes linguistic feedback useable. A principal objective of her book is '...to fit input, feedback and correction into a constrained theory of second language acquisition' (Carroll, 2001: 1). She proposes that interpreting any given feedback or correction requires a certain metalinguistic capacity on the part of the learner. As a result, and in line with conclusions drawn by Allwood (1993) and Havranek and Cesnik (2001), feedback and correction may not be useable in all situations:

> The interpretation of feedback and correction requires first of all a metalinguistic capacity since the correct construal of the corrective intention requires treating language itself as an object of thought. Feedback and correction would thus appear to be excluded in certain language learning situations because the learner has limited or no metalinguistic capacity (early L1 acquisition, possibly L2 acquisition in illiterates). (Carroll, 2001: 390)

Carroll distinguishes between two types of feedback: positive and negative. The former confirms that a given form, string or interpretation is possible in the language, whereas the latter confirms the contrary, that it is not possible in the language. Finally, she concludes that, '...the "best" feedback and correction is probably the most explicit – which is least likely to occur' (p. 390).

Interactionist research concerned with the very beginning stages of L2 acquisition, including studies on feedback and correction, is limited for the simple reason that collecting production data from 'true beginners' is extremely difficult. Although the current study does not explicitly examine the role of interaction in second language acquisition (cf. second section of Chapter 4), our results nonetheless contribute to interactionist debates involving the characterisation of 'intake'. Certain tests administered during the data collection period of this study required some form of 'intake' or 'prise' on the part of the learner, in particular the tasks requiring them to repeat TL words or to translate words or utterances from the TL into their NL. In some cases, the input was transmitted through a human being; in other cases it was transmitted by means of audio equipment. In both case scenarios, learners 'interacted' with TL input to accomplish the task. Although negotiation with an interlocutor during testing periods was not an option for our learners, we believe that the study of such negotiation merits attention in future research on the early stages of second language acquisition.

Research Related to the Notion of 'Comprehensible Input'

Numerous studies, many of which have been conducted in North America, have focused on the role that manipulation of the input plays in L2 acquisition. In a recent summary of the literature on the role of input in L2 acquisition, VanPatten (2000) identifies four kinds of input: *comprehensible, simplified, modified* and *enhanced*.

Introduced by Krashen (1978), the notion of 'comprehensible input' triggered an abundance of research responding to the question: does teaching have an effect on acquisition? Krashen (1985) proposes the 'input hypothesis', according to which the comprehension of a message is necessary for acquisition to take place. He claims that the acquisitional process is based on the rule 'i → i + 1', where 'i' represents the current state of the learner and 'i + 1' the following state.[5] For this rule to be operational, we would need a definition of state 'i', but Krashen fails to provide us with one. As a result, he fails to address the process by which a learner makes the input comprehensible.

Researchers working on the notion of 'simplified input' (cf. Meisel, 1977) have tried to identify the role that simplified input plays in the comprehension process. Hatch (1983) describes characteristics of the input that have been modified by a speaker (or writer) to facilitate an L2 learner's comprehension, such as speech rate, vocabulary and syntax, among others. The assumption is that better comprehension indirectly leads to acquisition; the more learners understand, the more they will acquire. This occurs because learners' developing linguistic systems are provided with more relevant linguistic information. Leow (1993: 335), however, poses an interesting question: '. . . learners may get more passage information from simplified input, as current research appears to indicate, but can they also take in more linguistic information from the input?' The notion of 'modified input' (cf. Long, 1983) encompasses simplified input, but goes beyond it. Long's study seeks to characterise not only the simplified input, but *all* the input directed at a language learner, including the input involved in interaction between a native speaker and learner. Such studies also attempt to discern whether modifications made to the input result in better comprehension.

Authors working on 'enhanced input' examine ways to manipulate the input in order to accelerate the acquisition process or to minimise problems. Sharwood Smith (1993) uses the term 'input enhancement' to include all external intervention, such as the instructor's input or the use of documents for the purpose of rendering the characteristics of the input more salient. Included in 'enhanced input' studies are the numerous studies attempting to discern the possible effects of focus-on-form teaching on acquisition (for an overview, see Doughty & Williams, 1998; Ellis, 2001). The basic premise of these studies is that redirecting learners' attention during input processing when they fail to notice a particular structure in the language may aid in the acquisition of that structure. According to Doughty (2003), it is still not clear what elements can effectively be brought into attentional focus during input processing, nor for which elements there is a long-term effect. Sharwood Smith (1996: 1) poses related questions: '...can focusing the learner's attention on the formal properties of language have some sort of beneficial effect after all? And, more crucially, if there *is* an observed effect, how are we to explain this?' It is the latter question that concerns us here, requiring investigation into the learners' own processes relative to the linguistic input provided.

The identification by VanPatten (2000) of these four types of input reflects the evolution of research concerned with the role input plays in L2 acquisition. More precisely, within this research perspective, the focus on 'comprehensible input' has progressively left its place to that of 'simplified input', which, in turn, has been replaced by 'modified input', followed by 'enhanced input', with each progression attempting to identify the language teaching methods and the kind of input that appear to be most effective for L2 acquisition. Taken as whole, these studies seem to imply that a learner's current L2 knowledge state is useful for L2 acquisition. We take this a step further and say that it is crucial. As Pienemann (1998) observes, there is a natural sequence for acquisition, and not all structures can be processed at any given time. Essentially, we need to know what the current (in our case, initial) knowledge state of an L2 learner allows as 'intake'.

VanPatten (1999: 44), for whom the study of input constitutes an essential area of research for SLA, seeks to clarify the distinction between input and intake: 'It is common knowledge in all circles that not all of input becomes intake; if this were true acquisition might as well be instantaneous'. According to VanPatten, intake is the result of input processing that occurs while the learner is focusing on form. VanPatten (2000: 295–296) provides three definitions of intake:

(1) *Intake as Incorporated Data*. This definition takes us back to Corder (1967: 165), who characterised 'intake' as 'what goes in'.
(2) *Intake as Process*. Intake is not a product, but rather the process of successively incorporating grammatical features into the linguistic system. Many stages of intake exist, such as 'initial intake' and 'final intake'.
(3) *Intake as a Filtered Subset of Input Before Incorporation*. Intake is the product of input processing; it is stored in working memory and available for subsequent processing.

The third definition represents VanPatten's own position on intake (1996, 2000). His principal questions are the following: what form-meaning connections do learners make? When do they make them? Why are certain connections made and not others? His model, *On-line Input Processing* (IP), attempts to respond to these questions, identifying five principal elements that influence the intake process: working memory, memory capacity limitations, communicative value, form-meaning connections and sentence processing. VanPatten (2000) proposes four principles for his model. Firstly, learners process input for meaning before form and lexical items before grammatical items. Consequently, priority is given to morphological items with higher communicative value. Secondly, for learners to treat form, the processing of the informational or communicative content must not pose a problem. Thirdly, an inherent first noun strategy leads learners to attribute the role of agent (or subject) to the first noun or noun phrase.[6] Learners will adopt other processing strategies once their developing linguistic system has incorporated new phenomena, such as case marking and acoustic stress (the Competition Model introduced in the second section of this chapter addresses similar questions). Lastly, learners process elements in initial sentence or utterance position first, while treating elements in final position before those in middle position (see also Slobin, 1985).

Following the work of Doughty (1991) and others (cf. Doughty & Williams, 1998; Ellis, 2001), VanPatten (1999: 48–49) elaborates the focus-on-form approach, posing the following questions: is there a way to enrich learners' intake using insights from IP? To what degree can we either manipulate learner attention during IP and/or manipulate input data so that more and better form-meaning connections are made? VanPatten has tested these questions by means of *Processing Instruction*, the objective of which is to modify processing strategies that learners use in comprehension tasks and to encourage them to make better form-meaning connections (cf. VanPatten, 1996, 2004; VanPatten & Cadierno, 1993; VanPatten & Oikkenon, 1996). After conducting five studies comparing groups who received processing instruction to those who did not, VanPatten (1996: 127) concludes, 'Not only do learners receiving processing instruction gain in the ability to process input better, but also their developing system is affected such that they can access the targeted linguistic features when making output'.

The work of VanPatten (1996) describes a methodology that highlights not only the importance of the instructor and the linguistic environment in instructed L2 acquisition, but also the essential work that learners themselves do on their input. Clearly, the more ways researchers discover to test what learners do with their linguistic environment, the more equipped we will be to comment on the effect of this environment on acquisition.

Generativist Models

Chomsky (1965, 1981, 1995) posits the theory of Universal Grammar (UG) for first language acquisition based on principles and parameters. Numerous SLA researchers working within the generativist framework have proposed the hypothesis that if UG is attested in L2 acquisition, then L2 learners will need to reset parameters that carry a different value from that of the L1 (cf. White, 1996, 2003). The current debate within the generativist framework centres on the factors that lead a learner to 'reset a parameter': is the resetting a consequence of the interaction between TL input and UG, as Epstein *et al.* (1998) propose, or of the interaction between TL input and the L1, as Bley-Vroman (1990) and Schachter (1988) propose, or is it rather a simultaneous interaction between TL input, UG and L1, as Eubank (1994) and White (1996) propose?

Adapting information provided by White (1989, 2003) and Gass (1997) in useful syntheses on L2 research within the UG perspective, we distinguish between the various positions taken with regard to input and UG:

(1) There is no access to UG. In other words, UG has 'disappeared'. The TL input passes directly into the L1 system (cf. Bley-Vroman, 1990; Schachter, 1988).
(2) UG is still available: the learner uses the L1 as a basis, but when the L1 proves insufficient for the task at hand, UG is accessed. The input passes first through the L1 system and progressively through UG as needed (cf. Schwartz & Sprouse, 1994).
(3) The input passes directly through UG without being filtered by the L1. It is UG that plays the role of filter (cf. Epstein *et al.*, 1998).
(4) UG, like L1, has an effect on the initial state of the L2. Certain aspects of the initial state are based on UG, others on L1. As a result, according to this model, TL input has two filters, UG and the L1 (cf. Eubank, 1994; Vainikka & Young-Scholten, 1994; White, 1996).

The majority of studies conducted within the UG framework focus on learners whose interlanguage is highly grammaticalised. Within this perspective, the term 'L2 initial state' is introduced in a special issue of *Second Language Research* in which Schwartz and Sprouse (1996) propose the Full Transfer/Full Access (FT/FA) hypothesis. They claim that the L1 grammar *is* the L2 initial state:

> This means that the starting point of L2 acquisition is quite distinct from that of L1 acquisition: in particular, it contends that all the principles and parameter values as instantiated in the L1 grammar immediately carry over as the initial state of a new grammatical system on first exposure to input from the target language. (Schwartz & Sprouse, 1996: 41)

According to these authors, when learners 'perceive' a discrepancy between the configuration of their grammars and the input, a restructuring of the L2 grammar, determined by UG, is triggered. They assume, for example, that the first utterances of an L1 Turkish speaker learning English would reflect an SOV order, the basic word order in Turkish (cf. Schwartz & Sprouse, 1994). In a more advanced stage, this grammar would be restructured and the SOV order would be replaced by SVO, basic word order in English.

In the introduction to a special issue of _Second Language Research_ on the 'L2 initial state', Schwartz and Eubank (1996: 1) offer another explanation of the L2 initial state: 'One of the more neglected topics in L2 acquisition research is the precise characterization of the L2 initial state, where "L2 initial state" refers to the starting point of non-native grammatical knowledge'. As mentioned above, researchers working in this perspective claim to study the _starting point_ of non-native grammatical knowledge, but their data come from learners who are capable of producing inflected verb forms in their L2, learners who are already beyond the _starting point_ of L2 acquisition. We hypothesise that the starting point of non-native grammatical knowledge may well be the starting point of non-native language acquisition, that is the moment a learner first comes into contact with the new TL.

Lalleman (1999) tested the FT/FA hypothesis using learners of Dutch from a variety of linguistic backgrounds. They were exposed to the TL for the first time at the onset of the study and for a subsequent period of 3–6 weeks. Informants were asked to judge Dutch sentences that contained different types of gapping, notably verb ellipsis in coordinate sentences, as in 'My mother sleeps badly and my children soundly' (Lalleman, 1999: 160). In Dutch, the verb can be eliminated in either the first or the second clause. In contrast, in the native languages of her informants, only one of these scenarios is possible: either verb ellipsis can occur in the first clause, but not in the second, or vice versa. Results suggest that the intuitions of all the learners as to the possibility of gapping in Dutch were much better than predicted by the FT/FA hypothesis. Contrary to Schwartz and Sprouse's (1996) claim, Lalleman concludes that, with respect to gapping, the final stage of L1 acquisition is _not_ equivalent to the initial stage of L2 acquisition.

The characterisation of the L2 initial state is controversial even within generativist circles, in large part due to the absence of suitable methodologies to collect data from learners at the initial stages of L2 acquisition. Vainikka and Young-Scholten (1998: 31) recognise the void: '...in order to make any claims about the learner's initial state, data need to be collected from learners at the earliest stages of acquisition'. To our knowledge, they have not as yet done this. The study described in this book was not conducted within a generativist framework as this would have been impossible. Rather, we propose methodologies that may prove useful for data collection at the early stages of second language acquisition regardless of one's theoretical framework.

Cognitivist Models

The Autonomous Induction Theory

Carroll (1999) raises the problem of distinguishing between input and intake in quantifiable terms. In her view, 'stimuli' are, in the case of speech, 'acoustic-phonetic events' or, in the case of written text, 'graphic objects'. Stimuli are observable and measurable with respect to objective properties: the signal frequency, length, amplitude, the spectral structure and so forth. Intake, on the other hand, '...is a mental representation of a physical stimulus' (Carroll, 1999: 8–9). Carroll claims that stimuli are converted into intake, and that intake from the speech signal serves *not* as input to learning mechanisms, but as input to speech parsers. Intake and input are therefore both viewed as mental constructs, whereas 'stimulus' is not. Carroll (1997, 1999, 2001) contrasts 'stimulus' and 'input', attributing a significance to the former that corresponds with what other SLA researchers generally refer to as 'input' (cf. Wong & Simard, 2000), that is, something in the external environment.

According to Carroll (1999), prior research on input processing has not responded to the question: how do stimuli become intake? She proposes that the question must be integrated into a conceptual framework that renders the nature of signal processing and linguistic parsing explicit. Once this has been done, the distinction between 'input to processing' and 'input to language learning' will become evident.

In her Autonomous Induction Theory, the objective of which is to explain how and why representation systems of a learner evolve over time, Carroll (2001) shows how speech processing and learning mechanisms interact with input processing. She examines the hypothesis that feedback and correction (two types of stimuli) can provoke a restructuring of interlanguage grammars. To show this, she adopts the theory of representational modularity (cf. Jackendoff, 1990), according to which only certain elements represented in our conceptual systems can be encoded in our phonological and morphological systems and vice versa. In fact, not everything can be encoded. According to Carroll (2001: 50), 'This means that there will be severe constraints on how conceptual information can interact with information encoded in the specialized representational systems'. As a result, one might assume that feedback and correction must then be limited in terms of the role they play in initiating grammatical restructuring. Carroll (2001: 50), however, insists that her theory is compatible with the hypothesis that feedback and correction, conceptually represented, can have an effect on grammatical restructuring: '...the investigation of exactly what the effects of feedback and correction are can shed light on the nature of modularity and information processing'.

In a summary of empirical research on input processing, Carroll (2001) cites studies that examine different types of metalinguistic information assumed to be able to trigger the restructuring of learners' psychogrammars, such as focus on form (cf. Doughty & Williams, 1998; Ellis, 2001), on-line input processing (cf. VanPatten, 1996) and methods using feedback and correction (cf. Carroll & Swain, 1993). The results of such studies are particularly conclusive: 'Although there are problems in the interpretations of each of the studies surveyed, taken together, they provide some evidence that metalinguistic instruction has a definite effect on learner behaviour with respect to a small number of linguistic phenomena which, nonetheless, cover a broad range of types of linguistic knowledge...' (Carroll, 2001: 312). Studies on feedback and correction reveal a teaching effect on the feedback items, but only certain types of feedback help learners generalise. Carroll (2001: 341) concludes that, 'Adult learners can learn abstract linguistic generalizations on the basis of various types of explicit and implicit feedback and are not restricted to instance-based learning or modeling'. It appears, therefore, that there is an effect of learning on feedback items, but that further research is needed to identify under what conditions feedback and correction lead to acquisition.

Carroll's work is crucial to our own for two main reasons. Firstly, she poses the same principal question, that is, what do learners do with the input (or stimuli) they receive? Secondly, she seeks to measure what we refer to as 'input': her approach consists of examining what learners *do* with feedback and correction, which, according to her, constitute two types of measurable stimuli.

The speech production model and the bilingual production model

Levelt's (1989) questions concerning 'information processing' are closely related to those of authors working on 'intake', although Levelt opts for other terminology. In Levelt's speech production model, the predecessor to input processing models (e.g. VanPatten, 2000) and cognitive representation models (e.g. Carroll, 1999), the 'output' of an item becomes 'input' for the following item. Levelt's model consists of four essential components: (1) conceptualising; (2) formulating: grammatical and phonological encoding; (3) articulating; and (4) self-monitoring. According to Levelt, the first stage of production is *conceptualising*, at which point pre-verbal messages are generated. To arrive at the pre-verbal message, the speaker must have access to two types of knowledge: declarative and procedural (organisational) knowledge. The former, which is stored in the speaker's long-term memory, refers to encyclopaedic knowledge developed over years of life experience. The latter corresponds to processing mechanisms involved in the act of speech production. This knowledge, which belongs to working memory, contains information that is *'attended to* by the speaker' (Levelt, 1989: 10).

The pre-verbal message, which is not linguistic in and of itself, contains necessary information for the following stage, that of *formulating*, where the conceptual structure is transformed into a linguistic structure. To convert the pre-verbal message into a phonetic plan, the lexical items are selected, and the corresponding grammatical and phonological rules are applied. During this operation, activation and encoding of morphophonological information of the lexical item is realised. This phonetic plan does not yet constitute *overt speech*, but rather, the internal representation referred to as *internal speech*. 'A more precise way to put things would be to say that internal speech is the phonetic plan as far as it is attended to and interpreted by the speaker – i.e., the phonetic plan as far as it is *parsed* by the speaker' (Levelt, 1989: 12). The product of this formulation then serves as input for the following stage, *articulating*, which brings the phonetic plan to life, resulting in *overt speech*. *Self-monitoring* is necessary during all of these operations. Speakers must systematically control the link between their own intention and their internal and overt speech.

De Bot (1992) proposes a bilingual speech production model based on Levelt's work, the principal difference between the two being that de Bot's model attempts to explain the selection or non-selection and the activation or non-activation of the speaker's known languages. Following Green (1986), de Bot assumes three levels of activation: selected, activated and dormant. The status of 'dormant' refers to the non-activation of one of the speaker's known languages. Activation and selection occur simultaneously, but the language in which the speaker produces (articulates) an utterance is referred to as the 'selected' language. The 'active' language does everything the selected language does, including making a phonetic plan, but this phonetic plan is not fed into the articulator. In other words, the selected language is both activated and articulated, whereas the active language is activated but not articulated.

Although Levelt and de Bot's models attempt to explain language production, the activity of perception may be viewed in these models as production in reverse. Internal speech can be viewed as needing to access the process of articulating in order to become overt speech. The latter constitutes the output from articulating, which is ready for the auditory step and for entry into the speech-comprehension system. Internal speech can obviously bypass this articulatory process and enter directly into the speech-comprehension system. Of importance here is the fact that in both internal and overt speech, the discourse is perceived and analysed by the speech-comprehension system. This is the case as well when comprehending the speech of others. As Levelt (1989: 469) explains, 'A speaker can attend to his own speech in just the same way as he can attend to the speech of others; the same devices for understanding language are involved'.

The main contribution of Levelt's model to the study of input processing at the beginning stages of acquisition lies in its ability to predict the information that will be processed by the speaker (or the learner in our case). What is important is not merely the linguistic environment, but also the interaction between this environment and the learner's stored knowledge, and the functioning of specific processes that are consciously or unconsciously managed by the learners themselves. De Bot's model makes an important contribution to the field in that it proposes an explanation for how learners' languages are selected and activated. What concerns us in the current study is how this selection or activation occurs as a result of exposure to specific TL input. In essence, what elements in the TL input provoke the selected, activated or dormant status of a speaker's known languages? We will return to this question in Chapter 5.

Processability Theory

Pienemann's (1998) *Processability Theory*, based on Levelt's speech production model, deals almost exclusively with constraints on learner productions. He states that, '...the key issues in language learnability are far from being resolved, and that every one of the major schools of thought has a number of shortcomings' (Pienemann, 1998: 32). His model, which examines language processing, and more specifically, L2 development, comprises principles that predict transitions in grammatical systems during development: '...it is the sole objective of Processability Theory to determine the sequence in which procedural skills develop in the learner' (p. 5).

For Pienemann (1998: 36), language learning is envisaged in terms of cognitive processes: 'One can no longer assume that the state of the learner's linguistic system can suddenly change fundamentally under the influence of social variables such as interactional parameters or formal learning environments'. In other words, we cannot expect a new situation to result in a beginning learner becoming an advanced learner without some sort of developmental process. The ZISA project (*Zweitspracherwerb italienischer und spanischer Arbeiter*) (cf. Meisel *et al.*, 1981; Pienemann *et al.*, 1988) identified a natural sequence for the acquisition of certain TL structures. Research on the acquisition of word order in German resulted in an implicational scale of structures which predicts developmental stages. During 'stage X' for example, canonical word order (SVO) is dominant in learners' productions; during 'stage X + 1', adverbs are found in sentence initial position, and so forth. We can therefore assume that the environment provokes a sequence of modifications in the learners' language processing that can gradually lead to the acquisition of capacities in advanced learners. Following Vygotsky's (1962) work on the zone of proximal development, the ZISA research programme also suggests that L2 development is based on the learner's capacity to process linguistic information, but that structures are learned in a strict order and that not all structures can be processed at any given time. This has strong implications for what can be 'taken in' at a given stage. Pienemann (1998) sets out to predict the structures that only learners at certain proficiency levels can process. He concludes that L2 acquisition is based on the development of the ability to process language. We take this to mean that, for Pienemann, the ability to process language leads to acquisition.

According to Pienemann (1998: 3, 90), any language learnability theory must include at least the following four elements:

(1) the target grammar;[7]
(2) the data input to the learner;
(3) the learning device that must acquire that grammar; and
(4) the initial state.

He states that, '...a learnability theory must specify how a learner develops from an initial state to the target grammar with the available input and the given learning device' (Pienemann, 1998: 3). It is important to note here that for Pienemann, the beginning of acquisition corresponds to an initial state, but he fails to specify what he means by 'initial state'. In his terms, 'The acquisition process starts at an initial state; this book refrains from speculating on the structure of that initial state' (p. 231). Although Processability Theory provides an interesting framework for how language learning might take place, Pienemann's failure to address the nature of the initial state is problematic. He rightly claims that a theory of learning must specify how a learner moves from the initial state to the TL grammar, but provides no indication as to what that initial state might look like. Pienemann's work raises similar questions to those raised in this book. We concur on the fact that a better understanding of L2 acquisition or development processes will depend on our understanding of a variety of factors, such as transfer, input, the learning mechanism and the initial state, and of how these factors interact. Through analysis of the data presented in this book, we attempt to provide further insight into the role these factors play in the L2 acquisition process.

Conclusion

The aim of this chapter was to provide an overview of SLA theories, models and frameworks concerned with the role played by the linguistic environment (input) in L2 acquisition and the learner's interaction with this input, that is, the transformation of this input into something that can be used for further processing. The perspectives presented here are vast and often lead to opposing predictions about second language acquisition. Some, however, overlap, resulting in similar predictions in spite of different frameworks. Although the field has made progress in the past 40 years, we are still faced with many unanswered questions. The remainder of this book addresses some of these, while also posing new ones. To move on now to a discussion of what learners bring to the L2 acquisition task, we introduce the reader, in the following chapter, to the objectives of the few 'first exposure studies' conducted until now, and we report results that are relevant to the current study.

Notes

1. Research in subsequent years has identified tasks that allow us, at least to some extent, to observe various language activities (cf. Frauenfelder & Porquier, 1980, for example).
2. The CHILDES database had only just been created in the 1980s. Taraban *et al.* use the reference MacWhinney and Snow (1985), but a more recent reference is MacWhinney (2000).
3. 'Bilingual' within the Competition Model refers to individuals who speak more than one language, regardless of their proficiency level.
4. The ESF project is a longitudinal and cross-linguistic study of second language acquisition by adults in a natural setting.
5. It is worth noting that Krashen's claim resembles the 'zone of proximal development' proposed by Vygotsky (1962).
6. Klein and Perdue's (1992) model *Basic Variety* claims this same phenomenon.
7. On page 3 of his book, Pienemann uses the expression 'target language grammar', whereas on page 90 he uses the term 'target language'. We assume that 'target language' refers to 'target language grammar' in that Pienemann's thesis concerns the 'processability of grammar'. This assumption is based as well on his analysis of 'learnability theory' within the rationalist tradition (cf. Pinker, 1979; Wexler & Culicover, 1980).

Chapter 2
First Exposure Studies

This chapter provides an overview of some common objectives of first exposure studies conducted in SLA and the sporadic results of such studies to date. The 'first exposure' designation applies to studies in which data are collected from the very first moment of contact with the TL and within the first seconds, minutes and hours of subsequent exposure, and in which all TL input is controlled. Researchers working at this early stage of L2 acquisition seek to learn more about the learner's pre-existing system, including the role that implicit and explicit knowledge and linguistic knowledge (L1 and other L2s) play in their ability to process elements of the new TL. In addition, such research investigates the influence of the linguistic environment (TL input) on the learners' processing of the new TL during specific language activities (perception, comprehension, grammatical analysis and production) and on their acquisition of the TL within the first seconds, minutes and hours of exposure to the given linguistic environment. Learner differences are also an area of investigation. We will begin with a discussion of general objectives of first exposure studies,[1] followed by a survey of the exiguous studies that have been conducted at this initial phase of L2 acquisition. This will set the stage for the presentation of our study on initial processing of foreign language input.

Objectives of First Exposure Studies

Knowledge brought to the acquisition task: The pre-existing system

Research conducted on first exposure to a TL shares the universal question: what do adult learners bring to this task of acquiring a new language? In this section we will explore what some SLA researchers have identified as factors of a 'prior system' (Giacobbe, 1992b), that is, the system that can be attributed to adult learners at the moment of first exposure to a new language. These factors, a number of which will be discussed to various extents in this book, include linguistic knowledge (L1 and other L2s) and implicit/explicit knowledge (Ellis, 1994; Hulstijn, 2005). The question of whether or not L2 learners have access to UG will not be explicitly treated in this book. We will, however, discuss potential methodology that may allow for an exploration of the question at earlier stages of L2 acquisition than is currently the norm.

According to Perdue (1996: 138), 'Far too little empirical attention has been paid to the very beginnings of the acquisition process'. In answer to the question, 'What does the adult absolute beginner bring to the learning task?', he assumes encyclopaedic knowledge, a properly functioning articulatory and perceptual system, accompanied by the ability to segment the speech stream and assign meaning to its segments. He also suggests that '...this useful knowledge consists of an at least partial understanding of the cognitive categories that universally receive grammatical expression in languages, and also a knowledge of how information is organised in different types of discourse' (Perdue, 1996: 138).

Giacobbe (1992b) refers to a 'prior system', which he defines as a linguistic and conceptual system that organises the learner's new linguistic material and by means of which learners can test hypotheses. According to Giacobbe (1992a, 1992b), it is the learner's L1 that provides this conceptual and linguistic framework. He claims that reliance on the L1 is fundamental in that the L1 represents the base of the new system under construction. The L1 is a 'filter' through which the TL input passes. Analysing the learners' first free productions in their study on Spanish *ser* and *estar*, Giacobbe and Lucas (1980) claim that the pre-existing system observed via these productions was derived from their learners' L1. It is important to note here that when Giacobbe and Lucas speak of learners' 'first free productions', they mean the first productions containing inflected forms of *ser* and *estar*, and this, independent of the learners' level of proficiency in Spanish. As seen in Chapter 1, this again evokes a problem rarely alluded to in the SLA literature, but a crucial one for our project on L2 initial processing, that of the difficulty of eliciting 'initial' free productions within the first hours of exposure.

Linguistic knowledge: The learners' L1

Studies focusing on the involvement of the L1 in the processing of TL input, whether referred to as cross-linguistic influence, transfer or activation of a learner's L1, are too numerous to cite here. In the field of SLA, we generally agree that the phenomenon most often referred to as 'L1 transfer' exists. This said, we do not agree on the conditions that trigger this transfer or on the types of transfer that take place.

The notion of transfer finds its origins in the work of Lado (1957). The premise is that TL structures that correspond to L1 structures are easily assimilated as a result of 'positive transfer', whereas TL structures that fail to coincide with corresponding structures of the L1 create difficulty and result in errors due to 'negative transfer' or 'interference'.

This approach fails on several accounts. In particular, it fails to recognise that it is the learner's processing of linguistic information during comprehension and production that counts, not whether a particular structure described by linguists is attested in the language or not.

Kellerman (1979) claims the existence of three principal interacting factors that control the use of transfer by learners: the learner's psychological structure of the NL, perception of NL-TL distance and actual knowledge of the TL. According to Kellerman (1983), not all forms of a language are transferable, and it is not necessarily the structure of the language that determines the limits of transferability. It is, rather, the linguistic judgement of the learners themselves. A given form in the L1 may be treated as neutral and is therefore transferable to the L2, or it may be treated as specific to the L1 and is therefore not transferable. This specificity may be related to the degree of markedness of a given L1 form (Kellerman, 1980). It follows then that the perceived distance between two languages (the learner's 'psychotypology') is not necessarily enough, in and of itself, for the transfer of a form to occur. Kellerman (1980) concludes, therefore, that the learners' judgements on the L1–L2 relation filter the L2 activity even in cases where the two languages share structures, and that the notion of transferability may vary from one learner to another. Giacobbe (1992a) acclaims Kellerman for advancing a welcomed view of transfer that focuses on the creative activity of the learners themselves when constructing an interlanguage.

Sharwood Smith (1986: 247) also attributes a certain creative activity to the learner: 'It is more a question of accepting input from their [learners'] L1 competence as part of the material with which they independently create the new L2 system'. He suggests that notions such as 'transfer', 'carry-over' and 'L1 dependence' are not necessarily the best metaphors for this creative process. Sharwood Smith and Kellerman (1986: 1) opt for the theory-neutral term 'cross-linguistic influence' to refer to 'the interplay between earlier and later acquired languages'. Selinker (1992: 208) adopts the term 'cross-linguistic influence' as well to refer to 'the influence and the use of prior linguistic knowledge, usually but not exclusively NL knowledge'.

The data from the current study will allow us to reflect on the notion of transfer and the processing of TL input as a function of the NL (French), the TL (Polish) and universals of information structure, such as scope properties. We will observe the interaction between learners' knowledge and TL input by analysing, in particular, cases where rules in the NL and TL differ. What do learners *do* when the structure in the input and the L1 structure differ? Chapter 3 provides a description of specific features in French and Polish to enable the reader to better understand the significance of our findings with respect to hypotheses about L1 influence at the very beginning of second language acquisition.

Linguistic knowledge: The learners' other L2s (L3 acquisition)

With regard to the terminology traditionally used in research on foreign language acquisition and multilingualism, 'L1' refers to the speaker's native language, that is, the first language acquired by the individual (balanced or early bilinguals may well have two L1s, trilinguals may have three and so forth) (cf. Safont Jordà, 2005). 'L2' generally refers to the non-native language being acquired when the other L2s known by the learner are not taken into consideration. When individuals learn a foreign language, be it their first foreign language, second, third or more, we generally refer to this process as 'second language acquisition'. This appears to be changing, however, at least for a certain group of SLA researchers (cf. Cenoz *et al.*, 2001; Trévisiol & Rast, 2006). The term 'L3 acquisition' is becoming more frequent, specifically referring to the acquisition of any given language after the L2. 'L3', therefore, usually encompasses L4, L5, L6 and so forth, unless otherwise specified (cf. Muñoz, 2006). This new perspective has resulted in a certain amount of terminological confusion. Fouser (2001: 150), for instance, proposes the term 'L ≥ 3' (more or equal to 3) to refer to post-L2 acquisition. Dimroth *et al.* (2006) introduce the term 'L2+' to refer to languages acquired after the L1. Several researchers have resorted to the designation L*n*, L*x*, L*y* or L*z* (cf. Flynn *et al.*, 2004; Leung, 2005). In fact, the lack of clarity in the terminology reflects our lack of understanding in the field about the effect of linguistic knowledge (not limited to L1 knowledge) on subsequent language acquisition.

In their introduction to a special issue on L3 acquisition, Trévisiol and Rast (2006) delineate the numerous factors investigated in studies of L3 acquisition, the interaction between these factors being of particular interest:

- L1 influence (cf. *supra*; Odlin, 1989, 2003; Ringbom, 1987, 2001);
- language typology (cf. Bardel, 2006; Cenoz, 2001; Ringbom, 1987);
- the 'psychotypology' of the learner (cf. *supra*): the learner's subjective evaluation of the difference between structures in the given languages (cf. Kellerman, 1983, and also Fouser, 2001; Ringbom, 2001; Singleton & Ó Laoire, 2006; Williams & Hammarberg, 1998);
- the 'recency' of the L2 (cf. Williams & Hammarberg, 1998);
- the learner's level of proficiency in the L2 and the L3 (cf. Bardel & Lindqvist, 2005; Muñoz, 2006);
- the frequency of use and the intensity of L2 study (cf. Dewaele, 2001);

- L2 status, or what is often referred to as the 'L2 factor' (cf. Cenoz, 2001; Dewaele, 2001; Hammarberg, 2006; Trévisiol, 2003, 2006; Williams & Hammarberg, 1998); and
- the positive and negative effects of knowing other L2s when acquiring subsequent languages (Cenoz, 1997; Klein, 1995; Nayak *et al.*, 1990).

In our current study, we have used the term 'L2' in its general sense when referring to the acquisition of any foreign language regardless of the chronology, and 'L3' when referring to Polish in cases where we consider the influence of learners' other L2s. 'L1' refers to our learners' native language, French.[2] It is important to note here that Polish was not the second language (chronologically speaking) of any of the informants of this study. In terms of chronology, it was anywhere from the third to the sixth. The nature of our study required us to take all languages known by our informants into consideration. As we will show, even limited contact with a language is sufficient reason to study its effects on the acquisition of other languages. As little research has been conducted on first contact with a new TL, we do not yet know at what moment a given piece of knowledge about a language, even if minimal, has an effect on the acquisition of another. This is one of our major areas of investigation in the current study.

Implicit and explicit knowledge

The distinctions between implicit and explicit knowledge and learning have been the focus of much SLA research in recent years. Hulstijn (2005: 130) implies that definitions of implicit and explicit *knowledge* are fairly standard: 'Explicit and implicit knowledge differ in the extent to which one has or has not (respectively) an awareness of the regularities underlying the information one has knowledge of, and to what extent one can or cannot (respectively) verbalize these regularities'. In contrast, Hulstijn notes that there is less consensus when it comes to definitions of implicit and explicit *learning*. Winter and Reber (1994: 117) describe the learning distinction as follows: 'Implicit learning refers, in the most basic sense, to the human ability to derive information about the world in an unconscious, non-reflective way. The common notion that people can under some circumstances "absorb" knowledge or information from the environment without awareness of the learning process captures the general spirit of this concept.' Explicit learning, on the other hand, represents a conscious process during which the individual forms and tests hypotheses with a view to finding the correct target structure (cf. Ellis, 1994: Introduction).

Hulstijn (2002: 206) describes explicit learning from a connectionist perspective as a 'conscious, deliberative process of concept formation and concept linking'. This type of learning may occur when learners are exposed to new concepts and rules, whether the information is provided by an instructor, in the form of a textbook, or by learners themselves when in a 'self-initiated searching mode'. Hulstijn continues by describing the link between this type of learning and explicit knowledge: 'When we learn a foreign language with the rules of a pedagogic grammar, we construct explicit knowledge consisting of concepts and rules'. In the same vein, Huot and Schmidt (1996) view explicit knowledge as reflected by the ability of learners to explain grammar rules verbally or in writing. It follows then that metalinguistic knowledge is a form of explicit knowledge.

Implicit knowledge, on the other hand, is viewed by Huot and Schmidt (1996) as the inferred knowledge of how grammatical items are used in communication. Some SLA studies have shown that implicit learning, and therefore the appropriation of implicit knowledge, takes place when a learner is exposed to a certain kind of input (cf. Ellis, 1994: Introduction; Reber, 1967).

Results of several studies conducted from a cognitive psychology perspective on implicit learning suggest that, '...stimuli are perceived even when observers are unaware of the stimuli' (cf. Merikle *et al.*, 2001: 115). In other words, perception can take place even when the individual makes no conscious cognitive effort. Whether this perception results in learning or whether learning results in implicit knowledge is not the focus of these studies, however. We cannot therefore assume from these results that the perceived item is necessarily available for further processing or represents what VanPatten (2000), for one, would call 'intake'. We will return to this point in Chapter 10.

This distinction between implicit and explicit knowledge is important for our study in that our informants were asked to perform tasks of a highly metalinguistic nature. We assume, therefore, that when performing tasks, their use of explicit knowledge was quite extensive.

The role of other factors

The linguistic environment (TL input)

As mentioned earlier, few studies have controlled and measured the input provided to learners. Of those that have, some are interested in the effect of non-linguistic input, such as visual highlighting (Zwitserlood *et al.*, 2000) or gestures (Dimroth *et al.*, 2006; see also Gullberg, 1998, 2006) on the processing of new information. Although we are cognisant of the importance of such studies, ours was not designed to account for such non-verbal phenomena and will focus rather on verbal and written input only.

We briefly return here to one of the principal objectives of this study, that is, to identify what aspects of the input are taken in by the learner, and to what extent they are subsequently used for further processing. In order to do this, we will analyse in detail features of the Polish input to which our informants were exposed. The following factors will be studied (cf. Chapter 7 for group results):

- word length;
- word stress;
- phonemic distance between the L1 and the TL;
- lexical transparency of a word with regard to the L1 and other L2s;
- word position (in a sentence or utterance);
- word frequency (in the input); and
- quantity of exposure (in hours).

We propose that the saliency of lexical items will need to be defined from the perspective of the learner (cf. Kellerman, 1983 on 'psychotypology'). The fact that a TL word is 'transparent' for us, researchers and observers, in no way implies that it is for the learner. Saliency of an input item for a learner at the very beginning of the L2 acquisition process may well depend on the knowledge the learner brings to the learning task. We will investigate this knowledge in Chapters 5 and 7.

Learner variability

Learner style and the relationship individuals have with their linguistic environments are also important factors to consider when investigating input processing. Meisel *et al.* (1981: 109) point out that, 'It is by now widely accepted that the learner takes an active part in the learning process'. The results of their study on the spontaneous acquisition of German suggest that sociopsychological factors greatly influence selective aspects of the L2 acquisition process.

Perdue and Klein (1992) discovered individual differences in the success of two learners of the ESF project, Andrea and Santo, both Italian beginning learners of English. Andrea's morphosyntactic system developed beyond the basic variety (cf. Klein & Perdue, 1992), but not Santo's. The data reveal differences in terms of how they negotiated and processed the L2 input. For instance, Andrea repeated pronouns used by his interlocutor, whereas Santo did not. The authors conclude that, 'Apparently, Andrea does pay more attention than Santo to the form of such input' (Perdue & Klein, 1992: 271).

According to Cammarota and Giacobbe (1986), different learners focus on different features in the input. They take, for example, the ESF data of two Spanish speakers learning French, BE and CA, to show the enormous difference in level of 'success' of these two learners in their acquisition of the TL. CA developed a hypothesis based on the similarity between NL and TL items, allowing the transformation of NL lexemes into TL lexemes. CA's hypothesis appeared to be the following: if I drop the final consonant of a Spanish word, the result will be a French word. This is illustrated below by comparing words in his interlanguage (in brackets) with Spanish (to the left of the arrow) and French equivalents (in parentheses). The hypothesis works in some cases as in Examples (1) and (2), but not in others (Example 3):

(1)   equipo → [ekip] (équipe 'team')
(2)   curso → [kurs] (cours 'course')
(3)   tengo → *[teng] (j'ai 'I have')

The other learner, BE, however, did not proceed in this manner. Interviews with BE revealed no such systematic NL–TL 'proximity hypothesis'. As Cammarota and Giacobbe (1986) point out, CA's development of his lexical construction system and the difficulties faced by BE during the same language production tasks reflect two different ways to establish one's first contact with a TL.

For the most part, the studies mentioned above report on interlearner differences. In Chapter 6 we will investigate not only inter-, but also intralearner variability through the case studies of two French learners of Polish.

An Overview of First Exposure Studies

This section provides an overview of first exposure studies already completed or in progress. As mentioned earlier, first exposure studies are sparse, leaving an unfortunate lacuna in the field of SLA in that such studies provide rich data for analysis of the underlying psycholinguistic processes involved in learning a non-native language. It is encouraging that researchers working within a variety of frameworks have at least begun to recognise the need for such studies. As White (1996: 8) points out, '...there may well be grammar acquisition in the "silent period" that precedes first productions.' Vainikka and Young-Scholten (1998), quoted in Chapter 1 (cf. the fourth section of Chapter 1), acknowledge that we cannot make claims about the L2 initial state without collecting data from learners at the earliest stages of acquisition. In her discussion of L2 linguistic development, Bardovi-Harlig (2004: 135) concludes, 'How they [learners] construct the initial stages and how the early systems expand toward target-like form-meaning associations is worthy of continued investigation'. Carroll (2006) emphasises the responsibility of any theory of SLA to describe all stages of L2 acquisition, including the very initial stage when a learner faced with TL input may hear nothing but 'noise'.

Although many researchers agree that the initial stages merit investigation, their recognition of this fact tends to appear in suggestions for future research; few have actually executed an investigation into the early stages of L2 acquisition. One intention of this book is to break the trend. We will begin by recognising those who have conducted research at the very beginning of L2 acquisition.

We mention briefly here a few psycholinguistic studies that are not generally considered 'first exposure' studies *per se*, although they control the language input and examine subjects' performance with regard to this input. These are often statistical learning studies designed to investigate learning and memory processes. They tend to use artificial language materials to control for prior learning and to have more precise control over the types of cues presented to learners (cf. Brooks *et al.*, 1993; Gómez, 2006; Hudson Kam & Newport, 2005; Mintz, 2002; Saffran, 2002, to mention a few). An early study of this kind was conducted by Reber (1967), who exposed subjects to an artificial syntactic language, a finite-state language constructed with a vocabulary using only five letters (P, S, T, V, X) and a grammar comprised of a set of sentence construction rules. He investigated the process by which subjects responded to implicit learning using memorisation tasks. Participants were presented with written stimulus items in the form of sentences under a time constraint of 5 seconds per sentence. One group was presented with 'grammatical' stimulus items, the other with randomly constructed items. They were then asked to reproduce the sentences in writing. The subjects received immediate feedback about the correctness of their responses following each training set. Results revealed a between-group difference as of Set 3, with the grammatical item group showing a significant improvement over the random item group. Subjects of the grammatical group learned one item at a time during initial training sets, becoming capable of learning two or three items on a single trial as of Set 3. The random group subjects, in contrast, rarely succeeded in correctly reproducing more than one item. Results suggest that information gathered about the grammar in such a memorisation task may be extended to a recognition task involving exposure to new stimuli.

Working on first exposure to a natural language, Henderson and Nelms (1980) examined the perceptual segmentation of speech in the absence of semantic and syntactic knowledge about the TL by exposing native English speakers to Czechoslovakian, a language with which they were 'unfamiliar'. Subjects heard 12-word strings in Czech. Six experimental conditions insured that the loudest speech sound was placed in such a way that it appeared in one of four locations relative to pause and intonation fall. Results revealed that intonation fall was a more helpful cue for subjects than was pause in the perceptual segmentation of speech.

One of the first clearly distinguishable SLA studies of this kind on natural language was conducted by Singleton and Little (1984), who examined the effect of L2 German on the comprehension of L3 Dutch by English native speakers who knew no Dutch at the time of the study.

Results show that informants with knowledge of German performed better on the oral/written comprehension test than those with no knowledge of German or another Germanic language, with the exception of English. The authors point out that informants were aware of their own strategy of using a language that was typologically close to Dutch (German in this case) to understand the Dutch text. In other words, learners were aware of the metalinguistic strategy involved in trying to understand a language they did not know.

Also using natural language as input, Zwitserlood *et al.* (2000) conducted a study in which native Dutch speakers were exposed to 15 minutes of Chinese input. The objective of the study was to discover under what conditions learners could recognise certain elements in the TL input and attribute meaning to them. Results showed that the frequency with which words were used by the Chinese speaker, in conjunction with the use of visual highlighting, had an effect on the recognition of words and their meaning. In addition, they found that informants were able to categorise as nonwords (i.e. words impossible in Chinese) those items that had correct Chinese segments in an incorrect position in the syllable. Zwitserlood and her colleagues conclude that, '...the striking result from our experiments is that our listeners, although in the traditional sense "understand" very little, can detect important regularities of the unknown language on the basis of so little input' (Zwitserlood *et al.*, 2000: 12). They showed that after only 15 minutes of exposure to Chinese their Dutch informants were able to recognise whether or not a combination of Chinese elements constitutes a Chinese word.

Following the Zwitserlood *et al.* (2000) study, Dimroth *et al.* (2006), reducing the time of exposure even more, examined lexical acquisition in terms of a sound and meaning connection, in this case after 7 minutes of exposure to spoken Chinese. Their results confirm those of Zwitserlood *et al.* Frequency or exposure alone had no effect on lexical acquisition, but frequency combined with either pre-exposure to a list of words in the input or highlighting of these words (using gestures) did have an effect. The authors conclude that pre-exposure boosts segmentation.

Also inspired by Zwitserlood *et al.* (2000), we conducted a pilot study to examine the first stages of acquisition in the case of French learners of Polish (Rast, 1998, 1999) in which the first 37.5 hours of Polish input (15 class periods) were recorded. Our research questions were of a broad nature:

(1) How does an L2 learner process the input of the target language environment?
(2) What knowledge is available to adult learners at the very beginning of the L2 acquisition process that will help them process the input?

(3) In what order are the target language items acquired? To what extent does this order reflect characteristics of the input?

As this was a pilot study, we were in search of an appropriate methodology to investigate these questions. Our principal methodological question was: what tasks administered to learners at this early stage could potentially reveal *how* they process the Polish input? The result was a battery of tests administered at various times over the 37.5 hours of instruction. We conducted a series of word order tests in which learners were asked to put the words of a decontextualised Polish sentence in the appropriate order. We also used grammaticality judgement tests, well aware of the fact that both test-types required extensive metalinguistic activity on the part of our learners. These tests were designed to provide information about our learners' syntactic preferences relative to their L1 knowledge and the TL input. We conducted a sentence repetition test based on methodology designed for the Heidelberg 'Pidgin-Deutsch' project (cf. HPD, 1979). Initially, our objective was to measure the learners' perception of Polish morphological markers. All words and forms in the test had appeared in the Polish input to learners sometime before the testing period. Analysis of these sentence repetitions revealed important information about saliency. Lexical transparency and word position in the sentence, for example, clearly played a role in the learners' ability to repeat the Polish words. Finally, we asked our learners to take two types of written production tests: one required writing a letter of introduction to a Polish speaker, the other a short story using 10 obligatory words.

Our pilot study provided crucial information for the study that would follow (the current study). It became evident that the most interesting information about the effect of prior knowledge and L1 influence was found in the first round of tests, after approximately five hours of exposure to Polish. Beyond this point, it became much more difficult to control the input, to measure it and to make claims about learners' performance relative to the input they had received. The written production data collected after 30 hours proved interesting in certain respects, but again, it was difficult to make claims about *what* exactly affected the learners' productions. We, therefore, made the decision to decrease the number of hours of exposure and to record only 6 class sessions (as opposed to 15) in our subsequent study. This would allow us to investigate both first exposure and the first hours of L2 development. For this reason, the current study examines the first 8 hours of exposure to the TL, the data presented in this book.

In an attempt to understand learners' processing of syntactic information at the early stages of acquisition, Hendriks and Prodeau (1999) examined the first 40 hours of acquisition of Dutch as a second language by two French native speakers, one of whom also had advanced knowledge of L2 German and the other of L2 English. The phenomenon studied was that of V2 (verb second) in Dutch, a feature that exists in German and Dutch, but not in English. They proposed the hypothesis that the learners would rely on knowledge of their L2 to analyse the L3 input. The nature of the linguistic environment was such that a native French speaker would have trouble recognising that Dutch was an L2 language in that the Dutch instructor provided no explicit rules or explanations about word order in Dutch. Data were collected by means of a variety of tasks: (1) spontaneous oral productions during unplanned in-class activities (answers to instructor's questions, questions about the material presented; (2) oral productions from prepared in-class activities (role-plays, such as introducing oneself); (3) oral productions from an unprepared poster description; and (4) written productions from word-order exercises, route directions and film retelling. The results indicate that the learner with knowledge of German hypothesised that 'Dutch is like German' with regard to the V2 rule, the result being that she produced sentences using the appropriate Dutch word order. The learner with knowledge of English, on the other hand, failed to produce the correct word order. These results suggest that prior knowledge of a specific L2 may have a facilitating effect on the acquisition of a third language (see Chapter 5 for further discussion of L3 acquisition), and that the input and the learner's knowledge interact in the process of language acquisition.

Lalleman's (1999) study, already introduced in Chapter 1 (cf. fourth section), should be mentioned here as well. Lalleman studied Dutch learners of numerous source languages who were exposed to Dutch for the first time during the study and for a subsequent period of 3–6 weeks. Her objective was to test Schwartz and Sprouse's (1996) FT/FA hypothesis. The object of her study was gapping, a grammatical phenomenon that occurs in ordinary spoken Dutch, but is not explicitly taught in beginning language courses. Learners from a variety of L1 backgrounds were asked to judge Dutch sentences with either forward or backward gapping. Both are possible in Dutch, but only one of the two is correct in the learners' native languages. Results show that her learners performed better than expected on the grammaticality judgement test. More importantly, they did not seem to use their knowledge of gapping possibilities in the native language to decide whether a Dutch sentence was correct or not. She concludes that a hypothesis of full L1 transfer fails to explain the data collected from her Dutch learners with regard to gapping.

Three other SLA studies merit discussion here: Yang and Givón (1997), de Graaff (1997) and DeKeyser (1997). These studies appeared together in a special issue of *Studies in Second Language Acquisition* on testing SLA theories in research laboratories. What interests us in these studies is their 'first exposure' nature in that the TL input was controlled from the moment of first exposure. Yang and Givón studied (1997) the first 50 hours of exposure to the artificial language 'Keki' by two groups of native English speakers. The first group (the pidgin group) received pidgin input, in which grammatical morphology was omitted, for 20 hours, followed by fully grammatical input for the remainder of the instructional period. The second group (the grammar group) was introduced to the grammar via fully grammatical input from the start. Using computer programs, the two groups received the same quantity of input, and the instruction for both groups was generally implicit in nature. Tasks consisted of repetition drills, matching sentences with pictures, comprehension tasks accompanying pictures and stories, picture-guided production tasks, and translation tasks in both directions. Results showed that 'Learners who received simplified pidgin input lagged behind learners who received fully grammatical input in both grammar acquisition and related comprehension skills' (Yang & Givón, 1997: 188). In the case of vocabulary acquisition, however, no significant difference was found between groups.

De Graaff (1997) examined the first 15 hours of exposure to the artificial language 'eXperanto' (a variation of Esperanto) by native Dutch speakers to investigate the effect of explicit grammar instruction and the complexity of structures on L2 acquisition. Complexity was measured as the number of grammatical concepts needed to correctly process or produce a structure. As in Yang and Givón's study, he divided his learners into two groups: the first received explicit grammar instruction with explanations about grammar rules after each activity; the second received no explicit grammar instruction, but rather participated in a series of exercises during which they were exposed implicitly to the grammar rules in question. Tasks included grammaticality judgements, gap-filling and vocabulary translation. Results confirmed the general hypothesis that explicit teaching facilitates L2 grammar acquisition. However, an effect of the variable 'complexity' on acquisition relative to the type of instruction was not confirmed. De Graaff concludes that to better understand the effect of 'complexity' in L2 acquisition, the number of criteria needed to process or produce a specific form, as well as the semantic saliency of these criteria, must be taken into consideration.

DeKeyser (1997) also developed an artificial language, 'Autopractan', an agglutinative language with flexible word order, in this case to investigate the effect of 'practice' on the acquisition of L2 morphology (within the context of the implicit/explicit learning debate). Initially, learners were exposed to vocabulary and grammar rules in Autopractan. They were then given computerised practice exercises in written comprehension and production. The total exposure period was approximately 22 hours. All subjects were taught the same rules and received the same amount of comprehension and production practice, but the groups varied in the rules practised for each skill. Tasks for practice and testing *comprehension* involved computerised picture – sentence matching; tasks for practice and testing *production* consisted of typing the correct sentence corresponding to the picture. Results showed that the learning of morphosyntactic rules is highly skill specific. DeKeyser (1997: 213) concludes that, 'Overall, our data lend strong support to the hypothesis that practice has skill-specific effect in the sense that performance in comprehension and production is severely reduced if only the opposite skill was practiced'.

These three exemplary studies conducted in a computer laboratory with learners exposed to an unknown language confirm the interest in examining this important stage in L2 acquisition, controlling the TL input and attempting to define what is 'taken in' and under what conditions. Studies such as these, where the TL input is controlled, described, qualified and quantified, are essential for the advancement of our understanding of what learners do with the input they receive. This said, SLA researchers are not always in agreement about the application of theories based on artificial languages to explain the acquisition of natural languages. Schmidt (1994: 166) remarks that, 'Learning an MAG [miniature artificial grammar] is unlike learning a natural second or foreign language in many respects, so it is not immediately obvious whether theories based on the results of learning MAGs may be relevant for theories of second language acquisition'. Yang and Givón (1997) conclude their article by saying that in spite of the temptation to generalise their results to real language learning, they are hesitant to do so. Subsequent studies using real languages are needed to add validity. We agree with this view inasmuch as theories based on studies of artificial languages can contribute to theories of SLA. The results of both taken together should allow us to make comparisons and come to conclusions about what learners *do* with their linguistic input, be it natural or artificial.

Now that we have taken a close look at first exposure studies and results to date, what can we say at this point about adult learners at initial exposure to a TL? Clearly we are unable to generalise the results with so few studies of this kind in existence. We can, however, summarise the findings thus far, including those using artificial languages, with respect to what learners appear to be capable of doing in the first seconds, minutes and hours of exposure, and to what affects this capacity. Firstly, in perceptual segmentation of speech, intonation fall was found to be a more important cue than was pause. Frequency and exposure alone had no effect on lexical acquisition in the first minutes of exposure; however, frequency and visual or gestural high-lighting affected the ability of subjects to recognise words and their meaning. Lexical transparency and the position of a lexical item in a sentence affected learners' ability to repeat the item in a sentence repetition task after limited exposure. Learners were found to use not only their L1 but also their L2 (in the case of L3 acquisition) when they perceived a similarity in the L2 and L3 items and structures in both oral and written tasks. Evidence of full L1 transfer was not found. Stimuli containing consistent grammatical information seemed to help informants memorise words in the new language. Finally, explicit grammar instruction was found to aid the acquisition of L2 grammar, and 'practice' (comprehension versus production) was found to be skill-specific.

Conclusion

This chapter has provided a comprehensive view of common objectives of first exposure studies and the few results of such studies that, to our knowledge, can be found in the SLA literature. This overview has shown that a variety of tasks can be used to observe various language activities at this early stage in L2 acquisition. Although data collection is challenging, we now know that it is by no means impossible. As argued in this chapter, first exposure studies can contribute to current debates about the knowledge learners bring to the L2 acquisition task, the role of linguistic (and non-linguistic) input, learner variability and how learners process information during different language activities. It is indeed first exposure studies that have the capacity to shed light on what learners bring to their L2 acquisition experience, and how they use what they bring to work on the TL input they receive. The following chapter will present a detailed description of the TL of our study (Polish) and the L1 of our learners (French), with a view to identifying similarities and differences between the two language systems and proposing hypotheses about L1 influence.

Notes

1. Although research objectives are often shared, first exposure studies are by no means conducted within a sole research framework. This will become evident later in the chapter (cf. second section), when the results of such studies are discussed.
2. The term 'L1' is also used to refer to both languages known by our balanced bilingual learners (cf. Chapter 9).

Part 2
The Study

Chapter 3
Polish–French Contrastive Analysis

Up to this point, we have scrutinised models and theories of SLA with respect to how they explain the constructs of input and intake and discussed first exposure studies and their objectives. We are now confronted with reality: our French NSs are expected to perceive, comprehend, analyse, process and acquire Polish, a language they know nothing about. What will they *do* and *how* will they do it? As we have seen in the preceding chapters, the extent to which learners use L1 knowledge when processing a TL is controversial. One way of testing its initial influence is to adopt a resolutely contrastive analysis attitude and to pinpoint differences between the two systems (NL and TL) that are testable. To this end, this chapter provides this type of analysis of Polish and French that will not only serve as a reference for readers who are unfamiliar with Polish and/or French, but will also illuminate differences between specific phenomena of the two systems that were tested in the current study.

An Introduction to Polish and French

Our reason for choosing Polish as the TL of this study is two-fold: (1) little research has been devoted to the study of adult acquisition of Polish; and (2) Polish is interestingly different from French in a variety of ways. Polish, for instance, is a highly inflected language with flexible pragmatic word order in which NP ellipsis is common. Person, number and gender are marked on the verb in Polish, so the syntactic subject of any given verb does not necessarily need to be made explicit. French, on the other hand, has relatively fixed SVO word order, has weak morphology and generally requires an explicit subject. Polish has no articles, but expresses determination by means of pronominal adjectives which agree in gender, number and case with the nouns they modify. Examples are possessives (*mój* 'my'), demonstratives (*ten* 'this') and numerals (*jeden* 'one'). In French, a common noun is normally preceded by a definite or indefinite article. Polish is aspect-prominent, whereas French is tense-prominent. In terms of their phonemic and phonological systems, Polish not only has sounds that are inexistent in French, but also has pronounced lexical stress. French is described as having phrasal stress. What follows is a more detailed description of the features tested in our study and those that are relevant for our data analyses.

Written and Spoken Forms

Both French and Polish writing systems have their origins in Latin, although Polish differs from French particularly in its diacritic features: accents (ś, ć, ź, dź, ń, ó), dots (dż, ż), hooks (ą , ę) and the slanting bar (ł). In addition, some letters shared by both languages are pronounced differently, as shown in Table 3.1. As in French and English, all Polish

Table 3.1 The Polish alphabet with approximative corresponding French and English pronunciation

Letter	Pronunciation in French	Pronunciation in English
a	*a* in *mal*	*a* in *father*
ą	similar to *on* in *bon*	no English equivalent
b	*b* in ballon	*b* in *bad*
c	*ts* in *tsé-tsé*	*ts* in *wits*
ć	similar to *ci* in Italian *ciao*	similar to *ci* in Italian *ciao*
cz	similar to *tch* in *tchèque*	similar to Cz in *Czech*
d	*d* in *date*	*d* in *day*
dz	similar to *zz* in *pizza*	*dz* in *adze*
dż	similar to *dj* in *Djakarta*	similar to *dj* in *sledge*
dź	no French equivalent	no English equivalent
e	*e* in *quelle*	*e* in *pet*
ę	similar to *ain* in *main*	no English equivalent
f	*f* in *femme*	*f* in *fall*
g	*g* in *gamme*	*g* in *game*
h	no French equivalent	*h* in *hat*
ch	no French equivalent	generally same as Polish *h*
i	*i* in *site*	*ee* in *meet*
j	*hi* in *hier*	*y* in *yes*
k	*q* in *craque*	*k* in *make*
l	*l* in *Sylvain*	*ll* in *million*
ł	*w* in *wallon*	*w* in *water*
m	*m* in *Marie*	*m* in *man*

Table 3.1 (*Continued*)

Letter	*Pronunciation in French*	*Pronunciation in English*
n	*n* in *non*	*n* in *no*
ń	*gn* in *cogner*	similar to *ng* in *sing*
o	similar to *o* in *poste*	similar to *ou* in *bought*
ó	*ou* in *ouvrir*	similar to *oo* in *moose*
p	*p* in *pâle*	*p* in *pan*
r	rolled *r* as in Italian or Spanish *r*	rolled *r* as in Italian or Spanish *r*
rz	similar to *j* in *je*	similar to *s* in *pleasure*
s	*s* in *seize*	*s* in *sit*
ś	no French equivalent	no English equivalent
sz	*ch* in *chaussure*	*sh* in *shoe*
t	*t* in *table*	*t* in *take*
u	same as Polish *ó*	same as Polish *ó*
w	*v* in *vin*	*v* in *vine*
y	no French equivalent	similar to *i* in *pin*
z	*z* in *zoo*	*z* in *zoo*
ż	same as Polish *rz*	same as Polish *rz*
ź	no French equivalent	no English equivalent

letters have a capital equivalent, which are generally used to begin sentences and to designate a proper noun.

The Polish alphabet

Table 3.1 shows the Polish alphabet with approximative corresponding standard French and English sounds (some English examples are taken from Paryski, 1938). A single letter in Polish may have several phonetic representations depending on place and manner of articulation. We have attempted to provide French and English words containing phonemes that *resemble* the Polish phoneme in question. This said, we offer no equivalent for consonants written with the diacritical mark (with the exception of ń), that is ś, ć, ź, dź. Dalewska-Greń (2002) points out that the diacritical accent provokes a 'soft' consonant as opposed to its 'hard' cohort signalled by means of a diacritic dot (i.e. dż, ż) or a succedent *z* (i.e. *sz*, *cz*). It is the 'hard' version that is found in French and English. The purpose of Table 3.1 is to indicate the Polish letters, sounds and pronunciations that may prove difficult for native French readers, hearers and speakers. Phonetic symbols are not included in the chart as such a detailed phonetic analysis was judged unnecessary for this study.

Consonants

The most obvious difference between the written and spoken systems of French and Polish is found in the rich consonant system of Polish. Polish consists of eleven fricatives and six affricates, whereas French has four fricatives and no affricates. In addition, plosives and nasals differ in the two languages. Many of the consonant sounds may be familiar to French speakers, but they generally only appear in words borrowed in French from other languages and are, therefore, relatively rare in spoken French. In addition, certain consonant clusters produce nothing comparable in written or spoken French, such as *šć* in the word *cześć* 'hello', pronounced like the *sh-ch* of 'fresh cheese' (Pogonowski, 1997), or even better, the word *bzdurstwo* 'nonsense' with the vowel–consonant structure CCCVRCCCV ('R' = sonorant). The difficulty French learners of Polish may have perceiving and producing these sounds should be evident.

Vowels

Only 7 vowels are found in Polish as opposed to 16 in French. The principal vowels, [i], [u], [ɛ], [ɔ], [a], are pronounced almost identically in French and Polish. Polish has two nasal vowels, *ę* and *ą*, that resemble respectively the French sounds [ɛ̃] or [ẽ] (as in French 'main') and [ɔ̃] (as in French 'bon'), but the degree of nasalisation is weaker in Polish. The coexistence of two vowels in Polish often leads to a phonetic change of the first vowel. For example, the endings -*ia* and -*io* are pronounced as one syllable as in [ja] and [jo]. The two Polish semi-vowels, [j] and [w], are found in French as well. A third semi-vowel exists in French, [ɥ] (the 'ui' as in 'h<u>ui</u>le' and 'l<u>ui</u>'), but not in Polish (Gniadek, 1979). Despite the difference in the written form of vowels in French and Polish, all Polish vowels have a relatively close French equivalent, a fact that should aid our French learners of Polish. There is one Polish vowel element, however, that could potentially pose a problem for the pronunciation and perception of our French learners: the *i*/*y* distinction. According to Gniadek (1979), in spite of contrary opinions proposed by phoneticians, the Polish *y* [ɨ] cannot be treated as a variant of *i* [i], as attested by the following minimal pair combinations: *bić/być, pisk/pysk, mi/my, miła/myła, wić/wyć*. The [ɨ] is not found in the French vowel system.

Prosody

Prosody differs as well in the two languages. French is considered a 'final-stress, phrase-stress language' (Harris, 1987: 215) and is not considered to have distinctive lexical stress (cf. Lacheret-Dujour & Beaugendre, 2002). Polish, in contrast, shows word stress, which is generally placed on the penultimate syllable, with rare exceptions (cf. Bielec, 1998). Results concerning the effect of lexical stress on a French learner's ability to perceive and reproduce Polish words after limited input are reported in Chapter 7.

Syntax: The Simple Declarative Sentence

Basic constituent word order

As mentioned earlier, due to the highly inflected nature of its verbal system, Polish shows flexible word order. French is similar to English in that it has relatively fixed canonical word order. The French sentence 'Grand-maman a fait un gâteau' and its English translation 'Grandma baked a cake' have a variety of Polish equivalents, as illustrated in the following sentences:

1) a) *Babcia* (Nom) *upiekła* (past, 3p sg, f) *ciasto* (Acc) (SVO)
      Grandma   baked   cake
   b) *Babcia* (Nom) *ciasto* (Acc) *upiekła* (past, 3p sg, f) (SOV)
      Grandma   cake   baked
   c) *Ciasto* (Acc) *babcia* (Nom) *upiekła* (past, 3p sg, f) (OSV)
      cake   Grandma   baked
   d) *Ciasto* (Acc) *upiekła* (past, 3p sg, f) *babcia* (Nom) (OVS)
      cake   baked   Grandma
   e) *Upiekła* (past, 3p sg, f) *ciasto* (Acc) *babcia* (Nom) (VOS)
      baked   cake   Grandma
   f) *Upiekła* (past, 3p sg, f) *babcia* (Nom) *ciasto* (Acc) (VSO)
      baked   Grandma   cake

All possible basic constituent word orders are found in Polish (SVO, SOV, OSV, OVS, VOS, VSO) in either affirmative or interrogative sentences or both, although some orders are more frequent than others. What is important to highlight here is that communication contexts impose constraints on Polish word order (cf. Labocha, 1996). The 'neutral' order is SVO; however, in a sentence family such as the one presented in Example (1), the appropriate word order will depend on the discourse context. Other orders can be viewed as textual variants of SVO, each responding to a different question. Often word order depends on the intentional link with the previous utterance or on the need for emphasis. Word order in Polish is, therefore, pragmatically determined in most cases.

In standard French, canonical word order (SVO) is generally fixed: the subject (usually obligatory) precedes the verb, which precedes the direct object in most indicative affirmative sentences. It is important to note, however, that other orders exist as well (in addition to interrogative forms), although they remain quite infrequent in written French. Grevisse (1993: 580) provides an example where the direct object is placed in initial sentence position for emphasis: 'Le chapeau qu'a choisi mon mari ne lui va pas' (The hat that chose my husband him suits not = The hat my husband chose does not suit him). In similar fashion, Trévise (1986: 187) points to 'non-neutral' canonical word order present in today's spoken French. French speakers make use of word order to express contrast, emphasis and the difference, for example, between new and maintained information. To illustrate the importance of topicalisation in spoken French, she provides hypothetical variations of the 'neutral' SVO utterance 'Jean aime les pommes' (John likes apples), of which we present only a few below:

2) *Jean il aime les pommes* (John he likes apples)
3) *Il aime les pommes Jean* (he likes apples John)
4) *Jean il les aime les pommes* (John he them likes apples)
5) *Les pommes Jean il aime ça* (apples John he likes that)

What is important to keep in mind here is that although non-SVO orders occur in colloquial French, the participants of our study were educated in the French system and have learned that French is an SVO language. We predict, therefore, that they may be influenced by their understanding of SVO as the 'norm' and by the predominance of SVO in written French. It follows that the Polish system of flexible word order could pose problems for the French learner in both comprehension and production. Take for example the following sentence provided by Gniadek (1979: 68):

(6) *matkę   kocha   syn*
    Acc   Vf   Nom
    mother   loves   son (= The son loves his mother)

Example (6) clearly shows how the role of declensions becomes crucial for the French learner of Polish who is accustomed to relying on word order for information about agent and patient. We hypothesise that when French learners who have not yet acquired nominal morphology hear or read a Polish sentence out of context, they will adopt the canonical SVO word order strategy of French to process the sentence, potentially posing problems of comprehension. Such learners are predicted to incorrectly interpret the sentence in Example (6) as 'The mother loves her son'.

The implicit subject in Polish

We mentioned above that the personal pronoun subject in Polish is often left implicit; in French it is generally required (especially in written French). As person, number and gender are marked on verbs in Polish, in many contexts an explicit subject would only create redundancy unless it were used for the purpose of emphasis or contrast, as in 'not A, but B' (cf. Stone, 1987), or to introduce a new referent. It follows that a subject must be made explicit when it is in focus (cf. von Stutterheim & Klein, 1989). The Polish particle *to*,[1] for instance, represents a strong focus marker as can be seen in the following context in which the questioner is attempting to find out who visited Agnieszka.

7) *Kto   był   wczoraj   u   Agnieszki?   Paweł czy Marek?*
   Who was yesterday at   Agnieszka's? Paweł or   Marek?

a) *To   Paweł   był   wczoraj   u   Agnieszki.*
   It is Paweł (who) was   yesterday at   Agnieszka's

The following example shows an alternative response to the same question (by a third party 'I') with a strong focus marking as well, this time using a personal pronoun in nominative case:

b) *To   ja   byłam*
   It is   I (who)   was

If we test the response to our original question without *to*, the focus marking is weaker, but still present:

c) *Ja   byłam*
   (It is) I (who)   was

There is no difference in the French or English translations of (b) and (c) (It is I who was...), but for a Polish native speaker, (b) and (c) represent different degrees of contrast. Because Polish permits NP ellipsis, we can logically also say:

d) *Byłam*
   (I) was

However, (d) fails to respond to the question in Example (7), which, in the context of contrast, imposes a response with an explicit subject in focus. The first person singular morphological marking on the verb alone is insufficient to express this contrast. This is all to say that certain contexts in Polish require an explicit subject; 'neutral' contexts do not. It follows then that French learners of Polish need to acquire not only the various degrees of contrast, but also the structures needed to express and understand these degrees. The challenge in production will be knowing when to make the subject explicit; the challenge in comprehension will be processing information about person and number provided in a Polish verb (in the absence of an overt subject) when the French speaker normally finds it in the subject. If a learner has not yet acquired Polish verb conjugations or when the endings are not particularly salient, learners may have problems discerning the implicit subject of the utterance. The following example reveals the difficulty in distinguishing between three conjugations of the verb *mówić*, especially in spoken communication:

8) *mówię* [muviẽ]   *mówi* [muvi]   *mówią* [muviɔ̃]
   (I) speak   (she/he) speaks   (they) speak

In situations where the referent must be made explicit, learners of both languages are confronted with a fairly complex pronominal system. In Polish, personal pronouns also carry strong case inflexion. French, on the other hand, has lost much of its declensional system over time; however, a distinction between nominative, dative and accusative appears in the personal pronoun system, depending on person and number.

In the input of our study, utterances in which the subject is left implicit are the norm. In our syntactical analyses, we make use of the symbol Ø to indicate an implicit subject. We regularly place the symbol in pre-verbal position as it is considered the most neutral position for the subject in Polish.

Negation

The Polish system of negation is less complex than that of French. In an indicative Polish sentence, the negator *nie* precedes the verb or the auxiliary except when it negates a sentence constituent, in which case it precedes the constituent. Smoczyńska (1985: 607) provides us with two clear examples of this:

9) a)   *Jan*   *NIE*   *idzie*   *do*   *szkoły*
         John   not   goes   to   school
         (= John doesn't go to school.)
   b)   *NIE*   *Jan*   *idzie*   *do*   *szkoły*
         not   John   goes   to   school
         (= (It is) not John (who) goes to school (but)...)

In (a), the action 'go to school' is negated, whereas in (b), the constituent *Jan* is negated. It is also important to note that in Polish the direct object of a negated verb stands in the genitive case, as in the following example taken from Smoczyńska (1985: 608):

10) *Czytam ksiązk-ę*   *Nie czytam ksiązk-i*
    (I) read book (Acc)   no (I) read book (Gen)

French has one of the more controversial negation systems, as can be witnessed by the many and varied analyses proposed in the literature, as we will see in the next few pages. In the standard French construction '*ne* + V_f + *pas*', the finite verb is enclosed by two negative morphemes *ne...pas*, as in:

11) Il   ne   vient   pas   'He isn't coming'
    S   ne   V$_f$ Neg

In spoken French, the pre-verbal particle *ne* is often omitted, as in the following utterance:

12) /ʃ sepa/   j' sais pas   'I don't know'
                S V$_f$ Neg   (examples adapted from Harris, 1987: 231)

This phenomenon can be explained in terms of Jespersen's (1917) work on diachronic analysis of negation in English and other Indo-European languages. Jespersen revealed a cycle whereby languages initially make use of a pre-verbal negative marker to express sentential negation. The following stage is characterised by the coexistence of the old pre-verbal marker and a new more heavily stressed post-verbal marker. Eventually, when the post-verbal marker comes to be used and understood as the 'negative proper', the original pre-verbal negative particle ceases to exist. This appears to be happening in French.

It is also worth noting that the particle *pas*, but not *ne*, can be replaced by another negative item, such as *rien* (nothing), *personne* (no one) or *jamais* (never):

13) Il   ne   connaît   *rien*
    He   ne   knows   nothing

Again, *ne* can be dropped in spoken French, but *rien* cannot, indicating the role of the post-verbal negator (generally *pas*) as principal carrier of the negative value of the verbal predicate:

14) Il   connaît   *rien*
    He   knows   nothing

In sum, the existence of *ne* alone is insufficient for rendering an utterance negative (cf. Giuliano, 2004).

From a generativist perspective, Zanuttini (1997) distinguishes between 'pre-verbal negative markers' and 'post-verbal negative markers' relative to the *finite* verb in Romance languages. (Pre-verbal negative markers may also precede the non-finite verb, but this is not their defining property.) She also makes a distinction between two types of pre-verbal negative markers, those that, alone, can negate a clause because they are the head of NegP, and those that cannot because they are not the head of NegP. As *ne* is not the head of NegP, according to Zanuttini's analysis, it cannot negate a clause on its own.[2] This provides further support for the position that *pas* is the principal French negator. In this book, we will apply the dominant analysis of clausal French negation, according to which *pas* is considered the principal negating element (cf. Gaatone, 1971; Harris, 1987).

What is of particular interest to us in this study is the choice that learners make with regard to the position of the negator relative to the finite verb. In this analysis, we use the abbreviation 'Neg' to represent both the Polish particle *nie* and the French particle *pas*. In Polish, sentence negator *nie* is placed in front of the finite verb, whereas in French, *pas* is placed after it. If French learners of Polish rely on their NL system of negation, they would likely place the Polish negator in the inappropriate post-verbal position. Some studies suggest, however, that the learners may rely on strategies other than simply resorting to forms in their NL. It has been shown that beginning adult learners produce the Neg-V order regardless of their NL or TL (cf. Hyltenstam, 1977; Meisel, 1997; Pienemann & Håkansson, 1999). For learners of Polish, this order (Neg-V) coincides with the order *nie*-V in Polish, the order present in the input. We therefore have the case of a syntactic phenomenon that differs in the NL and TL. If the learner places the negator after the verb, we can assume an NL influence. If the learner places the negator in front of the verb, we can assume either a pragmatic strategy, such as scope (i.e. place the negator in front of that which it negates) or the influence of the TL input. In order to eliminate the second possibility, we set out to test this phenomenon before the input could come into play, a testing scenario that clearly reflects one of the principal advantages of first exposure studies. Group results are presented in Chapter 9.

Reflexive verbs (the Polish reflexive pronoun *się*)

Three pertinent differences can be found between the French and Polish systems of reflexive verbs:

(1) The distribution of verbs requiring the reflexive pronoun in French and in Polish does not always coincide. In Polish, for example, the verb *wstawać* '<u>se</u> lever' (to get up) is not accompanied by a reflexive pronoun, whereas its French equivalent is. Likewise, the French verb 'boire' (to drink, in the sense of 'to have a drink') is generally not accompanied by a reflexive pronoun, but in Polish it is (*napić się*).

(2) In Polish, the reflexive pronoun *się* does not inflect for person or number, whereas in French the pronoun does: 'je <u>me</u> lave' (I wash), 'tu <u>te</u> laves' (you wash), 'nous <u>nous</u> lavons' (we wash), etc.

(3) The position of the reflexive pronoun is more variable in Polish than in French. In Polish the reflexive pronoun is generally found in pre- and post-verbal positions, with the post-verbal position being the most frequent and neutral. In French, the pronoun is found in pre-verbal position in simple declarative utterances (only imperatives have post-verbals). Grevisse (1993: 1133) analyses the reflexive pronoun as being either the direct object as in 'Elle <u>se</u> lave soigneusement' (She washes <u>herself</u> carefully) or the indirect object as in 'Je <u>me</u> coupe une tranche de jambon' (I cut a slice of ham for

myself). This analysis is interesting for our study of word order. Where normally an SVO language like French finds O in post-verbal position, this is not the case with French reflexive pronouns. They precede the verb, revealing a strong exception in French to canonical word order. This point will prove important in our syntactical analyses of the data containing *się* (cf. Chapters 6 and 9).

Weist (1990: 1337) states the rules for *się* placement: (1) if *się* follows the verb, it typically does so directly; and (2) there is an option to place *się* after the first stressed elements in the sentence; in other words, it needs an initial stressed element to follow. Take a look, for example, at several utterances produced by a Polish child (adapted from Weist, 1990: 1337):

15) a) *kręci się*
   turns Refl (= It is turning)
   b) *co się kręci*
   what Refl turns (= What is turning?)
   c) *czemu kręc-a się kółecz-k-a?*[3]
   why turns Refl wheel (= Why are the little wheels turning?)

In (a), the pronoun *się* appears after the verb with no option of movement because it cannot appear in initial position (for reasons stated above); in (b), *co* provides the option of movement and this option is taken; in (c), *czemu* provides the option of movement, but this option is not taken.

The expression *nazywam się* 'I am called' or 'my name is' appeared frequently in the input of our study and most often in the order V-Refl. The constraint preventing *się* from appearing in initial position applies to this expression as well, as seen in the following examples:

16) a) *Ja nazywam się*
   Me (I) call Refl (= Me, I am called)
   b) *Ja się nazywam*
   Me (I) Refl call (= Me, I am called)
   c) *Ø nazywam się*
   Ø (I) call Refl (= I am called)
   d) **Ø się nazywam*
   Ø Refl (I) call

The option of movement is not taken in (a), but is taken in (b). In (c) there is no option, which explains why (d) is not possible in Polish. This analysis implies that in the case of a structure with an implicit subject, the reflexive pronoun does not have the option of movement into initial position. The order V-Refl is therefore obligatory in such cases.

What interests us most about the reflexive pronoun *się* is its placement by our French learners in a Polish sentence. Will they select the pre-verbal position (that of their L1), the post-verbal position (one of the options in the input) or that which is most frequent in the input? What strategies will the learner of Polish put into place when faced with a choice of position for the reflexive pronoun? Would producing V-Refl, for example, be the result of a TL input effect or a meta-word-order strategy (cf. 'The Competition Model' in the second section of Chapter 1)? Would producing Refl-V be the result of the transfer of a particular L1 structure? In our syntactic analyses of reflexive verbs, we use the abbreviation 'Refl' to indicate the Polish pronoun *się*. Chapters 6 and 9 include results and discussion of this point.

Morphology

The noun

As mentioned earlier, the presence or absence of inflexion represents an important difference between Polish and French. In Polish, the noun declines for case and number, depending on gender. Gender serves as the basis for the classification of nouns, the three genders being masculine, feminine and neuter. Polish has seven cases: nominative, genitive, dative, accusative, locative, instrumental and vocative, all of which are formed by means of a suffix. In French, the only regular inflexional nominal marker is the final -s, which clearly marks the plural in the written language, but which is normally not pronounced in spoken French. Certain forms such as *-aux* mark the plural (e.g. 'cheval'–'chevaux') and are perceivable in both written and spoken language. Generally speaking, in French, gender is not marked by the noun *per se*, but rather by the determiner. However, there are certain regular form-gender correspondences for nouns, such as *-tion* (f) or *-age* (m). According to Miodunka and Wróbel (1986), in Polish the stem is the carrier of word meaning, and the word ending marks the grammatical function of the word within the sentence. In French, the word stem also carries the meaning, but function is determined by a number of factors, chiefly word order.

Smoczyńska (1985) points out that learners of Polish need to be able not only to recognise the specific function of the case in any given context, but also to identify the case on a formal level. French expresses a certain number of these functions by means of a preposition; for instance, the equivalent of Polish '*siostra Marka*' is French 'la soeur *de* Marc' (the sister of Mark = Mark's sister). The challenge for the learner of Polish, therefore, is not only to recognise and select the appropriate word ending, but also to modify the phonological form of the stem when certain rules are imposed (Smoczyńska, 1985). Table 3.2, an adaptation of Miodunka and Wróbel's (1986: 60–63) and Zaremba's (2001: 17–26) tables, shows the complexity of Polish nominal morphology.

As a consequence of this complexity, French learners of Polish are faced with a particularly arduous task. In interaction, learners must

Table 3.2 Nominal declensions in Polish

Case	Masculine		Neuter		Feminine	
	sing	*pl*	*sing*	*pl*	*sing*	*pl*
Nom	Ø, -a	-i, -y, -e, -owie	-o, -e, -ę, -um	-a	-a, -i, Ø	-y, -i, -e, -i
Gen	-a, -u	-ów, -i, -y	-a	Ø, -i, -y, -ow	-y, -i	Ø, -i, -y
Dat	-owi, -u	-om	-u	-om	-e, -i, -y	-om
Acc	-a	-ów, -i, -y, -e	-o, -e, -ę, -um	-a	-ę, -a, -i, Ø	= Nom
Instr	-em	-ami	-em	-ami	-ą	-ami
Loc	-e, -u	-ach	-e, -u	-ach	= Dat	-ach
Voc	= Loc	= Nom	= Loc, Nom	= Nom	-i, -y, -o, -u	= Nom

Ø denotes *no* marking. Exceptions do not appear in this table. Some cases also mark for animate, inanimate, personal and non-personal; the forms are included in the table, but the distinctions are not shown

choose the appropriate word endings in order to accurately communicate
their thoughts, while at the same time discerning endings produced by
their interlocutors in order to understand. To illustrate the problem, let us
return to a Polish sentence we analysed earlier:

17)

a) | *Syn* | *kocha* | *matkę.* | *Matkę* | *kocha* | *syn.* |
|---|---|---|---|---|---|
| son | loves | mother | mother | loves | son |
| Nom | Vf | Acc | Acc | Vf | Nom |

(= The son loves his mother.)

b) | *Matka* | *kocha* | *syna.* | *Syna* | *kocha* | *matka.* |
|---|---|---|---|---|---|
| mother | loves | son | son | loves | mother |
| Nom | Vf | Acc | Acc | Vf | Nom |

(= The mother loves her son.)

(Gniadek, 1979: 68)

The obvious problem is how the learner will come to understand or
express *who* loves *whom*. To take this a step further, imagine a hypothetical utterance in the interlanguage of the learner:

c) | **Matka* | *kocha* | *syn.* |
|---|---|---|
| mother | loves | son |
| Nom | Vf | Nom |

(= either 'The son loves his mother.' or 'The mother loves her son.')

The use of a nominative form for both nouns ('mother' and 'son')
provokes the ungrammaticality of this sentence.

The Polish adjective agrees with its noun in number, gender and case,
but adjective morphology is less complex than nominal morphology in
that fewer endings are attested. The adjective normally precedes the
noun in Polish. The French adjective agrees with its noun in gender and
number and is generally placed after the noun.

The verb

In this study, we are most interested in verbal morphology as it
relates to person, number and gender[4] (i.e. typical verb conjugations).
Before we present this information, however, we need to briefly
introduce the Polish system of aspect as some verbs appeared in the
input of our study in either or both of their perfective or imperfective
aspectual forms.

Although linguists have not yet reached a consensus as to how to best
describe the systems of aspect in languages in general, we can safely say
that the French and Polish systems differ in the formation of the inflected
verb and in their aspectual distinctions. The two aspects in Polish, the
imperfective and the perfective, are generally expressed by morphological means (prefixes and occasionally suffixes) or by modifying the

verbal stem. Take for example the verb *czytać* 'to read' in its two aspectual forms:

18) *czytać* (imperfective)   *przeczytać* (perfective)

Based on the simple infinitive form, the Polish speaker is able to convey the meaning of a completed or not completed event merely by means of the presence or absence of a prefix. It sounds easy, but there are of course complications for the French learner.

The first challenge is on a formal level, that is, to learn all the affixes (there are approximately 15 prefixes and several suffixes) and how they combine with verbs. Any given verb can take the majority of these affixes, but the learner needs to know which affixes can be attached to which verbs. In addition, there are imperfective verbs in Polish that have no corresponding perfective form, such as *rozpaczać* 'to despair' and *znać się* 'to know each other'. Likewise, there are perfective verbs that have no corresponding imperfective forms, such as *zdołać* 'to manage to do something'. French learners need to learn these groupings. Karolak (1995) claims that in many cases a perfective verb stem expresses aspect without an aspectual affix and that when an affix with the same aspectual value is added, it is neutralised and becomes redundant. Learners need to be aware of this as well.

French learners of Polish above all need to understand the semantic distinction between imperfective and perfective. Generally the perfective aspect designates a punctual event, while the imperfective designates a continued action or a durative habitual state, as shown below by means of suffixes:

19)
(perfective)   X *krzyknął* = X cried out
(imperfective) X *krzyczał* = 1. X was crying out
                                2. X cried out repeatedly (in adapted situations), implying that he would continue.

(adapted from Karolak, 1995: 72)

According to Karolak, once French learners of Polish are aware of the biaspectual nature of Polish, their problems lie in the fact that they seek the perfective equivalent to an imperfective when such an equivalent often fails to exist.

One final point on Polish aspect which may prove helpful to the reader is that the future imperfective is formed by using the verb *być* 'to be', an auxiliary followed by an infinitive, as in *będę śpiewać* '(I) will be singing', where first person singular (I) is marked on *będę* (Gniadek, 1979: 99). Its perfective counterpart is *zaśpiewam* '(I) will sing' without *będę* and where first person singular is marked on the lexical verb *zaśpiewam*.

Our learners were confronted with problems of Polish aspect quite early in the study. During comprehension tasks in particular, they were asked to interpret both perfective and imperfective verb forms (cf. Chapter 8 for results). Two pairs appeared quite frequently in the input of our study: (1) *pić* 'to drink' (imperfective) and *napić się* 'to drink' (perfective); (2) *jeść* 'to eat' (imperfective) and *zjeść* 'to eat' (perfective). A contextual framework is generally necessary for an accurate translation of these verbs; however, as the acquisition of Polish aspect was not the focus of our study, adequate context was not always provided to our informants. Consequently, in our French and English glosses of these verbs, we specify the aspectual designation (perfective or imperfective) only in cases where such a distinction is necessary.

In terms of verb conjugations, in Polish the verb conjugates for person, number, tense, mode, voice and gender. In French, the verb receives markers indicating person, number, tense, mode and voice. Table 3.3 lists the present indicative conjugations of the three groups of Polish verbs. Stone (1987) identifies a fourth group that consists of only four verbs: *umieć* 'to be able', *śmieć* 'to dare', *wiedzieć* 'to know' and *jeść* 'to eat'. These do not appear in the table, but we mention them because several appeared in the input of our study.

Table 3.3 Verb conjugations in Polish (present tense)

	Group 1	*Group 2*	*Group 3a*	*Group 3b*
1p sg	pisz-ę	lub-ię	pad-am	rozumi-em
2p sg	pisz-esz	lub-isz	pad-asz	rozumi-esz
3p sg	pisz-e	lub-i	pad-a	rozumi-e
1p pl	pisz-emy	lub-imy	pad-amy	rozumi-emy
2p pl	pisz-ecie	lub-icie	pad-acie	rozumi-ecie
3p pl	pisz-ą	lub-ią	pad-ają	rozumi-eją

Adapted from Stone (1987: 361)

Although we predict that the form of Polish verbal endings will prove challenging to our Polish learners, particularly for production, it is NP ellipsis that will likely cause problems for comprehension.

Expressions Using *Po*

In the data and input of our study, the expressions *po polsku* 'in Polish', *po francusku* 'in French' and *po włosku* 'in Italian' were frequent. The French sentence 'je parle le polonais' (I speak Polish) (S-V-O) translates as *mówię po polsku* '(je) parle en polonais' ([I] speak in Polish) (S-V-PP/Adv). An extensive search through Polish grammar texts revealed no explicit explanation of the structure '*po* + language' (analysed here as PP/Adv). Bielec (1998), however, includes a list of contexts in which *po* is classified as a preposition. We will use this interpretation of *po* as well, following the example below adapted from Bielec (1998), *po* + loc (in a certain manner/language):

20) *nie mówię po polsku, tylko po angielsku*
    pas (je) parle en polonais, seulement en anglais
    'not (I) speak in Polish, only in English'

Bielec (1998) notes that expressions with the preposition *po* are often idiomatic. We predict that the learners of our study will perceive this structure as formulaic speech and will process it as they would a lexical item.

Summary and Hypotheses

As mentioned in Chapter 1, we in SLA seem to be in agreement that some sort of L1 'transfer' exists, but we differ with respect to the nature of this transfer and to the role attributed to it in the L2 acquisition process. Two prominent perspectives on L1 transfer can be identified in the SLA literature: (1) the L1 constitutes the foundation or the basis of L2 acquisition; and (2) the L1 plays an important role in L2 acquisition, but it is the L1 combined with other factors that constitutes the foundation or basis for L2 acquisition.

If we accept the existence of L1 transfer in some form or another, regardless of the degree of influence attributed to the L1 in this process, what might we expect from our French learners of Polish upon first exposure to Polish and within the few hours that follow? By analysing certain features of French and Polish and identifying recurring points of contrast as we have done in this section, we can anticipate certain initial hypotheses formulated by our beginning learners, that is, if they indeed resort to properties of their L1.

With regard to phonetic and phonological analysis, it is Polish consonants in particular that will pose problems for French speakers. As certain Polish sounds have no equivalent in French, a hypothesis of L1 transfer predicts that the French learner will have difficulty both perceiving (including segmenting the speech signal) and producing such sounds in Polish. It follows that problems of perception will affect the comprehension of Polish as well.

On the syntactic level, we predict that the order of basic sentence constituents will pose more problems for perception and comprehension than for production. In the absence of knowledge about the Polish morphological system, beginning French learners of Polish will rely on

SVO order to comprehend the pre-verbal and post-verbal noun phrases of an utterance. Hypotheses proposed within the Competition Model framework (Bates & MacWhinney, 1987) predict that the French learner will rely on word order to interpret the subject (agent) and the direct object (patient) of an utterance. In production, however, learners will choose the order of their L1 (SVO in this case), one of many orders attested in Polish. This follows the alternation hypothesis proposed by Jansen *et al.* (1981), according to which learners look for familiar patterns (i.e. L1 patterns) in the L2 input. The alternation hypothesis states that when faced with two preponderant orders in the TL, one of which is possible in the L1, learners will opt for the L1 order.

With regard to negation in Polish, as discussed earlier, the question of L1 transfer is a complex one. Clearly if we follow the predominant syntactic analysis that Polish is a Neg-V language and French is V-Neg (cf. 'Negation' in the third section of Chapter 3 and the second section of Chapter 9 for a detailed discussion of this feature), then a hypothesis of L1 transfer predicts that our learners will place the Polish negator in the inappropriate post-verbal position from the very beginning.

A hypothesis of L1 transfer, however, should not predict serious difficulty with the processing of the Polish reflexive pronoun *się*. Firstly, *się* does not decline for person and number as its French equivalent does. Secondly, it can be placed in either pre-verbal or post-verbal position. Applying the alternation hypothesis once again to the performance of our learners, this hypothesis predicts that they will choose the order Refl-V, that of their L1, an order that is also possible in Polish.

With regard to verbal morphology, the educated French speaker has learned that the French verb is generally marked for person and number. Due to the fact that these markers are not always perceptible, however, the French NS relies on word order and/or an overt subject to comprehend and communicate information about the agent of an utterance. A hypothesis of L1 transfer would then predict that French NSs will apply such a reliance strategy when performing a task in Polish.

But what if there is no overt subject, as is often the case in Polish utterances? The Polish implicit subject, as with flexible Polish word order, is predicted to pose more problems for perception and compre-hension than for production. In the absence of knowledge about Polish verbal morphology, what strategies will our learners use to understand a Polish utterance that is void of an explicit subject? If they rely on their L1, they will use word order to interpret who does what, the first noun phrase acting as the agent. If they attempt to identify the agent by analysing the context of the utterance, they will rely on lexical items already acquired or on those in which the *signifiant* is similar to its equivalent in French. Obviously the latter of these two strategies will only be effective if the *signifié* is the same in both languages.

Conclusion

To conclude this chapter, we have closely examined the features of French and Polish that are pertinent to our study in order to formulate hypotheses about L1 transfer in particular. We return to these hypotheses in relevant sections throughout the book, providing a general discussion, in light of our results, in Chapter 10. Our question now is the following: how do we go about testing our participants if we want to know under what conditions and to what extent French learners of Polish rely on their L1 (or on other factors) to accomplish a task in Polish? The following chapter provides details of our research methodology, and throughout the book we make recommendations as to how this methodology might be ameliorated or expanded.

Notes

1. *to* also has the function of demonstrative pronoun (*ten/ta/to*).
2. Pollock (1989) and others (Rowlett, 1993; Rule & Marsden, 2006) analyse *ne* as being head of NegP.
3. It is important to note here that this example, taken from the production data of a child, reflects incorrect case markings. The correct sentence in Polish would be *Czemu kręci się kółeczko?*
4. Gender in Polish appears on past tense, but not present tense verbs.

Chapter 4
Research Methodology

This chapter provides a detailed description of our research methodo-logy. To the extent that limited research has been conducted on the early stages of L2 acquisition, as shown in Chapter 2, identifying appropriate tasks to elicit useful data was one of our foremost challenges. As this is a study of how L2 learners work on the linguistic input they receive, we were concerned not only with collecting data from the participants of the study, but also from the Polish instructor. In other words, we developed techniques to compare the performance of the learners in the TL with the quantity and quality of TL input received. Although we are limited in the amount of raw data we can include here due to space constraints, the original tests administered to our participants that are discussed in this book appear in the appendices. For more detailed information regarding the methodology of the study, consult Volume II of Rast (2003).

Participants

The primary data collection for this study was conducted at the Université Paris VIII in Saint-Denis, France, following a pilot study two years prior (cf. Rast, 1998). The learners were French native speakers who attended a specially designed Polish course, in which only students with absolutely no knowledge of the Polish language were permitted to enrol. Data were also collected from groups of native French speakers who did not participate in the Polish course and for whom one task in Polish represented their first exposure to the Polish language.

A total of 127 informants, constituting three distinct groups, partici-pated in the study:

(1) French learners of Polish attending the Polish course ($n = 19$) – a subgroup of this group consisted of 8 monolingual French learn-ers who attended all class sessions.
(2) French informants for whom the only Polish input was that provided during the language task ($n = 96$) – they are referred to as our 'first exposure' group.
(3) Native Polish speakers who served as a control group ($n = 12$).

No informants in the first two groups had had contact with Polish at the onset of the study.

The first group, the learners of Polish, comprised students in the *French as a Second Language* programme at the Université Paris VIII, training to become language instructors. The Polish course fulfilled a requirement of this programme, a component of a course entitled *Learning and Self-Observation*, in which participants study an unknown language and observe their own second language acquisition process.

Table 4.1 presents the language profile of our learners[1] and their attendance record.

Table 4.1 Language profile of learners and their class attendance

Informants	Other L2s (1-5)[a]	Class session absence[b]	Subgroups[c]
Adib	En-3	3,5,6	B (Ar/Be)
Alice	Por-4, Sp-3, En-2	6	M (Sp/Por)
Ana	En-2	3	B (Sp/Por)
Carole	En-4, Sp-2.5, Ch-1	4,6	M (En)
Cécile	Ge-3, En-2, *Ru-1*	6	M (*Ru*)
Celia	It-4, En-3, *Ru-2*	*present*	B (Sp/Por/*Ru*)
Dalia	En-4, Sp-3, Ge-1, Ar-1	*present*	*M (En)*
Emma	En-3/4, Ge-1.5, Gr-.5	*present*	*M (En)*
Eva	En-4, Hi-3, *Ru-2*	4	M (*Ru*)
Gilles	En-5	*present*	*M (En)*
Julie	En-4, Sp-2, Cr-2, FSL-2	*present*	*M (En)*
Luc	En-2	*present*	*M (En)*
Maria	Sp-4/5, En-2/3	*present*	B (Sp/Por)
Nadine	En-3.5, Sp-2.5	*present*	*M (En)*
Romain	Sp-4.5, En-3.5	3-6	M (Sp/Por)
Sabine	Ge-4, En-2, Ka-1	*present*	*M (Ge)*
Samia	En-1	*present*	B (Ar/Be)
Sandra	Ge-4, En-3	*present*	*M (Ge)*
Sonia	Por-4, Sp-3, En-3	4	M (Sp/Por)

[a]Other L2s – language rating on self-evaluation from 1 to 5, where 1 is little knowledge and 5 is fluent: (En) English, (Ge) German, (Sp) Spanish, (Ar) Arabic, (Por) Portuguese, (Ka) Kabyle, (Ch) Chinese, (Gr) Greek, (It) Italian, (FSL) French Sign Language, (Hi) Hindi, (Cr) Creole, (*Ru*) Russian
[b]Attendance: the class session not attended (1–6), *present* = no absences
[c]Information about native languages: (M) monolingual, (*M*) monolingual who attended all 6 Polish classes, (B) bilingual, (Ar) Arabic, (Be) Berber, (Sp) Spanish, (Por) Portuguese

Learners who attended all class sessions are identified as *'present'* in Table 4.1. Biographical data were collected by means of a questionnaire intended to identify the native and dominant language(s) of the learners, their previous knowledge of other non-native languages and their approximate proficiency levels in the respective languages according to their own self-evaluation. The group was first divided into two subgroups: monolinguals (M) and bilinguals (B). 'Monolinguals' were those who used only French on a daily basis, whereas 'bilinguals' used French and at least one other language regularly. Learners were also categorised by the knowledge they had of other L2s. The language subgroups that appear in Table 4.1 take into account the learners' proficiency in their L2s according to their self-evaluations and whether or not a learner had had exposure to another Slavic language (Russian in this case). A detailed list appears below:

> M(En) – 'monolingual' with an advanced level of L2 English[2]
> M(Ge) – 'monolingual' with an advanced level of L2 German
> M(Sp/Por) – 'monolingual' with an advanced level of L2 Spanish or Portuguese
> M/B(*Ru*) – 'monolingual' or 'bilingual' with knowledge of L2 Russian
> B(Ar/Be) – 'bilingual', French–Arabic and/or Berber
> B(Sp/Por) – 'bilingual', French–Spanish and/or Portuguese

This subdivision will allow us to investigate the influence of other L2s on our learners' acquisition of an L3 (cf. Chapter 5 for a discussion of the data in light of L3 acquisition research).

Attendance is obviously crucial in a longitudinal study of input processing in which the input itself is highly controlled. We analysed certain aspects of the data from all 19 learners, both monolinguals and bilinguals, who attended the first class session in Polish. However, after this first session, if learners missed a class or even part of a class, their data were excluded from subsequent analyses. At the end of the data collection period, that is after six class sessions, eight participants in the M(En) or M(Ge) subgroups had been present at all sessions. They had therefore all been exposed to the Polish input provided by the instructor in its entirety and had taken part in all the language tasks. In the longitudinal analyses of this study, these eight learners make up the core group of monolingual French learners who received 8 hours of Polish input.

The group of 'first exposure' informants comprised 96 monolingual French informants who resembled the learners of Polish with regard to gender, age, language background and other sociobiographical parameters.[3] As with our group of learners, they had no knowledge of Polish at the time of the study. Members of this group are identifiable in the analyses by their initials, in contrast to our learners to whom we assigned first name pseudonyms. Tasks administered to these informants were designed to collect data at the moment of first exposure to the TL (Polish). For this reason, each informant of the 'first exposure' group performed only one task in Polish. Having completed the task, the informant was considered as having been 'exposed' to the Polish language, and was therefore no longer eligible to perform another 'first exposure' task.

The final group of informants, a control group, included 12 native Polish speakers who had no knowledge of French.[4] The purpose of having a control group was to collect data that could confirm our hypotheses about Polish native speaker preferences with regard to word order in Polish.

All of our participants, with the exception of the control group, came to this project with a high level of metalinguistic knowledge, capable of using this knowledge to describe their experience in language learning and testing. They knew the concepts and terminology to speak about the agent, action and patient, and to assign grammatical functions such as subject, verb, object. They were French university students who shared French as their NL and were raised in the French educational system in which they learned *about* French during their many years of French schooling. They were taught, for example, that French is SVO in spite of the fact that there are many pragmatic word order possibilities in colloquial French (cf. Trévise, 1986). This academic *norm* is important for the interpretation of our results presented in the following chapters of this book.

The L2 Input

Monitoring the input

In order for a study of input processing in the early stages of SLA to provide contributive results, the input must be meticulously controlled. For this reason, the Polish instructor wore a microphone, and all class sessions were recorded in their entirety. A native Polish speaker transcribed the instructor's productions to assure a precise and authentic transcription of the input for analysis. The verbal input of the first class session was analysed in detail using the CHILDES programs (*The Child Language Data Exchange System*, MacWhinney, 2000).

Written input appeared in two forms: on the blackboard and/or in photocopied handouts provided by the instructor. All Polish written on the board was recorded, and all photocopies were classified as to the moment, relative to class session and testing, when the instructor handed them out. With respect to the objectives of this study, at times, we recognised a need to differentiate between the written and oral input, whereas at others, it was judged less crucial. For instance, when speaking of overall input received by the learners in terms of 'hours' of instruction, both types of input are included. When speaking of 'frequency' of a word in the input, however, we are referring to *oral* input only. We will call attention to specific written input in our discussion of results when relevant.

We remind the reader that 'input' in this study refers to the Polish that the learners heard and/or read. We were initially interested in recording the learners' verbal utterances in addition to those of the instructor; however, problems with the physical nature of the classroom and equipment limitations rendered potential recordings unreliable. For this reason, transcriptions of the input include the instructor's productions only. This said, during the data collection period, the instructor made a concerted effort to repeat learners' interventions, in a sense indirectly recording them and ensuring that all participants could benefit from this input. It follows then that when we calculated numbers of tokens of a form in the input, this calculation was based only on the instructor's productions and not on those of the learners. In sum, we chose to concentrate on what was measurably common in the input to all learners.[5]

To insure that the input learners received remained strictly monitored, the Polish instructor asked students not to consult dictionaries, grammar books or any outside input for the duration of the data collection period. She gave precise homework assignments based on photocopied materials with strict instructions and time limitations. As the learners were all enrolled in a programme for language teachers, they were intrigued by the scientific aspect of the course, which, to our knowledge, encouraged them to respect the imposed conditions.

In addition to studying an unknown language for their course *Learning and Self-Observation*, the students were also required to keep a journal. These provided us with useful information about learners' motivation, physical and psychological states, hypotheses, strategies, reactions to various aspects of the course and reflections on their own language learning. We will include excerpts of these journals when deemed relevant to empirical findings.

It is important to note here that the input to which the learners were exposed did not consist of 'pure' Polish, but rather of a slightly manipulated form of Polish. Occasional sentences were judged by native Polish speakers as grammatically or pragmatically unacceptable. As one of our Polish transcribers remarked, 'This is an odd kind of Polish'. The manipulations concerned the area of syntax in particular. As mentioned earlier, Polish is quite flexible when it comes to word order, and all configurations of the principal sentence constituents (S,V,O) are possible. It is not, however, as flexible as it looks on the surface. Precise contexts impose the use of certain word orders. The instructor of the Polish course identified necessary contexts for each of the basic constituent orders and tried to make use of these in class. Obviously this proved a formidable task within the first hours of exposure to the language and explains why she occasionally produced sentences that are considered inappropriate by native Polish speakers. Throughout this book, we describe the nature of the input in detail within the context of our interpretations of specific data collected.

The Polish instruction

The Polish instructor was a native Polish speaker with an excellent command of French, trained in the teaching and acquisition of language. To create an environment that simulated as closely as possible that of non-guided learners, the Polish instructor used the communicative approach in the classroom and avoided using metalanguage. The class met once a week for two and a half hour sessions over a period of 15 weeks. The present study is concerned with the first six class sessions only. These correspond to 8 hours of total input, not including testing time. Once the data collection period had ended, the Polish classes continued without the input constraints. When we make mention of the number of hours of input to which learners have been exposed, we use the European coding for hours (i.e. 1h00 refers to one hour, 2h00 to two hours, 3h30 to three and a half hours and so forth).

As an example of how classes were conducted, the first session began with 'introductions'. The instructor introduced herself and then introduced a female colleague present in the classroom, juxtaposing the Polish first and third person singular subject pronouns and verb forms. The choice of this theme was a deliberate one, intended to incite the use of names, nationalities, cities and countries of origin or residence, professions and languages spoken. We had established a list of verbs to appear in the input and had identified the theme of 'introductions' as one that would naturally elicit these verbs. Verbs such as *mieszkać* 'to live', *pochodzić* 'to come from', *mówić* 'to speak', *pracować* 'to work' and *lubić* 'to like' were chosen to study word order. The transitive verb *lubić*, for instance, allowed us to put cues of word order and nominal morphology in competition with each other in simple NVN or NNV sentences (e.g. 'Mark likes ice cream' versus 'Ice cream likes Mark') (cf. Bates & MacWhinney, 1987). The verb *nazywać się* 'to be called' (as in 'She is called Ewa' or 'Her name is Ewa') allowed us to observe the acquisition of the reflexive pronoun *się*. Following the introductions of herself and her colleague, the instructor then compared the information about herself and her colleague, as in the following excerpt taken from the transcription of the first class session:

1) *jest Amerykanką.*
   '(she) is American.'

2) *i pochodzi ze Stanów Zjednoczonych.*
'and (she) comes from the United States.'
3) *ja jestem Polką.*
'I am Polish.'
4) *i pochodzę z Polski.*
'and (I) come from Poland.'

This comparison provided the context necessary to use word orders other than SVO and to use an explicit contrastive subject, as in utterance (3). The instructor then introduced a male colleague (also present in class), implicitly introducing Polish gender. She made more comparisons and concluded with a general summary about the three people she had just introduced: herself and her two colleagues.

The instructor then encouraged the students to participate by asking them questions about the three people previously introduced, as shown in the following examples ('Refl' denotes the Polish reflexive pronoun *się*):

5) *jak nazywa się moja koleżanka?*
'how is called Refl my colleague?' (= What is my colleague's name?)
6) *gdzie mieszka?*
'where (she) lives?' (= Where does she live?)

The questions were asked in such a way that learners could reply with one-word responses, keeping the potential anxiety level low. The instructor also asked the learners questions about themselves, again expecting one-word responses only. Each response was immediately repeated by the instructor. If a learner was unable to respond, the instructor prompted with a cue. If this was insufficient, the instructor provided the correct answer. No grammatical or metalinguistic explanations were given, with the exception of a few minutes spent on the pronunciation of Polish. Following this question–answer period, she handed out a written text containing example questions, such as *Jak się nazywasz?* 'What is your name?', and three sample introductions: one of herself (first person), of her female colleague (third person, feminine) and of her male colleague (third person, masculine). To aid the learners with pronunciation, she also handed out a list of Polish letters (accompanied by phonetic symbols) for which the sounds differ from the corresponding French sounds and she then modelled the sounds. Finally, she gave the learners 10 minutes to interview a fellow student and to prepare an introduction of this person to the class using the written models. After the preparation period, learners introduced each other in Polish.

We should also mention here that in our data analyses references are occasionally made to a segment of the Charlie Chaplin film *Modern Times*. During the fourth Polish class, learners listened to and read a dialogue about four friends discussing various topics over dinner in which one of the characters describes a scene from *Modern Times*. Learners reviewed the vocabulary in the subsequent class in preparation for tests designed to investigate basic constituent word order preference. Although references to the film appear in these tests, the learners did not actually view the segment from *Modern Times* until *after* the 8-hour experimental period.

Transcription of the verbal input

The verbal input from the first six Polish class sessions, a total of 8 hours, was thoroughly transcribed by a native Polish speaker using the programs and format of the CHILDES project (MacWhinney, 2000). The advantage of this system for a detailed analysis of the input is two-fold: firstly, it provides standardised conventions, such as those found in CHAT, for transcription and coding; secondly, programs like CLAN assist in analysing and describing with quality precision the language to which learners are exposed.

We chose to segment the instructor's productions into phrases and clauses with a view to analysing syntax at the level of the basic sentence constituents for which we created a syntactic tier (%syn). We decided against developing a morphological tier because the input analysis concerns only NS data (the instructor), not learner data. Instead of coding for morphology, we used CLAN to calculate frequencies of whole words (stem and affixes included). For instance, we were given the number of tokens in the input of the nominative/accusative form *język* 'language' and its genitive counterpart *języka*. In this way, we could comment on learners' performance relative to the frequency of one or both of these forms in the input. What follows is a short excerpt of the syntactically analysed oral input from the first Polish lesson. The symbol Ø denotes an implicit subject.

*TEA: *jestem Polką.*
%fre: (je) suis polonaise. '(I) am Polish'
%syn: < Ø Cop C >.
*TEA: *i pochodzę z Polski.*
%fre: et (je) viens de Pologne. 'and come from Poland'
%syn: < Conj Ø V PP/Adv >.
*TEA: *ale mieszkam w Paryżu we Francji.*
%fre: mais (je) habite à Paris en France. 'but (I) live in Paris in France'
%syn: < Conj Ø V PP/Adv PP/Adv >.
*TEA: *lubię Paryż.*
%fre: (je) aime Paris. '(I) like Paris'
%syn: < Ø V O >.
*TEA: *wykładowcą jestem.*

%fre: professeur (je) suis. 'professor (I) am'
%syn: < C Ø Cop > .

Data Collection Procedures

Data collected from our French learners of Polish

Our informants performed a wide variety of tests, resulting in a battery
of tests that contain data relevant to the initial processing of foreign
language input. Some of the data collected have not yet been analysed or
were not exploitable. The current presentation and description of tests
administered to our participants therefore includes only those tests that
are discussed in this book. The list below itemises the tests taken by
participants who attended the Polish course (i.e. the 'learners'):

- word order test (Appendix 4),
- grammaticality judgement test (Appendix 5),
- written translation of the grammaticality judgement test (Appendix 5),
- oral sentence translation test (Appendix 3) and
- sentence repetition test (Appendix 2).

Learners took the first four tests (word order, grammaticality judgement, and written and oral translation tests) at three different periods,
after a cumulative input of 1h30, 3h30 and 7h00. Different versions of the
tests were administered at each period. The form of these tests remained
the same throughout the period of data collection, but questions were
modified according to the new input received. In contrast, we designed
only one version of the sentence repetition test. Table 4.2 summarises
time intervals for testing relative to time of input exposure. The 'period
of exposure' (henceforth 'period') corresponds to the cumulative hours of
instruction the learners had received at any given time. Note that 'period'
is therefore equal to 'cumulative input'.

It is important to highlight here the unique challenge for both learners
and researchers when involved in a study of early L2 acquisition. We
knew that the learners could easily lose their motivation if we did not
proceed with caution. As one of our learners, Sandra, described in her
journal, '. . . the class is quite exhausting because it requires constant
attention. In addition, the quantity of vocabulary items seems impress-
ive. This is why I felt a bit unmotivated before the third class. I was afraid
of not being able to keep up with the pace throughout the semester.' The
testing undoubtedly added to this pressure. Our tests, therefore, needed
to be economical. There were times when we wished to add more items
to enrich our data, but we ultimately decided that beyond a certain
number of items we would be asking too much of our learners and
would risk taking too much time away from learning and exposure. Data

Table 4.2 Tests administered to our learners relative to hours of instruction

Class session	Input received	Cumulative input	Period of exposure	Tests taken
1	1h30	1h30	1h30	Word order, grammaticality judgements, written translation, oral sentence translation
2	1h30	3h00	Not relevant	No relevant testing
3a	0h30	3h30	3h30	Word order, grammaticality judgements, written translation, oral sentence translation
3b	0h30	4h00	4h00	Sentence repetition
4	1h45	5h45	Not relevant	No relevant testing
5	1h15	7h00	7h00	Word order, grammaticality judgements, written translation, oral sentence translation
6	1h00	8h00	8h00	Sentence repetition

presented in the following chapters are therefore limited in terms of quantity of test items and cannot be used to generalise. They do, however, reveal certain tendencies and provide a solid methodological launching pad for future studies of this kind. It goes without saying that replication studies are welcome.

To return to the description of our tests, the word order tests involved reading a sentence that provided context and then putting the scrambled words of the subsequent sentence in order. Data collected from these tests reflected the learners' choice of word order and, therefore, allowed us to analyse their preferences relative to factors such as input, L1, other L2s and individual strategies.

The grammaticality judgement tests were designed for learners to make judgements within the context of a short paragraph. The texts consisted of anecdotes incorporating vocabulary used in previous Polish classes. The learners were asked to read the text, find the ungrammatical forms and correct them. Our objective was to observe learners' perception of and sensibility to morphological markers, diverse constituent word orders and implicit versus explicit subjects.

The written translation tests required informants to translate the Polish text of the grammaticality judgement tests into French. This allowed us to control for our learners' comprehension of the written vocabulary used in the grammaticality judgement series.[6]

During the oral translation tests, learners listened to sentences in Polish and translated them into written French. Each sentence was repeated once. After only 1h30 of Polish input, this proved to be a difficult task; however, it provided us with interesting data as to what elements of the input learners perceived and comprehended (or failed to perceive and comprehend).

During the sentence repetition test, learners listened to 20 Polish sentences comprising between 3 and 12 words each, recorded by their Polish instructor (the 3-word sentences were eliminated in the final analysis, resulting in a total of 17 sentences). Sentences were only spoken once, and learners were asked to repeat them as best they could. This task was used to determine how a learner perceives and memorises, in the short term, an expression in the TL. The data collected from the Polish sentence repetitions allowed us to examine the relevance of certain factors to the learners' ability to correctly repeat a word; factors such as the quantity (in hours) of TL input, word length, word stress, phonemic distance relative to French, lexical transparency relative to French, the position of the word in a sentence and the frequency of the word in the input.

Data collected from 'first exposure' informants

As mentioned earlier, the 'first exposure' groups comprised the participants of our study who were unfamiliar with Polish and who did *not* take the Polish course. They differ from our learner group in that they were not learners of Polish; they were merely exposed to Polish for the duration of one first exposure task only. The following is a list of tests taken by groups of 'first exposure' informants:

- sentence repetition test (Appendix 2),
- oral word translation test (Appendix 1) and
- written word translation test (Appendix 1)

The same sentence repetition test taken at two distinct periods by our learners was also administered to a group of 'first exposure' informants. This allowed us to compare participants' ability to repeat Polish sentences correctly at three periods: Period 0 ('first exposure' group), Period 4h00 (the learners of Polish after 4 hours of instruction) and Period 8h00 (the learners of Polish after 8 hours of instruction).

The oral and written word translation tests were designed for two reasons: (1) to assign a transparency score to words in the sentence repetition test (cf. 'Hypotheses' in the first section of Chapter 7 for calculating transparency scores); and (2) to investigate how learners process isolated words in an unfamiliar language. In the written version of the test, informants *read* 119 Polish words and were asked to translate what they thought they understood into written French. In the oral version, another group of informants was asked to *listen* to the same 119 words and were also asked to translate what they thought they understood into written French. In the oral version, the words were recorded by a native Polish speaker and a 3-second period was left between each spoken word for the informants to respond. The words were identical in both tests and were presented in the same order. Those that shared the same stem but not the same word ending were distanced from each other by at least 10 words. The words were selected from the first ten minutes of the first session of our Polish course (as described in 'The Polish instruction' in the second section of this chapter). These data provide information about the knowledge learners initially bring to the L2 acquisition process.

Data collected from the Polish native speaker control group

Our Polish NS group served to confirm our hypotheses about NS preferences regarding word order in Polish. Two series of tests taken by our learners were also administered to this group: the word order tests and the grammaticality judgement tests. Both series of tests provided context and allowed our NSs to formulate sentences using specific basic constituent word orders based on the context. We will report results of this data collection when relevant.

Data Analysis and Interpretation

The data of our study will be presented in the following chapters of this book. Before we move on, however, one important methodological point needs highlighting, that of 'task'. The tasks used in this study differed not only in terms of whether they were written or oral, but also in terms of the specific language activity being observed. Frauenfelder and Porquier (1980) rightly point out that it is as difficult to tease out the different language activities involved when performing a given task as it is to identify which tasks are capable of eliciting a specific language activity. A task designed to elicit production, for example, could require comprehension and vice versa. In the study presented here, we will examine in detail elements of speech perception, speech comprehension and grammatical analysis. We emphasise, however, that our categorisation of language activities when analysing learner data does not by any means imply that these processes are independent of each other. On the contrary, the interaction between these linguistic activities is not only evident, but also crucial for language acquisition and for overall communication. This categorisation, however, helps us describe hypotheses formulated by learners, as well as strategies they use when faced with a given task in the TL.

As an indication of how we interpreted our data, we now complete this chapter with a brief description of the language activities discussed in this book and with questions of interest that pertain to a specific activity.

Speech perception

We can assume that learners who attempt to process an unknown TL are faced with what Klein (1986) refers to as the 'problem of analysis', that is, the problem of segmenting the stream of acoustic signals into constituent units. Carroll (2001, 2006) claims that L1-specific pre-lexical processing procedures are applied when analysing the speech signal. Her prediction is that when segmenting the speech signal of an unknown language, listeners will create initial analyses of sound units based on L1 phonetic and phonological knowledge, which will constitute the basis for storing phonetic and phonological information in memory. A logical methodological question is then: how do we capture the moment of 'perception', that is the moment when the learner 'perceives' the TL item and has not yet necessarily comprehended it? And how do we come to understand the functioning of this process? As Carroll (2006) suggests, we need empirical data on pre-lexical speech processing to discover the difference between the case scenario in which learners exposed to a new TL for the first time hear incomprehensible noise that they appear to be unable to process, and the scenario in which the same such learners hear recognisable sounds that they somehow manage to reproduce. Our discussion of these questions will continue in further detail in Chapters 5 and 7.

Comprehension

Lambert and Voutsinas (2001) identify two distinct perspectives in current L2 speech comprehension research: (1) an interactionist approach that investigates comprehension within the context of communication and interaction (cf. Bremer *et al.*, 1996; Færch & Kasper, 1986; Matthey, 1996); and (2) a cognitivist approach that seeks to describe the modes of information processing (cf. Bates & MacWhinney, 1987; Gaonac'h, 1990; Lambert, 1994a; Roberts, 2007). Although we recognise the former as being crucial to understanding L2 acquisition processes, the focus of this study is the latter.

Gaonac'h (1990), working within the latter of the two perspectives, identifies processes subsumed under the category of language comprehension, such as activating the *signifiant*, making inferences, searching memory, activating schemas and constructing representations linked to global meaning. These processes reflect numerous characteristics and notions, two of which interest us here: processing 'level' and automatisation. With regard to the former, research in L2 comprehension often makes use of the bottom-up and top-down distinction, the former constituting phonemic and graphemic processes and the latter the textual and contextual processing. Regarding automatisation, in a summary of research conducted on automatisation processes, Gaonac'h explains that cognitive activities assume the functioning of numerous operations. Some of these require a high level of attention on the part of the informant, while others can be performed automatically. This automatisation should facilitate comprehension, rendering the process more efficient and economical. It follows then that executing a task in the TL could be more or less costly on a cognitive level. In situations of rapid speech, Lambert and Voutsinas (2001) claim that the success of processing activities depends on the automatisation of these activities, or as Levelt (1989) puts it, the 'high level' versus 'low level' processing. In fact, the efficiency of L2 processing could depend on the degree of automatisation of the operations and on the flexibility of the strategies put into place (i.e. top-down and bottom-up), both of which influence the cognitive cost of the task.

Language recognition studies investigate both perception and comprehension. In Zwitserlood's (1989) terms, three functions are attributed to the general process of word recognition: access, selection and integration. In order to interpret a message transmitted by means of a spoken utterance, the listener must identify the words (or forms) of the utterance and be able to access the meaning of these words. To do this, the sensory input is linked to the representations of the mental lexicon. The semantic and syntactic characteristics of stored words in the mental lexicon serve as fundamental elements for the construction of a structural and semantic interpretation of the utterance. It follows that a pertinent question for our study of speech comprehension is, in fact, the second case scenario envisaged by Carroll (2006) above: how does the L2 listener faced with a new TL manage to 'identify' words or forms as something that could be recognisable?

Research on comprehension at the *initial* stages of L2 acquisition is needed. In our analyses of L2 comprehension upon first contact and in the hours that follow (cf. Chapters 5 and 8), we will provide insight into how learners comprehend elements of an unknown language, and we will return to the question of 'cognitive', or rather, 'processing', cost and its influence on the ability of the learner to accomplish the task at hand.

Grammatical analysis

The European Science Foundation research team (cf. Perdue, 1993), who focused predominantly on production, provided us with important information about syntactic structures at the beginning of L2 acquisition. Klein and Perdue (1992) identify a relatively stable system, referred to as the 'basic variety', in which organisational principles of a semantic and pragmatic nature can be observed. They also present data from their 'beginner' group of informants. Examination of the profiles of these informants reveals that all of them had already been exposed to a significant amount of input before the onset of data collection and that they had already lived in the TL country for anywhere from one month to one year. One informant had studied the TL formally in a course for refugees, while another had worked in the host country for almost a year. Although these informants were already well beyond the level of acquisition we are interested in here, the data of these learners provide evidence for a 'pre-basic variety', the first early systematic stage SLA research has, as of yet, been able to identify (cf. also Bernini, 1995; Giuliano, 2004). These are tightly structured systems in terms of topic-focus and are for the most part independent of the specificities of the NL or the TL.

Bernini (1995), who studied four learners of Italian at what he calls the 'initial' state of L2 acquisition, identifies pragmatic principles as the foundation for the pre-basic variety. According to Bernini, a learner who has minimal knowledge of the TL is forced to create (or access) linguistic strategies to communicate with an interlocutor. Bernini's claim is based on analysis of oral production data, whereas our study focuses rather on grammatical analysis in the written form, examining the hypothesis that the adult learner will look for a way to resolve syntactic problems and to analyse grammatical structures from the very first moment of contact with the TL. The adult is capable of this metalinguistic activity, and the knowledge base allowing it is claimed to be either L1 (cf. Schwartz & Sprouse, 1996) or language-neutral information structure (cf. Klein & Perdue, 1992). Analysis of data collected in the first stages of L2 acquisition should shed light on these claims.

In a study such as ours on the first hours of L2 acquisition, models of production are difficult to apply. We collected limited data on free production for the simple reason that 8 hours of exposure to the TL is generally insufficient for learners to be able to freely express themselves using structures other than those that are formulaic or memorised. As we believe that production data serve to partially reveal information about other language activities, such as perception, comprehension and grammatical analysis (cf. Frauenfelder & Porquier, 1980), methodologies for free production data collection at this early stage need to be carefully designed. This is clearly an area for future research. We would like to point out, however, that many of our tasks required 'production' in the written form. So as not to confuse learners' oral productions with data elicited by means of written tasks such as word order tests and grammaticality judgement tests, we chose to describe our learners' activity as 'grammatical analysis'. Results of this activity appear in Chapter 9.

Conclusion

This study of initial processing of L2 input in an instructional setting attempts to find a balance between control and naturalness (cf. Bialystok & Swain, 1978). Our aim was to replicate a 'natural' adult L2 classroom situation, hence our choice of a 'real' language, Polish in this case, as opposed to an artificial language. Conducting a study of this kind in which the TL input is controlled from the moment of first exposure proved challenging within the context of an institutional setting. Controlling the linguistic input in a natural setting, however, would prove close to impossible. This said, an attempt to solicit production data in a natural setting in combination with controlled input is an approach to consider for future research. The input, for example, could be controlled within the classroom, while production data are collected through a variety of tasks, such as natural interviews or role-play situations in which there are fewer methodological constraints.

In the chapters that follow, we will present results of the data collected by means of methods described in this chapter. When necessary, we will briefly remind the reader of the data collection procedures used to obtain these results, referring the reader back to this chapter for a more detailed explanation of methodological issues. We proceed now to Chapter 5 in which we investigate the role of prior linguistic knowledge in the ability of our 'first exposure' informants to translate Polish words. We will complicate matters by investigating not only the role of the L1, but also that of our informants' other L2s. It is a fact, after all, that many of the L2 learners from whom we in SLA collect language data are acquiring their L3 (or more). We will look at this more closely in what follows.

Notes

1. Pseudonyms replace real names in all examples.
2. Note that we placed Luc into the M(En) even though he gave himself a rating of 2 in English. An oral interview in English revealed that his English was significantly stronger than he had thought.
3. Informants were students in the *French as a Second Language* (FLE) programme at the Université Paris VIII, Saint-Denis, the FLE programme at the Université François Rabelais in Tours and the English Department of the Faculté des Lettres of the Institut Catholique de Paris. They responded to an abridged version of our questionnaire.

4. Informants were students at a professional high school in Nowa Huta, Poland, Zespól Szkoł Gastronomicznych w Nowej Hucie.
5. Another type of input one could attempt to study is inner speech. One of our learners wrote, 'I try to construct simple sentences in my head. I imagine simple communicative situations and try to find corresponding words'. As this form of input is not 'common' to all of our learners, we will not discuss it here.
6. In hindsight, had learners translated the sentences in the word order tests as well, we could have avoided certain problems of interpretation of the data.

Chapter 5

The Adult's Available Knowledge at First Exposure to an Unknown Language

In this chapter, we present the results of 'first exposure' comprehension tasks in which we investigate the strategies used by French NSs when confronted for the first time with written or spoken words in an unknown language, Polish in this case.[1] The term 'strategy' here refers to the way our informants proceed, in the absence of pertinent knowledge about Polish, when asked to perform a task in Polish. The general question that guides this chapter is the following: what knowledge is brought to the L2 acquisitional process from the very beginning and how is this knowledge applied at the moment of initial processing of foreign language input? More specifically, we pose the question: what knowledge sources help the learner associate a meaning to a word presented out of context? In other words, how will a learner go about finding a *signifié* for a decontextualised *signifiant*? The results presented in this chapter provide insights into whether or not the L1 alone serves as the basis for L2 acquisition, leading us to extend our investigation to the role played by learners' other L2s in this process. What if a learner has knowledge of another language, such as Italian, German or Russian? Would this knowledge help the learner process the new Polish words?

We administered word translation tests to two groups of 'first exposure' informants (see Appendix 1 for test items). Participants of one group took the written form of the test in which they were asked to translate the words they *read* into French; members of the other group took the oral form in which they were asked to translate the words they *heard* into French. In the oral test condition, informants were given 3 seconds between each word to respond. Unless signalled otherwise, we performed group analyses of the data (i.e. written and oral data combined). We mention modality only when separate analyses were conducted on the written and oral data.

The goal of these tests was to access the intuitions of informants with regard to the meaning of a given Polish word. A translation task requires certain semantic choices, but the question is whether or not it can also lead to decisions made based on morphological features. Jakobson (1963) claims that languages essentially differ in what they must express, not in what they can express. French nouns are marked for gender and number. The marking of gender in French is linked to the lexeme, but is often marked by an article. French native speakers, for example, would say 'une échelle' and not 'un échelle' because they know that 'échelle' is feminine. Suppose now that French learners are confronted with a TL word, *studentem*, which they think could refer to either a man or a woman. Such cases are interesting because they allow us to see if our French translators look for indications about gender in the Polish word because the marking is required in French, as in French 'étudiant' (student-masculine) or 'étudiante' (student-feminine).

It is important to note here that during the oral test, response time was limited to 3 seconds, a short amount of time if one needs to write a response (the case with our informants), but too long if the objective is to test on-line processing. It would therefore be inappropriate to compare the data of this study with those measuring reaction time in milliseconds (*cf.* Dijkstra *et al.*, 1999; Marslen-Wilson & Tyler, 1980; Schulpen *et al.*, 2003). Nevertheless, our task does impose a constraint (3 seconds) and therefore the informant's response will be a strategic one. Our question is the following: considering the highly metalinguistic nature of our task (our judgements are based on decontextualised linguistic objects) and the 3-second restriction, what knowledge do learners manage to mobilise in order to give a response?

Prior Linguistic Knowledge and Hypotheses

The informants for the oral and written translation tasks ($n = 34$; 18 written, 16 oral) had had no contact with the Polish language before the onset of the study. They were monolingual French native speakers with an advanced level of English (principal L2), academic knowledge of Latin (academic L2), as well as knowledge of German or Dutch (only one informant had studied Dutch), Spanish and/or Italian (secondary L2s). Four informants had studied one year of Russian. With this information we identified four linguistic groups, presented in Table 5.1. Informants who knew languages other than those mentioned in Table 5.1 were excluded from the analysis. All 6 L2 German informants took the written test (none took the oral test), one L2 Russian informant took the written test (3 took the oral test) and the other two groups were fairly well balanced.

The languages that concern us here are French (L1), Polish (L3) and English, Latin, German, Spanish, Italian and Russian (L2). Rather than speaking of the typological closeness or distance between languages, we simply propose a comparative analysis between the Polish lexical items that appear in the translation test and their L1 and L2 equivalents. Tradition induces us to speak of 'cognates' when commenting on lexical cross-linguistic influence; however, in this section we will distance ourselves somewhat from this tradition and speak in terms of formal

Table 5.1 Linguistic groups as defined by informants' L2s*

Groups	*Other L2s*	*No. informants*		
		Written test	*Oral test*	*Group total*
German	German	6	0	6
Romance	Spanish and/or Italian	5	5	10
Mixed	German or Dutch *and* Spanish or Italian	6	8	14
Russian	Russian (1 year of study)	1	3	4
Total		18	16	34

*All informants also had an advanced level of English and had studied Latin

features of words in the different languages concerned (L1, L2s and L3) that a learner might perceive as similar. In other words, it is not the fact that *collègue* in French and *colleague* in English have their etymological roots in the Latin *colligare* that interests us here. It is, rather, the morphophonological features perceived as similar in the three words *collègue*, *colleague* and *colligare* that are important for our analysis.

Singleton (1993–94: 22) makes the observation that from the moment of very first contact with a new word in an L2, whether one's intention is to memorise or simply understand it, both semantic and formal processes are engaged. At the same time, Singleton (1999) underlines the importance of the semantic process, arguing that words are stored according to both their semantic and phonological/orthographic representations. If this is the case, we would expect the task proposed here to require activation of both formal and semantic representations.

A hypothesis of L1 transfer predicts a reliance on the L1 when attempting to perceive, comprehend and translate a given Polish word. We extend this hypothesis to a common one found in recent L3 acquisition research which predicts a reliance on *all* known languages (not just the L1) to identify similarities between at least one formal element in the heard or read Polish word (i.e. a phoneme/grapheme, morpheme, or even the word in its entirety) and a formal element found in one of the informants' known languages. For this strategy to be effective, these formal elements must also have the possibility of being linked to meaning.

With regard to morphological nominal inflexion, Polish, Russian and Latin share the fact that they are highly inflected languages. Nouns in these three languages are marked for gender and decline for case and number. German nouns also decline for case and number, but German nouns show inflexion for fewer cases than Polish, Russian and Latin nouns. In French, Spanish, Italian and English, nouns do not decline for case, with the exception of personal pronouns and the genitive final '-s' in English. Nouns do not mark gender in English. Generally speaking, this is the case in German, French, Spanish and Italian as well; however, gender is marked by the determiner and can occasionally be deduced from the lexical item, as for example in French forms that end in '-tion' (f) or '-age' (m). With regard to plural marking, English, German and Romance languages mark plural by means of a suffix, generally a simple morpheme (/s/, /z/, /iz/ or /ɛn/ (*oxen*) in English; /ɛn/ in German; /i/ in Italian).

The L1/L2 transfer hypothesis then predicts that when French NSs who know other L2s are confronted with a translation task in which they hear or read a word that appears to consist of a stem and a suffix, they will activate all their linguistic knowledge in order to categorise the word in terms of its part of speech. If it is categorised as a noun, for instance, learners will turn to their other languages to discern whether the morphological marking indicates case, gender or number. If it is a verb, learners will seek to identify the person and number, and maybe even tense and aspect.

Word Recognition

We begin this section by looking at words that were either recognised or not recognised by all of the informants in both testing conditions, the criteria for 'recognised' being the following: when the translation carries the same meaning as the Polish word, regardless of its grammatical form, the word is judged as 'recognised'. For example, if an informant hears the Polish word *studentem*, which means 'étudiant' (student), and responds 'étudie' (study), the response is coded as 'recognised' even if the word class is incorrect. False cognates, however, are not counted as 'recognised' words.

Taking the 119 translation opportunities of the 34 informants, over a total of 4046 recognition possibilities, we found an 18% rate of recognition, a fairly high rate for informants who were hearing and seeing Polish for the first time.[2] What helped the French informants translate these words? In order to respond to this question, in the following sections we will analyse the translations in terms of different percentages of recognition.

90–100% rate of recognition

Table 5.2 presents words recognised by 90–100% of the informants.[3] The translations presented in Table 5.2 show that the three Polish words recognised at a rate of 90–100% have quasi-identical French equivalents. In addition, the word *mama* has similar phonological and orthographic

Table 5.2 Polish words recognised by 90–100% of the informants and their translations in the languages of the study

Polish	*French*	*English*	*German*	*Spanish*	*Italian*	*Russian*
film	film	film/ movie	film	película	film	film
mama	maman/ mère	mom/ mommy/ mother	mama/ mutti/ mutter	mamá/ madre	mamma/ madre	mama
informa-tykę	informa-tique	computer program-ming/ informatics	elektro-nische datenverar-beitung/ EDV	informá-tica	informa-tica	informa-tyku

features in all the languages ('ma' or 'mo' followed in most cases by another 'm'), *film* is identical in all the languages except for Spanish and *informatykę* is close to identical in the romance languages, Russian and English. In the case of these three Polish words, informants' L1 knowledge combined with knowledge of their L2s may have aided them in their translations. From this information, we thus hypothesise that two factors play an important role in the recognition of words in a novel TL: (1) the degree of resemblance between the Polish word and its equivalents in L1 and L2s; and (2) the number of languages known to the learner where an equivalent to the Polish word exists. These will need to be tested in future research with a larger selection of lexical items.

76–82% recognition rate

Table 5.3 presents Polish words recognised by 76–82% of our 34 informants. Analysis of the words in Table 5.3 reveals important similarities between the Polish words and their French equivalents. This said, we find fewer identical or quasi-identical phonological or orthographic forms in Table 5.3 than in Table 5.2, which may explain a somewhat reduced rate of recognition of the words in Table 5.3 compared to those in Table 5.2. With the exception of *kolega*, no equivalent in Table 5.3 ends with the same sounds or letters as the Polish word. This suggests that the degree of transparency and the number of languages in which an equivalent to the Polish word exists may play an important role in the recognition of unknown words, and illustrates Singleton's (1999) line of thinking *supra* concerning the involvement of both semantic and formal processes.

Table 5.3 Polish words recognised by 76–82% of the informants and their translations in the languages of the study

Polish	French	English	German	Spanish	Italian	Russian
francji (82%)	France	France	Frank- reich	Francia	Francia	francii
francusku (79%)	français	French	franzö- sisch	francés	francese	franzus- kim
amery- kańskim (79%)	américain	American	Amerika- ner	améri- cano	ameri- cano	amery- kanskym
studiuje (79%)	étudie	studies	studiert	estudia	studia	izuchaju
studentem (76%)	étudiant	student	Student	estu- diante	studente	student
kolega (76%)	collègue	colleague	Kolege	colega	collega	kolega

18–74% rate of recognition

In order to understand why certain words are better recognised than others, we need to fine-tune our notion of 'resemblance' between words in different languages. How is it that a foreign word encountered for the first time can be recognisable? The information provided in Table 5.4 may provide us with some clues.

We mentioned earlier the importance of a form-meaning mapping in a task of word recognition such as ours. A total of 26 words from the list of 119 were recognised at a rate of 18–74%. Table 5.4 only presents three of these for analysis. Let us take the word *angielsku*, for example, recognised by 26% of our informants. We continue to observe certain similarities, such as the formal relation between the Polish word *angielsku* and its French translation 'anglais'. The initial three phonemes are similar in the two

Table 5.4 A selection of Polish words recognised by 18–74% of the informants and their translations in the languages of the study

Polish	French	English	German	Spanish	Italian	Russian
hiszpański (59%)	espagnol	Spanish	Spanisch	español	spagnolo	ispanskij
paryżu (41%)	Paris	Paris	Paris	París	Pariggi	Parizhe
angielsku (26%)	anglais	English	Englisch	inglés	inglese	aglijskim

languages; however, beyond that the forms show no resemblance. Translation equivalents in English, German, Spanish and Italian share even fewer features with the Polish word, although it is worth noting that the German word 'Anglistik' (English studies) exists and could have had an influence on our L2 German informants' translations (3 of the 6 informants in this group translated it correctly). In similar fashion, *hiszpański* 'Spanish' (as in the 'Spanish' language) was translated by 59% of our informants. Although none of the translation equivalents are exact replicas of the Polish form, we can find formally and semantically related forms in several of the L2s that may account for this fairly high percentage of correct translations, such as French 'hispanophone' (Spanish speaker), English 'Hispanic' and German 'hispanisch' (Hispanic). If we analyse the word *paryżu*, we observe that 41% of the informants translated it as 'Paris'. The equivalents in all the languages begin in a similar fashion with 'par', followed by 'i' in the written form and [i], [I] or [ɨ] in spoken. Again, it appears that Polish words that share similar *initial* phonemes with words in other of our informants' known languages may have been more easily recognisable (cf. Marslen-Wilson's, 1987 cohort-based model of word recognition).

To verify whether a specific combination of languages had more influence than another in this task, we examined the responses according to linguistic group (cf. Table 5.1 for group profiles). Table 5.5 shows the recognition of these same words as a function of linguistic group.

We calculated the total percentage of recognitions by linguistic group of the 26 words recognised by all informants (words varied between 18% and 74% correct recognition).[4] The results by group, given in Table 5.5, suggest that the German and Russian groups have some advantage; however, we are unable to provide a sound statistical analysis for the results presented here as such an analysis would require groups of

Table 5.5 Number of informants in each linguistic group who recognised the words in Table 5.4

Polish word	Translation	German, n=6 informants	Romance, n=10 informants	Mixed, n=14 informants	Russian, n=4 informants
hiszpański (59%)	Spanish	6	5	6	3
paryżu (41%)	Paris	3	0	4	3
angielsku (26%)	English	3	2	3	1
Total recognition		67%	23%	31%	58%

similar size and more informants. Clearly future research of this kind is needed and would no doubt benefit from converging evidence drawn from different corpora and methods.

While looking at lower percentages of recognition, as shown in Tables 5.6–5.11 (9%, 6% and 3%), it becomes more and more evident that neither French nor English (our informants' principal L2) sufficed when translating the Polish words.

9% rate of recognition

Table 5.6 and Table 5.7 list words that were recognised at a rate of 9% by our 34 informants. Results presented in Table 5.7 suggest an expected tendency, that knowledge of Russian helps the recognition of Polish words. Those who had studied Russian, even if only for one year, tended to recognise some Polish words more easily than those who had not studied Russian: 31% of the informants in the Russian group as opposed to 5%, 4% and 2.5% of informants in the other groups. Let us now

Table 5.6 Polish words recognised by 9% of the informants and their translations in the languages of the study

Polish	French	English	German	Spanish	Italian	Russian
i	et	and	und	y	e	i
mnie	moi	me	meiner	yo	io	mne
ja	je	I	ich	yo	io	ja
mój	mon	my	mein	mi	mio	moj

Table 5.7 Number of informants in each linguistic group who recognised the words in Table 5.6

Polish word	Translation	German, n=6 informants	Romance, n=10 informants	Mixed, n=14 informants	Russian, n=4 informants
i	and	0	0	2	1
mnie	me	0	0	0	1
ja	I	1	1	1	0
mój	my	0	0	0	3
Total recognition		4%	2.5%	5%	31%

Table 5.8 Polish words recognised by 6% of informants and their translations in the languages of the study

Polish	*French*	*English*	*German*	*Spanish*	*Italian*	*Russian*
lubi	aime	likes	liebt	ama/le gusta	ama	ljubit
ona	elle	she	sie	ella	lei	ona
brat	frère	brother	Bruder	hermano	fratello	brat
marka	Marc	Mark	Marks	Marcos	Màrco	Marka

examine words that were recognised by only 6% of our 34 informants (see Table 5.8).

6% rate of recognition

As can be seen in Table 5.8, analysis of the Polish words in light of their equivalents in other languages shows a growing distance between forms, with the exception of Russian. Consequences for our informants are shown in Table 5.9.

With the exception of the first name *marka* 'Mark', the other words were recognised by members of the Russian group only (the average for the 4 informants was 37%). This is not surprising as the words *ona* and *brat* are identical in Polish and Russian, and *lubi* and *ljubit* share phonological and orthographic features. We observe some beneficial effect of Russian on the translation task in that members of the Russian group were the only informants who managed to find some sort of resemblance between the given Polish word and something that already existed in their lexical stores.

Table 5.9 Number of informants in each linguistic group who recognised the words in Table 5.8

Polish word	*Translation*	*German,* **n=6** *informants*	*Romance,* **n=10** *informants*	*Mixed,* **n=14** *informants*	*Russian,* **n=4** *informants*
lubi	likes (3p, sg)	0	0	0	2
ona	she	0	0	0	2
brat	brother	0	0	0	2
marka	Mark	0	0	2	0
Total recognition		0%	0%	3%	37%

Let us return briefly to the word *marka*. Two informants from the Mixed group recognised *marka* as being the first name 'Marc' (Mark), and most of the informants offered a translation, even if not the correct one: 'marque' (mark/grade) (21 responses, or 62% of the informants), 'note' (grade) (4 responses), 'marché' (market) (1 response). The resemblance between the forms *marka* and 'marque' is obvious. Given that the word *marka* was presented to the informants in isolation and without a capital letter (in the written test), informants had only the form of the word itself from which to deduce a translation. This suggests that in the absence of context and in the case of homophony and homography, constructing a semantic representation from the input requires specific cues, such as a capital letter (in written text) or a morphological marker.

3% rate of recognition

The beneficial effect of Russian is again confirmed in Table 5.10 and Table 5.11, where we see words recognised by 3% of the informants of our study, although to a lesser extent.

Table 5.10 Polish words recognised by 3% of informants and their translations in the languages of the study

Polish	French	English	German	Spanish	Italian	Russian
jackowi	Jacques	Jack	Jakob	Jaime/ Santiago	Giacomo	Jakowa
lekcji	leçon	lesson	Lektion	lección	lezione	lekzii
koleżanka	collègue	colleague	Kollegin	colega	collega	kolegi
kelner	serveur	waiter/ server	Kellner	camarero	cameriere	ofizianta
lubię	aime	like (1p, sg)	liebe	amo/me gusta	amo	ljublju
dobrze	bien	good	gut	bien	bene	horosho
zna	connaît	knows	kennt	conoce	conosce	znaet
znają	connaissent	know (3p, pl)	kennen	conocen	conoscono	znajut
osiem	huit	eight	acht	ocho	otto	vosem
język	langue	language/ tongue	Sprache/ Zunge	lengua	lingua	jazyk
moja	ma	my	meine	mi	mia	moja
piwa	bière	beer	Bieres	cerveza	birra	piwa

Table 5.11 The number of informants in each linguistic group who recognised words in Table 5.10

Polish word	Translation	German, n=6 informants	Romance, n=10 informants	Mixed, n=14 informants	Russian, n=4 informants
jackowi	Jack	0	1	0	0
lekcji	lesson	0	1	0	0
koleżanka	colleague	1	0	0	0
kelner	waiter/server	1	0	0	0
lubię	like (1p, sg)	0	0	0	1
dobrze	good	0	0	0	1
zna	knows	0	0	0	1
znają	know (3p, pl)	0	0	0	1
osiem	eight	0	0	0	1
język	language/tongue	0	0	0	1
moja	my	0	0	0	1
piwa	beer	0	0	0	1
Total recognition		3%	2%	0%	18%

Clearly we are unable to claim absolute conclusions with such a small informant sample; however, tendencies emerge. The Russian group consistently shows some advantage over the others: the average recognition is 18% in contrast to 3%, 2% and 0% in the other groups. This advantage manifests itself in spite of the fact that this group only studied one year of Russian and that Russian was the fourth language chronologically speaking for most of them. We imagine that these two factors play a role as well in the activation, or lack thereof, of linguistic knowledge. Nevertheless, it is worth pointing out that the potential for activation depends on the individual knowledge a learner has acquired in any given language. If, for example, learners of the Russian group are unfamiliar with the word *piwa* in Russian, their knowledge of Russian will prove less than pertinent when trying to comprehend the word *piwa* in Polish.

A continuum of lexical transparency

To summarise the results of the data presented up until now, we calculated the percentage of all recognised words in both tests according

Table 5.12 Percent recognised words (based on 119 words)

Linguistic group	% Recognised words (maximum possible)	Global rank order[c]
Russian[b] ($n = 4$)	22.5% (476)	1
German[a] ($n = 6$)	21.3% (714)	2
Mixed ($n = 14$)	17.5% (1666)	3
Romance ($n = 10$)	15.1% (1190)	4

[a]Written only (no German group for the oral test)
[b]Primarily oral
[c]1, best recognition results; 4, poorest recognition results

to linguistic groups, as shown in Table 5.12. Table 5.12 shows a slight advantage for the Russian and German groups (see global rank order), suggesting that knowledge of Russian and German helped French informants in their task of processing Polish more than did knowledge of Spanish and Italian, and that even as little as one year of Russian made a difference in terms of their success in the translation task. Table 5.13 shows the individual percentages and the average rank order associated with the four linguistic groups for the word translation test. More specifically, Table 5.13 presents rank orders corresponding to the raw data shown in Table 5.5, Table 5.7, Table 5.9 and Table 5.11.[5] Given the difficulty of computing sound statistics from such raw data (small groups of unequal size), we made the decision to gather recognition rank orders associated with each linguistic profile and the global rank order within a single table. Our data indicate that German and Russian tended to be the two most helpful languages for the recognition of Polish words.

These results taken as a whole lead us to propose a continuum of lexical transparency where TL words are placed according to their degree

Table 5.13 Recognised words (partial results) and the corresponding average rank order of data presented in Tables 5.5, 5.7, 5.9 and 5.11

	18–74% rank order	9% rank order	6% rank order	3% rank order	Global average rank order[a]
German	1	3	1	1	1.5
Russian	2	1	3.5	2	2.1
Mixed	3	2	2	4	2.8
Romance	4	4	3.5	3	3.6

[a]1, best recognition results; 4, poorest recognition results

of phonological and orthographic similarity to words in the learners' L1 or L2s. In Chapter 7, we will propose that transparency depends on features of the languages in question (L1, L2, L3, etc.) and that the learner will focus on the words in the input that contain an easily identifiable form-meaning mapping. In the same manner, the results presented above underline the important role that a high level of transparency (as defined in the first section of Chapter 7) plays in the translation task. Observing the similarity or distance between Polish forms and their equivalents in two or more languages and their rate of recognition, we propose a continuum of transparency, as shown in Figure 5.1, that will allow us to predict to what extent an L1 or an L2 form will help assign a meaning to the TL form. Two factors are considered in this continuum: (1) the number of languages known by the informant; and (2) the degree of transparency between the target word and words in the known languages that share the same *signifié* (cf. below 'false cognates'). The words of all languages known to the learner could appear on such a continuum.

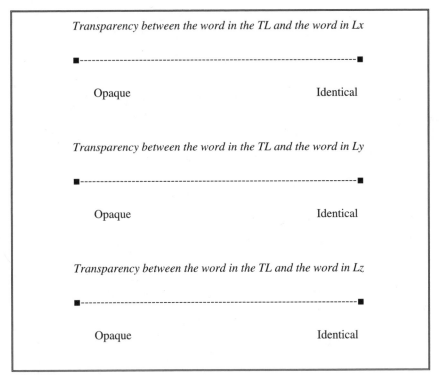

Figure 5.1 Continuum of lexical transparency

Three principles apply:

(1)   The closer to 'identical' the word in the informant's known language is, the higher the chances that it will be recognised.
(2)   The more known languages there are that contain formal equivalents with some resemblance to the target word, the higher the chances that it will be recognised.
(3)   Points 1 and 2 are only true in cases where an equivalent form-meaning mapping occurs (the problem of false cognates).

To sum up, 'correct' comprehension will take place when a connection is made between the form (phonetic/phonological and/or orthographic) of the target word and the forms already known in the given languages (regardless of what they are) *and* when an equivalent form-meaning mapping occurs.

Incorrect Word Recognition

Up to this point we have examined the recognition of words in cases where the informants translated the Polish word correctly. The translations discussed in this section, however, reflect the *unsuccessful* attempts of our informants, the result often being a French word that shares no resemblance with the Polish word either formally or semantically. Table 5.14 shows, for example, the 34 informants' translations of the Polish word *mówi*.

Table 5.14 Translations of *mówi* 'he/she speaks'

Translations	Number of informants, n =34 informants	Corresponding percentage
film/cinéma 'film/cinema'	16	47
mouvement 'movement'	2	6
nouveau 'new'	1	3
No response	15	44

Table 5.14 reveals a case of clear English influence on the translations of our French informants. Their processing began with the reading or hearing of a Polish word (in this case *mówi*) which activated their English (*movie*) and resulted in the French translation *film* or *cinéma*. We observe the same phenomenon with L2 German in Table 5.15.

Table 5.15 shows that 11 informants, all of whom had knowledge of German, translated *jeden* 'one' as either 'chaque' (each) (29.5%), or 'tous' (all) (3%), correct translations of German 'jeden'. Considering that

Table 5.15 Translations of *jeden* 'one'

Translations	Number of informants, n = 34 informants	Corresponding percentage
chaque 'each'	10	29
rien 'nothing'	3	9
jardin 'garden'	3	9
jeune 'young'	2	6
tous 'all'	1	3
No response	15	44

Polish and German show the identical form *jeden*, it is not surprising that those who knew German applied this knowledge to Polish. Here we see a convincing case of L2 German activation. In the cases of both *mówi* and *jeden* it appears that the informants linked a Polish *signifiant* to an English or German *signifiant*, the result being a French *signifié* (one that differs from the original Polish *signifié*). If this is in fact the case, such a process is unique to L3 acquisition. Although it may function properly in some cases, here the result is an incorrect hypothesis about the new language.

Processing Morphosyntactic Markers

Accuracy of translation

Until now we have focused on similarities between Polish lexical items and their equivalents in the languages of the study. To obtain a finer reading of our results, we analysed the data in a different light, posing the question as to whether the factor 'linguistic group' had an effect on the accuracy of the translation. As mentioned earlier, Jakobson (1963) makes the observation that when faced with a translation task, translators must make decisions based on features of the language into which they are translating, French in our case. A logical prediction, therefore, would be that French speakers will look for grammatical information in the Polish word when such information has to be coded in the French equivalent. Take the Polish word *studentem* 'student' for example. In order to translate the word *studentem* with any precision, French translators would need to consider the following: what word class does the given word belong to? Is the proper translation 'étudier' (to study), 'étudie' (study) or 'étudiant(e)(s)' (student[s])? If one decides it is a noun, is it singular or plural? If one decides it is a verb, is it the infinitive form, or is it first, second or third person? Because a correct translation in French of *studentem* 'étudiant' requires information about the gender, this type of word allows us to investigate whether or not our informants searched for this type of information in the Polish word and if so, whether linguistic group had an effect on this process.

In order to investigate the phenomenon of grammatical accuracy, we created two categories of recognised words. The first, referred to as 'R+', comprises *accurate* translations of the Polish word, that is, when the informant correctly translated not only the meaning of the word, but also the grammatical information. The second, called 'R–', consists of French translations that share the same meaning with the Polish word, but not the same grammatical information. Both categories, R+ and R–, grouped as one, is referred to as 'R' (all word recognitions whether grammatical or not). Table 5.16 shows the percentage of word recognitions as a function of linguistic group and accuracy.

Table 5.16 Percentage of word recognitions according to linguistic group and accuracy, including corresponding rank order of the *total* percentage

Linguistic group	R+ (%)	R– (%)	R (total) (%)	Corresponding rank order[a]
Russian	17.4	5.1	22.5	1
German	18.1	3.2	21.3	2
Mixed	13	4.5	17.5	3
Romance	12	3.1	15.1	4

[a]1, best recognition results; 4, poorest recognition results

There seems to be converging evidence that Russian and German were the most helpful languages (cf. Table 5.13 and Table 5.16). In other words, knowledge of German (when it is not mixed with that of Spanish and Italian) and knowledge of Russian (even if limited) appeared to help the French informant upon first contact with the TL to effectuate a word recognition task in Polish with some grammatical accuracy.

As mentioned earlier, 18 informants took the written test and 16 took the oral test. When separating the data of these two test types, we found a slight advantage for those who read the written word over those who heard the spoken word: 20% rate of word recognition on the written test ($n = 18$) versus 15.5% rate of recognition on the oral test ($n = 16$). Given the fact that we were unable to administer an oral test to a German group, we predicted that the higher success rate of the German group seen in Table 5.16 was possibly linked to the written test advantage. To eliminate the effect of test type, we analysed the written data alone across

Table 5.17 Percentage of word recognitions during written test

Linguistic group	Written test R+ (%)	Written test R total (%)	Corresponding rank order[a]
German	18.1	21.3	1
Mixed	15	20.3	2
Romance	14.2	18.8	3
Russian[b]	–	–	

[a]1, best recognition results; 3, poorest recognition results
[b]Results of the Russian group are excluded as only one informant took the written test

linguistic groups, with the exception of the Russian group which comprised a sole informant for the written test. The results appear in Table 5.17.

The results presented in Table 5.17 continue to show that the German group translated grammatical information more accurately than did the other groups even when results from the oral test were removed from the analysis. This leads us to the hypothesis formulated above, that the learners with a highly inflected L1 or L2 may be more sensitive to morphological markers than those who have no knowledge of this type of language. Despite typological differences between German and Polish, they both have inflexional systems that make use of suffixes to express information about case, gender and number. It is possible that learners with knowledge of German were more liable to look out for morphological cues in the Polish input because of this resemblance.

Analysis of translations of three forms of '*koleg-*'

In order to better understand how the informants processed grammatical information at the moment of first exposure to Polish, we examined their translations of three forms in Polish: *kolega, kolegi* and *kolegę*. All three forms signify 'collègue' (colleague) and are marked for masculine singular. They differ, however, in their case markings, respectively marked for nominative, genitive and accusative. The translations of the nominative form, *kolega*, appear in Table 5.18.

The ending *-a* in *kolega* signals nominative, masculine, singular. What interests us in particular here is the fact that three informants translated *kolega* using one of three feminine forms: (1) 'collègue', specifying the feminine form by adding '(f)'; (2) 'amie' – the feminine equivalent of the masculine 'ami' (friend); and (3) 'collégienne' – the feminine equivalent of the masculine 'collégien' (pupil). This implies that some informants are sensitive to morphological forms from the very beginning. They analysed both the lexical item and its morphology in order to discover

Table 5.18 Translations of *kolega* 'colleague' (Nom, m, sg)

Translations	Number of informants (n =34 informants)	Corresponding percentage
collègue 'colleague'	25	73.5
collègue (f)/amie/collègienne 'colleague/friend/pupil' (all f)	3	9
collège 'secondary school'	1	3
No response	5	14.5

Table 5.19 Translations of *kolegi* 'colleague' (Gen, m, sg)

Translations	Number of informants, n =34 informants	Corresponding percentage
collègue 'colleague'	14	41
collègues 'colleagues'	6	17.5
collège 'secondary school'	5	15
collègienne 'pupil'	1	3
No response	8	23.5

the most thorough meaning of the Polish word, and all of this within the first *minutes* of contact with the new TL.

Comparable working hypotheses such as those identified above can be observed in the informants' interpretation of *-i* in *kolegi* as an indicator of number, as shown in Table 5.19.

A total of six informants translated the form *kolegi* 'collègue' (colleague) (Gen, m, sg) with the plural form in French 'collègues'. Three of these informants belonged to the Russian group. Russian shows a plural noun marker -i as in the following examples: *knig-i* 'books', *det-i* 'children', *krask-i* 'colours'. We can only speculate with so few tokens that this is a case of informants who know something about Russian generalising their knowledge of Russian plural to Polish.

Before we continue, however, it is important to remind the reader that although we see processing of inflexional markers in action, this does not mean that this processing actually *helps* the informant for the particular task at hand. As a reminder, the Polish suffixes in question here, *-a/-i/-ę*, do not correspond in any direct way to the markers of gender and number in Polish. To illustrate, the ending *-a* can mark a singular

Table 5.20 Translations of *kolegę* 'colleague' (Acc, m, sg)

Translations	Number of informants, n =34 informants	Corresponding percentage
collègue 'colleague'	17	50
collège 'secondary school'	13	38
connaissance/savoir 'knowledge'	1	3
No response	3	9

masculine noun for nominative, genitive or accusative case, or a plural neutral noun for nominative or accusative case. Other possibilities exist as well. Informants' hypotheses described above can therefore be viewed as interesting working hypotheses, but they remain incorrect.

In Table 5.20, the form *kolegę* signifies 'collègue' (colleague) as well (Acc, m, sg). As can be seen in Table 5.20, 13 of the 34 informants (or 38%) translated *kolegę* with 'collège' (secondary school). We have a clear case here of a false cognate: based on the identity of a *signifiant*, the informants came to a false conclusion about the identity of the *signifié*. The 13 informants who did this, however, were all provided with a written stimulus. No informant taking the oral test responded with this translation. This can be taken as a reminder of the importance of distinguishing between phonological and orthographic processing of information. For those taking the oral test, the sounds [g] in *kolegę* and [ž] in 'collège' were clearly distinct. For those taking the written test, however, the orthographic resemblance between the written words *kolegę* and 'collège' was, understandably, quite strong.

We conducted one final analysis on our *kolega/i/ę* data to investigate individual performance. As mentioned above, three informants interpreted the -*a* in *kolega* as a feminine marker, and six interpreted the -*i* in *kolegi* as a plural marker. Only one of these informants responded with *both* of these interpretations. The remaining informants provided only one such grammatical analysis. In sum, 8 of our 34 informants (or 24%) attempted to interpret Polish endings in some way.

We return to our findings presented earlier, that is, that the Russian and German groups translated grammatical information slightly more accurately than did other groups. Is it possible that knowledge of an inflected language may have served as a signal to the informant to focus on morphology (word endings in particular) when processing a foreign word? It may be that the actual form of the TL word-ending itself does not determine whether or not it is a potential object of transfer, but rather the informant's basic knowledge of how noun morphology works, possibly combined with the experience an informant has had with various inflexional systems. If this is true, it appears then that previous linguistic knowledge and metalinguistic strategies are part of what makes up what Kellerman (1983) refers to as a learner's 'psychotypology'.

A continuum of morphological transparency

Our data show quite convincingly that grammatical analysis of TL words may well take place already at first exposure. As we did for lexical items, we propose a continuum of morphological transparency, shown in Figure 5.2, which involves three factors: (1) the number of languages known by the learner; (2) the degree of transparency between the given word ending in the TL and those in the known languages; and (3) the degree of morphological inflexion of each known language. The

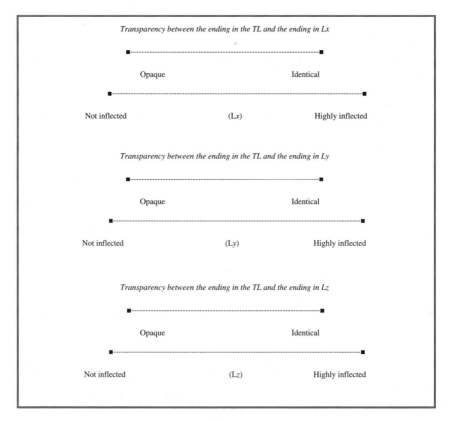

Figure 5.2 Continuum of morphological transparency

morphological forms of all known languages could appear on such a continuum.

Two principles apply:

(1) The closer a word ending in a known language is to that of the given word ending in the TL, the more likely it is that the ending will be perceived (and possibly recognised).
(2) The more known languages there are that present an equivalent with some resemblance to the ending in the TL, the more likely it is that the ending will be perceived (and possibly recognised).

The 'correct' comprehension of morphological markers will only take place when a connection is confirmed between the form of the TL word and the forms already known (phonetic/phonological and/or ortho-graphic), independent of the languages in question *and* when a form-meaning mapping occurs. This latter constraint is rarely fulfilled, which explains why this kind of transfer often results in false hypotheses. What is more pertinent and interesting is the attempt made by informants to understand morphological markers. How did some of our informants manage to extract grammatical information from a Polish word? They focused their attention on the end of the word where morphological markers can be found in the languages of this study. They seem to have transferred the automatism of looking for grammatical information in the word endings, using it as a strategy to process the Polish word. A future study of the processing of a new TL whose morphological markers appear as prefixes or infixes would provide an interesting comparison to the data collected here.

Before concluding this section, we acknowledge the fact that most of our informants did not mark the distinction between gender and number in their translations (although some did, which is quite amazing). We suppose that these informants translated the words using a 'neutral' form, that is the singular masculine form in French. We could have modified the task by asking them to specify gender and number, but in doing this, we would have lost the natural traces of the initial processing of Polish input. These traces are essential for our understanding of the processes implicated from the moment of first exposure to a new TL.

Discussion

The informants discussed in this chapter were confronted with a word translation test under time pressure (3 seconds for the oral group) in an unknown language. The data suggest that in order to accomplish such a task, informants made use of all of their available linguistic knowledge. In his work on lexical influence of L1 on L2, Hall (2002) proposes that L2 learners use their existing store of knowledge (the L1 lexicon in his study) to create a new store of L2 knowledge. Referring to his model, *Parasitic Strategy,* he claims that learners who are confronted with an L2 word for the first time will automatically detect similarities with existing forms, which for him means L1 forms. Ecke (2001) confirms this strategy and extends it to L3 acquisition. He found that in the search and extraction of their L3 lexicons, beginning learners of L3 German (Spanish L1 and English L2) used strategies of association and categorisation with words from their L1 and L2. He points out that few intralingual synonyms have the potential to be activated by beginning learners. Obviously for participants of our study who were exposed to the new TL for the first time, intralingual synonymy was not an option. They naturally activated their other languages.

Our results also show that knowledge of other L2s, in particular German and Russian, prompted these informants to formulate hypotheses in terms of the lexicon and morphology. When all is said and done, however, this prior linguistic knowledge also posed problems, such as false cognates, a problem that is well known in the research on lexical L2 acquisition (cf. Laufer, 1993–4). Singleton (1999: 218) notes that, '... the relative importance of form and meaning in lexical acquisition and processing is a function of the degree of familiarity/unfamiliarity of the item(s) in question rather than of the status (L1 or L2) of the language concerned'. In other words, learners either 'know' the TL word and there is no problem, or they do not know it and, consequently, they look for similarities to something that they do know, namely an element in one of their known languages (L1 or another L2).

Regarding morphology, some informants formulated working hypotheses about word class, gender and number of a Polish word, the result being, often but not always, an incorrect hypothesis. In fact, the results reveal an elaborate grammatical processing on the part of the informants. Such a result, if it is generalisable, has implications for all research on an L2 learner's grammatical knowledge. In Chapter 1 we introduced Schwartz and Eubank's (1996: 1) definition of the 'L2 initial state[6]': 'One of the more neglected topics in L2 acquisition research is the precise characterization of the L2 initial state, where "L2 initial state" refers to the starting point of non-native *grammatical* knowledge' (our emphasis). Schwartz and Sprouse (1996: 41) claim that everything is potentially transferable, but qualify the statement in a footnote: '... the phonetic matrices of lexical/morphological items are assumed not to transfer'. Perdue (1996) disputes the qualifying statement for production when closely related languages are involved and uses the productions of CA (Cacho), a Spanish learner of French, to argue his point. Examples are cited in Chapter 2 (cf. 'The role of other factors' in the first section of Chapter 2). We dispute Schwartz and Sprouse's qualifying statement for perception and comprehension. When faced with a decontextualised metalinguistic task such as the one discussed in this chapter, our learners tried to apply aspects of their L1 and L2 morphophonological systems to their TL, Polish, which is not even necessarily closely related to their L1 and L2s.

Referring once again to Jakobson (1963), we point out that when faced with a translation task in which the informant is translating into a language that marks the noun for gender and number (French in this case), the informant must attempt to decipher the TL word in order to find signs of grammatical category. SLA research on learners' productions has shown that acquisitional grammaticalisation consists of a process of convergence whereby the learner's interlanguage gradually approaches the TL system (cf. Giacalone-Ramat, 1992; Klein & Perdue, 1992). If comprehension follows a similar process of convergence, our results (keeping in mind that our task was of a highly metalinguistic nature) would suggest that this process begins already upon first exposure to the TL. Learners formulate hypotheses about the meaning and the grammatical categories of TL lexical items with the help of their linguistic knowledge base. Obviously, the more languages learners know, the more linguistic knowledge they will bring to the task of learning a new language.

In order to predict to what extent certain phenomena of known languages can be transferred, we have proposed a continuum of transparency for lexical items and morphological markers. In fact, the data presented here suggest that beginning learners, faced with a translation task, activate all their languages in search of something 'familiar'. Our data confirm Kellerman's (1983) thesis on psychotypology, showing that it is the learners themselves and their perception of the relationship between their known languages (L1 and L2s) that determine what will be transferred. Even if French and Polish or English and Polish are traditionally considered 'distant' languages from a typological point of view, this in no way prevents 'transfer' from occurring between the two languages. In the absence of other useful information, learners will resort to their knowledge stores of even those languages that are typologically distant from the TL.

This claim applies to the acquisition of any new TL in that the lexical and morphological memory is composed of mental lexemes and morphological forms of the L1 and all L2s of the learner. As we have seen, this memory, or knowledge, provides the basis on which adult learners develop strategies to formulate hypotheses about language. We can no longer treat the transfer of L2s as negligible. The process is much more complex. Hall (2002: 83) was correct in concluding that, 'In applied linguistics and language pedagogy, we often underestimate how much learners bring to the learning task'.

Conclusion

This chapter presented data that contribute to our in-depth analysis of an adult learner's performance when faced with a task in an unknown language. Our results show that our informants made use of all pertinent linguistic knowledge (whether helpful or not) to accomplish the task in an unknown TL. In order to translate the Polish words and to identify the gender, number and part of speech of the target word, informants used not only their L1, but also their L2s. Their hypotheses were often incorrect, but as Cenoz (1997) rightly points out, plurilingualism considerably increases the range of possible hypotheses. The plurilingual learner, endowed with more linguistic knowledge than a monolingual, will have more operative hypotheses to formulate that can later be confirmed or rejected. According to Giacobbe (1992a), it is through this type of cognitive work that acquisition takes place.

In future studies, we plan to refine our research methods, measuring reaction times in milliseconds, for example, as inspired by psycholinguistic studies such as Dijkstra *et al.* (1999) and Schulpen *et al.* (2003). Such methods can be used to investigate the responses of multilinguals upon first contact with a new TL as a function of their first, second, third, fourth language, and so forth. Would it take longer for them to activate another L2 than it would an L1? This would allow us to test, for instance, whether or not a learner's L1 is activated *first*, that is, *before* other known language systems are activated, the strategy being if L1 fails to work, then try L2. Such data would contribute to our understanding of the selection and activation processes involved when learners know more than one language, and the interaction between these languages (if there is any) during these processes.

In the following chapter, we present two case studies using the data collected from two of our French learners of Polish with quasi-identical profiles. A comparison of their data will allow us to continue our observation of what learners actually *do* with TL input, while investigating whether learners with similar profiles work on the same input in the same way and articulating hypotheses that can be confirmed or rejected by the group data presented in Chapters 7–9.

Notes

1. A French version of the information presented in this section first appeared in Rast (2006) and is included here with the permission of the executive committee of *Acquisition et Interaction en Langue Étrangère (AILE)*.
2. It is important to remind the reader that the 119 Polish words selected for the word recognition task originate from a recording of the first 10 minutes of an initial Polish class. In fact, the Polish instructor, a NS of Polish, had an excellent grasp of the French language and therefore may have, even if unconsciously, presented a fair number of French–Polish 'cognates' in order

to help the learners better understand her first utterances in Polish. This is a well known strategy in language teaching and could explain the high success rate of word recognition upon first exposure to Polish. Our aim, however, is to investigate what it is about these 'cognates' (and non-cognates) that led to word recognition on the part of our informants.

3. We excluded Latin in the tables for the simple reason that our informants learned literary and not conversational vocabulary in their Latin classes. The words chosen for this study include only words that one would find in a typical conversation involving introductions.

4. The percentage of total recognition equals the number of recognitions in a given group of informants divided by the total number of possible responses of that group (i.e. $n \times$ the number of words), multiplied by 100.

5. This partial analysis is intended to serve as merely an indication of differences in linguistic group.

6. Note that Leung (2005), working from the generativist perspective as well, raises the question of 'L3 initial state', showing that transfer originates not only from L1, but also from L2.

Chapter 6

Case Studies: Two Learners with Similar Linguistic Profiles

The objective of this chapter is to describe and compare the interlanguage development of two learners during the first 8 hours of instructed L2 acquisition in an unknown language (Polish). The two learners in question, Gilles and Luc, had nearly identical linguistic profiles (French L1, English L2), were of the same gender (male) and age (26 and 27), and received identical Polish language input. We analysed the performance of Gilles and Luc at different 'periods' of TL exposition with respect to the input processing activities of speech perception, speech comprehension and grammatical analysis. Each 'period' coincides with the number of hours of Polish input the learners were exposed to (e.g. 'Period 1h30' refers to the point in time when the learners had been exposed to a total of one hour and thirty minutes of Polish input). As we are interested in L1 (French) influence on the learners' performance, we have glossed the Polish sentences in French, followed by an English gloss. The same is true with all results presented in this book. This allowed us to maintain a natural means of observation, that of the acquisition of Polish through the eyes and ears of the French speaker-reader-hearer. As mentioned earlier, the learners of our study kept journals during the observation period. We will use remarks from these journals when pertinent. Quotations will be translated into English from the original French versions.

The organisation of this chapter is as follows. We begin with a detailed description of Gilles' data collected from tests at distinct periods between 1h30 and 8h00, followed by Luc's data collected during the same time periods. Our discussion of Luc's data includes comparisons with Gilles' data. Results are reported chronologically, that is, beginning with results at Period 1h30 (the first testing session for our learners) and concluding with Period 8h00 (the final testing session). Within each time period, we report on language activities separately, beginning with speech perception, followed by speech comprehension and then grammatical analysis. We follow this order when all language activities were tested during one given time period; however, if this is not the case, we report on the language activity observed in the tests administered at the given time period. We introduce each time period with observations made by Gilles and Luc in their journals.

Case Study 1: Gilles

Gilles was born and raised in France as an only child by French-speaking parents. At the time of our study, he was 26 years old and working on a 'licence' (a French degree approximately equivalent to an American Bachelor's Degree) in FLE (Français Langue Etrangère 'French as a Foreign Language'). His reason for learning Polish was two-fold: to engage in the observation of his own learning of a foreign language while also fulfilling one of the requirements for the course entitled *Apprentissage et auto-observation* (*Learning and Self-Evaluation*), that of studying an unknown foreign language. In addition, his motivation for learning the language was heightened by the fact that he was interested in discovering Poland, a country he claimed to know nothing about. His knowledge of languages other than French was limited to English. On the self-evaluation questionnaire in which all participants were asked to assign themselves to a level of 0 to 5 (5 being 'fluent') for all of their known non-native languages, Gilles rated himself as a 5 in English. During a personal interview conducted in English, we found that he was a strong English speaker, but not fluent, and assigned him the rating of 4. This rating, along with the fact that he did not use English on a daily basis, placed him into the monolingual group of learners for the purpose of this study.

Gilles: Period 1h30

In a journal entry after the first Polish class (1h30), Gilles recognises what may be a classic problem of phonemic recognition in the early stages of adult language acquisition: 'We understand nothing in detail; we associate a group of indistinct phonemes to a more or less specific meaning'. With regard to grammar, he claims to be able to distinguish between markers of first, second and third person singular, but remarks that 'everything is still vague and it all goes very fast'. At one point he realises that the instructor's gestures and rising intonation mean she is asking a question and expecting a response. These observations reveal a certain metalinguistic awareness on the part of Gilles. In response to how he felt about the tests taken at the end of the first Polish lesson, Gilles seemed satisfied with his performance. As no test of perception was administered to our learners at Period 1h30, we begin our discussion with an analysis of Gilles' *comprehension* of Polish by means of data collected during an oral sentence translation test in which our learners were asked to translate into written French the sentences they *heard* in Polish.

Gilles: Speech comprehension at Period 1h30

During the first oral translation test of the project (cf. the third section of Chapter 4 for a list and description of test types), Gilles correctly translated all SVO and most OVS-type sentences. His translation of a C-Cop-S sentence provides interesting information about his processing of a Polish sentence:

1) Sentence heard: *inżynierem jest on w fabryce*
                            ingénieur est il à usine (engineer is he at factory)
    Gilles' translation: Fabrice il est ingénieur dans une usine.
                            (Fabrice he is engineer in a factory.)

Gilles first processed *fabryce* 'factory' as 'Fabrice'. This could be a result of the processing of formal information only: *fabryce* and 'Fabrice' resemble each other on the phonemic level. When processing grammatical information, however, Gilles may have been in search of a subject for the sentence, and 'Fabrice' filled this function. He then correctly processed *fabryce* as 'usine' (factory) on the semantic level, having apparently recalled the meaning of the Polish lexeme.

Of the two sentences in VSO order, he had no trouble with one, but translated the other with the form of a question in French:

2) Sentence heard: *Nazywa się on Marek.*
                            appelle se il Marc
                            (is called Refl he Mark = His name is Mark)
                            V Refl S C

Gilles' translation: Comment s'appelle Marek? (How is called Mark?)

There were few occurrences of this word order (V-S-C/O) in the input, which could account for Gilles' confusion. An explanation for this translation might be that in order to understand the sentence, Gilles relied on word order in his L1, French, a language in which a sentence-initial verb generally signifies either a question or an imperative.

Gilles: Grammatical analysis at Period 1h30

   Gilles: Constituent word order at Period 1h30.   During the first word order test, Gilles responded correctly to 7 of 10 sentences. Two of the three incorrect responses were, without a doubt, incorrect, while the third was described as 'strange', but not necessarily 'incorrect', by several native speakers of Polish. The first incorrect response was an inappropriate placement of *się*. The second was an ungrammatical construction in which an attributive adjective was separated from its noun, generally an unacceptable structure in Polish. The third consisted of a sentence in which a noun phrase needed to be formed with the words *język* 'language' and *angielski* 'English'. Normally in Polish, as in French, the appropriate order is *język angielski* (langue anglaise 'language English') and all of our Polish informants responded in this manner. Gilles, however, supplied the order *angielski język* 'English language', an acceptable word order in English, but not in Polish or French. His choice of order was apparently not influenced by the TL input nor by his L1, but may have been influenced by another L2 (English for instance). In the seven correct sentences, Gilles opted for SVO.

The first grammaticality judgement test contained three clauses in which the word order was not SVO. In two of these, Gilles changed the order from the original to SVO:

3) Original clause: *Nazywa się ona Mary*

   appelle se elle Mary (is called Refl she Mary)

   V Refl S C

Gilles' response: *Ona nazywa się Mary*

   elle appelle se Mary (she is called Refl Mary)

   S V Refl C

4) Original clause: **Mieszkam[1] ona w Chicago*

   (je) habite elle à Chicago (live she in Chicago)

   V-1p sg S PP/Adv

Gilles' response: *Ona mieszka w Chicago*

   Elle habite à Chicago (she lives in Chicago)

   S V-3p sg PP/Adv

In the third clause, however, he accepted the order C-Cop, making no modification to the original order *Architektką jest* (architecte est 'architect is'), an utterance that 100% of our Polish control group informants changed to Cop-C, *jest architektką* '(she) is architect'. He translated the clause, 'Elle est architecte' (She is an architect), revealing that he understood its meaning. In another clause with an implicit subject, Gilles accepted the order OV. The data from these two tests reveal Gilles' preference for the order SVO at this early point in L2 acquisition, a result that is not surprising given that the input was primarily presented in the order SVO (92% of the declarative sentences showed SVO constituent word order) and his L1 is an SVO language.

Gilles: Placing the negative particle nie *at Period 1h30.*   Gilles found the correct position for the Polish negator *nie* early on as seen in his responses to the three sentences in the first word order test that required the placement of *nie*. He placed them all correctly in pre-verbal position, suggesting that after very limited exposure to Polish *nie*, he had already formulated an effective hypothesis concerning the placement of *nie*, one that shows no reliance on his L1.

Gilles: Placing the reflexive pronoun się *at Period 1h30.*   In the first word order test, Gilles placed the two possible tokens of *się* in pre-verbal position. An analysis of the first 1h30 of Polish input reveals that *się* appeared in both pre- and post-verbal positions with approximately identical frequency (51% Refl-V, 49% V-Refl). Given that the analogous French reflexive pronoun appears in pre-verbal position, this suggests an L1 influence on his placement of *się*. Further examination of the input, however, discloses the fact that the Polish instructor generally used Refl-V in questions and V-Refl in statements. We will discuss this point in detail during our analysis of the group data in Chapter 9 (cf. third section of Chapter 9).

During the grammaticality judgements, Gilles accepted an occurrence of *się* in post-verbal position, as seen below:

5) Original clause: *Nazywa się ona Mary*
             appelle se elle Mary (is called Refl she Mary)
             V Refl S C

  Gilles' response: *Ona nazywa się Mary*
             elle appelle se Mary (she is called Refl Mary)
             S V Refl C

Gilles changed the basic constituent word order in favour of SVO, replacing V-Refl-S-C with S-V-Refl-C and translated the structure as 'Elle s'appelle Mary' (She is called Mary), confirming his correct comprehension of the sentence elements. The data from both tests taken together suggest that Gilles has an early preference for the order Refl-V; however, he appears undisturbed by the order V-Refl.

Gilles: Verbal morphology at Period 1h30

The first grammaticality judgement test contained three errors of verbal morphology. Gilles found and corrected two of them:

6) **pochodzisz* (2p sg) → *pochodzi* (3p sg)
   (tu) proviens (de) → (elle) provient (de)
   ([you] come [from] → [she] comes [from])
7) **mieszkam* (1p sg) → *mieszka* (3p sg)
   (je) habite → (elle) habite ([I] live → [she] lives)

Gilles' modifications suggest that he perceived some Polish verbal morphology from the beginning. He was not always consistent, however, as we see in Example (8) below, where he failed to replace the second person verbal form *znasz* (connais 'know'-2p sg) with third person *zna* (connaît 'knows' – 3p sg) as required by the context.

8) *i *znasz dobrze język hiszpański*
   et (tu) connais bien langue espagnol
   (and [you] know well language Spanish)

The semantic processing of (8) may have required a greater cognitive effort for Gilles than did his processing of (6) and (7). This is evidenced by the follow-up translation test in which Gilles had no difficulty translating (6) and (7). He translated (8) above, however, as 'et elle parle bien espagnol' (and she speaks well Spanish). In our global analyses of the data collected from our learners during the grammaticality judgement test, we observed a number of French equivalents used by our informants to translate *znać* (connaître 'to know'). During this first period of acquisition, Gilles regularly translated *znać* as 'parler' (to speak).

However, in the Polish input, the verb *mówić* (parler 'to speak'/dire 'to say') was normally used to express the meaning 'to speak' (as in 'to speak a language'). The presence of synonyms in the input may have complicated Gilles' access to pertinent semantic information. In addition, the clause in Example (8) contained the word *język* 'language', a word he did not explicitly translate during the translation test. He translated *język hiszpański* 'langue espagnole' (Spanish language) as 'espagnol' (Spanish).

Another explanation for Gilles' accurate corrections of (6) and (7) may be found in the frequency effect of items in the input. Table 6.1 shows the frequency of the verb forms in the three clauses in question and their grammatical variants in the first 1h30 of Polish instruction.

Table 6.1 Gilles' responses to grammaticality judgements and frequency of verb forms in the input at Period 1h30

Appropriate variant (not in test)	Corrected	Inappropriate variant in test	Tokens in the input (1h30)
pochodzi (3p sg)	Yes		52
		pochodzisz (2p sg)	16
mieszka (3p sg)	Yes		41
		mieszkam (1p sg)	19
zna (3p sg)	No		11
		znasz (2p sg)	17

In Table 6.1, we observe that the forms required by the context in clauses (6) and (7), *pochodzi* and *mieszka*, were more frequent in the input than their grammatical variants. The contrary was true in (8), where Gilles failed to find and correct the morphological error. Clearly with such little data we cannot conclude an effect of item frequency in the input here, nor can we generalise any such effect to other learners. This is a crucial question for our study of initial processing of a foreign language, however, and will therefore be analysed in explicit detail in our group results (Chapters 7–9).

To conclude this section, we observe that after 1h30 of exposure to Polish, Gilles appeared to already have the capacity to perceive, judge and correct certain incorrect third person singular forms, provided that the sentence presented no difficulty on the semantic level.

Gilles: Period 3h30

Period 3h30 includes the first 30 minutes of input of the third Polish lesson, a 30-minute period that served as a warm-up in Polish before our learners took a second series of tests. It allowed them to review the vocabulary encountered during the first two lessons with a view to avoiding misinterpretations that could falsify results.

As stated in his journal entry, Gilles found the second word order test 'quite easy' and the oral translation test 'very easy'. The grammaticality judgement test and its translation apparently posed more problems: 'This exercise disturbs me a bit; I doubt that I did very well'.

Gilles: Speech comprehension at Period 3h30

During the oral translation test, Gilles encountered few problems of comprehension. Basic constituent word order in simple Polish sentences apparently posed little problem for him. He translated both sentences *'Anna lubi lody'* (Anna likes ice cream) (SVO) and *'lody lubi Anna'* (ice cream likes Anna) (OVS) correctly with 'Anna aime les glaces' (Anna likes ice cream). The only sentence that posed a problem of comprehension was Sentence (9) below:

> 9) Sentence heard: *ja również zjem deser*
>   je/moi aussi mangerai dessert
>   (I/me too will eat dessert)
>   Gilles' translation:... mange dessert (...eat dessert)

This sentence contains an explicit subject, *ja* 'I/me', as the focus element of the sentence. In the input sentences with an implicit subject were much more frequent than those with an explicit subject. We are unable to verify whether Gilles understood the first person nature of the verb *zjem* as he translated it into French with 'mange' (eat), a form that reflects either first or third person. His translation, however, leads us to believe that he understood neither the word *również* 'too/also' nor the pragmatics of the sentence, that is, the emphasis expressed by the explicit subject.

Gilles: Grammatical analysis at Period 3h30

Gilles: Basic constituent word order at Period 3h30.   The data from period 3h30 continue to confirm Gilles' preference for the order SVO. He chose the correct word order for all 10 sentences in the second word order test, replying in all cases with the order SVO, as did all the informants of our Polish native speaker control group.

Of the 6 clauses in the second grammaticality judgement test, Gilles allowed only one non-canonical word order, as seen in Example (10):

> 10) Preceding clause: *Piotr jest w restauracji*
>   Pierre est à restaurant (Peter is at restaurant)
>   Clause in question: *piwa   napije   się   on*
>   bière   boira   se   il (beer will drink Refl he)

This clause was poorly accepted by our Polish informants. Ten of our 12 NS informants changed the order to SVO: *on napije się piwa* 'il boira se bière' (he will drink Refl beer). Two modified the aspect as well: *pije piwo* '(il) boit bière' (he drinks beer) (imperfective). Gilles, however, accepted this OVS structure and translated it as 'il boit de la bière' (he drinks beer), demonstrating that he understood the individual elements, with the possible exception of aspect, the perfective aspect being marked by *na* on the verb *pije* (cf. 'The verb' in the fourth section of Chapter 3 for analysis of aspect in Polish). Does this acceptance of an OVS structure suggest a certain sensitivity on the part of Gilles to non-SVO word orders in Polish? We will return to this question in our group analyses (cf. 9.1).

Gilles: Placing the negator nie *at Period 3h30.* Before analysing the data concerning the placement of the negator at this period, we remind the reader that Gilles showed signs of understanding the system of negating the Polish predicate already at Period 1h30. Analysis of the data collected at Period 3h30 confirms this understanding. In the four sentences containing *nie* in the second word order test, Gilles placed the negator in its appropriate position, pre-verbal.

The negator *nie* also appeared in two of the grammaticality judgement sentences. In one, *nie* was well placed and Gilles accepted it. In the other, *nie* was incorrectly placed in the post-verbal position, and Gilles moved it into pre-verbal position.

These results provide convincing evidence that Gilles has formulated a successful hypothesis concerning clausal negation in Polish. After only 3h30 of exposure to Polish, his NL appears not to intervene with his hypothesis on negation. Other factors, such as the input, seem to play a stronger role. We will return to Gilles' preferences concerning the position of *nie* again at Period 7h00.

Gilles: Placing the reflexive pronoun się *at Period 3h30.* At Period 1h30, Gilles showed a preference for the order Refl-V, that of his NL. Interestingly enough, at Period 3h30, this pattern reversed. In the three sentences of the word order test that contain a reflexive pronoun, Gilles consistently placed the pronoun in post-verbal position. An analysis of the input shows that pre-verbal *się* was less frequent in the cumulative input at Period 3h30 than was post-verbal *się* (41% and 58% respectively). This would suggest that Gilles' responses (V-Refl) reflect an influence of frequency in the input already after 3h30 of exposure to Polish. At the same time, they fail to confirm the alternation hypothesis (Jansen *et al.*, 1981), which states that when two phenomena alternate in the input (e.g. in our case Refl-V and V-Refl), the structure selected by the learner will be that of the L1. This hypothesis was indeed confirmed by Gilles' responses at Period 1h30, but not at Period 3h30. Two related interpretations may explain this result. It is possible that the alternation hypothesis is only valid for certain periods of acquisition or that its validity may be dependent on the quantity of input received for each alternative in question. If, for example, the alternative that differs from the L1 structure is more frequent in the input than the alternative that resembles the L1 structure, it could be that this frequency is in fact a more viable cue than the presence of an equivalent form in the L1. We will analyse this phenomenon further in our group results (cf. third section of Chapter 9).

Gilles: Verbal morphology at Period 3h30

We inserted three ungrammatical verb forms in the second grammaticality judgement test, two of which Gilles found and corrected. His responses and word frequency are shown in Table 6.2.

We see in Table 6.2 that the appropriate forms were more frequent in the input than the inappropriate variants. It seems that the input played an important role in Gilles' ability to identify and correct inappropriate forms in the text. He did not, however, signal a problem or replace the incorrect form *zjem* (mangerai 'will eat' – 1p sg) with *zje* (mangera 'will eat' – 3p sg), which, after all, appeared 56 times in the input. We suggested in Period 1h30 that the level of semantic difficulty of the given sentence items may have had an effect on Gilles' ability to process the grammatical information. Looking at the clause in question, Example (11), we can imagine this being the case here as well.

11) Original clause: *i *zjem kotlet schabowy*
            et (je) mangerai côtelette
            (and [I] will eat pork chops)

Gilles made no modification to this structure; however, his translation shows signs of processing difficulty in that he originally translated the form *zjem* with 'prend' (take), crossed it out and replaced it with 'mange' (eat). Could it be that the cognitive effort needed to comprehend the sentence left insufficient resources for grammatical analysis in the form of a correction?

Table 6.2 Gilles' responses to grammaticality judgements and frequency of verb forms in the input at Period 3h30

Appropriate variant (not in test)	Corrected	Inappropriate variant in test	Tokens in cumulative input (3h30)
chce (3p sg)	Yes		**75**
		chcą (3p pl)	23
zje (3p sg)	No		**56**
		zjem (1p sg)	18
lubi (3p sg)	Yes		**41**
		lubię (1p sg)	8

Gilles: Period 4h00

Following an additional 30 minutes of Polish input, we administered the first sentence repetition test in which our learners were asked to repeat the Polish sentences they heard. Gilles, seemingly discouraged, made the following comment about his performance: 'I couldn't do it at all'.

Gilles: Speech perception/sentence repetitions at Period 4h00

Analysis of 17 Polish sentence repetitions allowed us to identify certain strategies used by beginning learners to respond to such a task (see Chapter 7 for group results). After 4h00 of input, Gilles was able to accurately repeat three of the four 4-word sentences. In the fourth sentence, Gilles failed to repeat the word in sentence-final position *chętnie* (volontiers 'with pleasure'), a word that was categorised as phonemically distant. The other sentence he repeated in its entirety was a 7-word sentence presented below in which the words were either frequent in the input or had a fairly high transparency rating. The word order was SVO and the sentence contained no Polish consonants that present particular difficulty for French speakers (cf. Chapter 7 for criteria used to measure frequency, transparency and phonemic distance).

12) Original sentence and Gilles' repetition:

Marek jest studentem, i mieszka w Krakowie

Marc est étudiant et habite à Cracovie

(Mark is student and lives in Krakow)

In one case, Gilles' word order differed from that of the original sentence, suggesting an attempt at comprehension:

13) Original sentence:

książkę mojego kolegi, zna Piotr bardzo dobrze

livre mon collègue connaît Pierre très bien

(book my colleague knows Peter very well = Peter knows my colleague's book very well)

Gilles' repetition: *zna mój kolegi*

          connaît mon collègue (knows my colleague)

Of the 17 sentences, Gilles repeated nothing in only three sentences. In the vast majority of cases, he repeated the first few words of the sentence only. Looking at these results in terms of correct word repetitions (cf. 'Hypotheses' in the first section of Chapter 7 for criteria used to judge repetitions), we found that Gilles repeated 40 of the 113 words correctly, that is, 35% of all the words, as shown in Table 6.3.

Returning to Gilles' comment in his journal, 'I couldn't do it at all', we conclude that he performed better on the sentence repetition test than he had apparently thought.

Table 6.3 Results of Gilles' sentence repetitions (measured in words) at Period 4h00

Total words repeated		Words repeated correctly	
Raw score (n =113)	*Percentage*	*Raw score* (n =113)	*Percentage*
45	40	40	35

Gilles: Period 7h00

Period 7h00 includes tests of comprehension and grammatical analysis administered to learners during the fifth class session.

Gilles: Speech comprehension at Period 7h00

The results of the third oral translation test show no sign of Gilles being disturbed by the order of basic sentence constituents in his comprehension of simple sentences in Polish. In the test, '*Marek lubi zupę*' (Marc aime soupe 'Mark likes soup' – SVO) is juxtaposed with '*zupę lubi Marek*' (soupe aime Marc 'soup likes Mark' – OVS). Gilles gave the same accurate translation for both sentences: 'Marek aime la soupe' (Mark likes the soup). In the same manner, '*Jacek zna restaurację*' (Jacques connaît restaurant 'John knows restaurant' – SVO) was contrasted with '*restaurację zna Jacek*' (restaurant connaît Jacques 'restaurant knows John' – OVS). Gilles was correct in translating both with 'Jacek connaît le restaurant' (John knows the restaurant). Although these results seem to suggest that the order OVS does not affect Gilles' aural comprehension, we return to the research programme of those working in the Competition Model framework (cf. Bates & MacWhinney, 1987). Even for a speaker of an SVO language, the order OVS should not necessarily present problems of comprehension if one argument is animate and the other is not; we do not say 'The soup likes Mark'. The problem becomes serious when both arguments are animate as in 'Anna likes Mark' or 'the girl likes the boy'. Our selection of lexical items in the input did not permit us to test this hypothesis, but this will be a priority in a future study of early L2 acquisition.

When comparing Gilles' responses during the oral translation tests at Periods 3h30 and 7h00, we see some amelioration in his ability to comprehend Polish structures that make use of an explicit subject to place the referent in focus. At Period 3h30, Gilles failed to translate the following sentence in its entirety:

Example (9) repeated here:
    Sentence heard: *ja również zjem deser*
                        moi aussi mangerai dessert (I too will eat dessert)
    Gilles' translation:... mange dessert (... eat dessert)

At Period 7h00, however, he came closer to a correct translation of a similar sentence:

14) Sentence heard: *ja również napiję się piwa*
                moi aussi boirai Refl bière
                (I too will drink Refl beer)

Gilles' translation: Moi aussi je bois de la bière (Me too I drink beer).

The explicit subject did not seem to disturb him here as it did during the previous translation test. Missing from his translation, however, is a sign that he understood the Polish perfective aspect. The correct translation of this sentence is, 'moi aussi je prendrai une bière' (me too I'll take/have a beer), the logical context being that of ordering a beer in a bar or restaurant, and the speaker is not yet drinking the beer. Gilles' translation fails to communicate this. As we mentioned in our analysis of Polish aspect in Chapter 3, we did not focus on this phenomenon in our study. We simply wish to point out that even at the very first stages of L2 acquisition, adult learners need to understand and communicate such complex semantic and pragmatic notions. Extensive research focusing on this question has been conducted using production data (cf. Bardovi-Harlig, 2000; Starren, 2001), but future research in the area of comprehension is needed as well.

Gilles: Grammatical analysis at Period 7h00

In Gilles' final journal entry, he comments on his difficulty with Polish grammar: 'This aspect of language was not treated succinctly. Is it because it was not dealt with in detail that it appears to be the most difficult area for me?'

    Gilles: Basic constituent word order at Period 7h00. Canonical SVO word order was dominant in Gilles' responses in Polish as of the first round of tests. This dominance continued at Period 7h00. In the word order test, Gilles opted for SVO order in 12 of the 13 sentences. The remaining sentence reflects a case of predicate coordination, comprising two verbs to be linked by means of a conjunction as shown below:

15) Context sentence: *Charlot nie płaci w restauracji.*
                  Charlot pas paye au restaurant
                  (Charlie not pays at restaurant)

Words to put in order:
              policja – i – zabiera – Charlot – przyjeżdża – do więzienia
              police – et – amène – Charlie – arrive – en prison
              (police – and – take away – Charlie – arrive – to prison)

Gilles' response: *przyjeżdża policja i Charlot zabiera do wiezienia*
                  arrive police et Charlot emmène en prison
                  (arrive police and Charlie take away to prison)

Gilles provided a correct response for the first predicate, *przyjeżdża policja* 'arrive police', selecting the order V-S, the preferred order of 11 of our 12 Polish NSs. The second predicate, however, posed a problem. This may be due to Gilles' miscomprehension of the verb *zabiera* (emmène 'take away'). In a subsequent task, Gilles translated '*i zabiera Charlot znowu więzienia*' (et emmène Charlot à nouveau en prison 'and take away Charlie again to prison') as 'et Charlot *retourne* en prison' (and Charlie *returns* to prison). If in fact Gilles thought *zabiera* meant 'returns', it follows that he probably interpreted *Charlot* as the subject of the verb *zabiera*, formulating a compound sentence. In a French compound sentence, as in English, an overt subject is required for both predicates unless the first subject is coreferential with the second, in which case ellipsis is allowed, as in 'La police arrive et amène Charlot en prison' (The police arrive and take Charlie away to prison). If, however, the subjects of the two verbs are not coreferential (as appears to be the case in Gilles' interpretation), then French requires two overt subjects, normally placed in front of their respective verbs. This would explain Gilles' placement of *Charlot* in pre-verbal position, having assigned it subject status. Gilles' confusion can be highlighted by his lack of modification to the following clause in the grammaticality judgement test:

16) Original clause: *i zabiera Charlot znowu do więzienia*
      et emmène Charlot à nouveau en prison
      (and takes Charlie again to prison)

Gilles' translation: et Charlot retourne en prison
      (and Charlie returns to prison)

Gilles accepted the V-S word order and made no modification to this structure. We will return to these sentences in our analyses of the group data to examine the responses of our other learners (cf. the first section of Chapter 9).

Gilles: Placing the negator nie *at Period 7h00.* The word order test at Period 7h00 comprised five sentences that required the placement of *nie*. Gilles responded accurately in all cases by consistently placing the negator in pre-verbal position, even in a sentence that posed problems for him on the semantic level. The negator appeared only once in the grammaticality judgement test, in post-verbal position. Gilles found and corrected this error.

Gilles: Placing the reflexive pronoun się *at Period 7h00.* After 3h30 of input, we observed that Gilles favoured the post-verbal position for the reflexive pronoun *się*. This preference was confirmed after 7h00 of input. In the three sentences containing the reflexive pronoun in the word order test, Gilles responded with the order V-Refl. There were no occurrences of *się* in the grammaticality judgement test. An analysis of this phenomenon in the input reveals the same pattern as was found at

Period 3h30, that is, that the order V-Refl was significantly more frequent in the cumulative input than was Refl-V (66% and 33% respectively). This analysis suggests that, with respect to this phenomenon, Gilles conforms more to the pattern of the input than he does to the pattern of his L1.

Gilles: Verbal morphology at Period 7h00

The grammaticality judgement test administered during Period 7h00 contained only two incorrect verb forms, as shown in Table 6.4.

Table 6.4 Gilles' responses to grammaticality judgements and frequency of verb forms in the input at Period 7h00

Appropriate variant (not in test)	Corrected	Inappropriate variant in test	Tokens in cumulative input (7h00)
jest (3p sg)	Yes		556
		jestem (1p sg)	78
pije (3p sg)	No		44
		piją (3p pl)	10

Finding the correct form *jest* posed no problem for Gilles, possibly due to its high score of frequency in the input (556 tokens). The second error, which he did not correct, requires a more detailed analysis. It involved a one-word proposition *piją* (boivent 'drink'– 3p pl):

17) Original clause: *piją

(ils) boivent ([they]) drink)

Gilles' translation: il boit (he drinks)

The context required the form *pije* (boit 'drinks' – 3p sg). In fact, Gilles' translation 'il boit' (he drinks) demonstrates his comprehension of semantic information. Although he failed to provide an overt correction of the morphological error, he apparently processed the verb correctly.

Gilles: Period 8h00

Gilles: Speech perception/sentence repetitions at Period 8h00

The results of the sentence repetitions after 8h00 of input demonstrate a development in Gilles' capacity to repeat Polish words. Table 6.5 shows that Gilles repeated 40% of the words at Period 4h00 (35% were correct repetitions) and 59% at Period 8h00 (53% were correct repetitions). As we observed in the first sentence repetition test administered after 4h00 of input, at Period 8h00 Gilles changed the word order from the original

Table 6.5 Results of Gilles' sentence repetitions (measured in words) at Periods 4h00 and 8h00

Period 4h00				Period 8h00			
Total words repeated		Words repeated correctly		Total words repeated		Words repeated correctly	
Raw score (n =113)	%	Raw score (n =113)	%	Raw score (n =113)	%	Raw score (n =113)	%
45	40	40	35	67	59	60	53

order he heard in two sentences, suggesting a strategy of attempting to understand before repeating.

Gilles: Summary of development

In terms of perception, the results of the two sentence repetition tests show a clear development in Gilles' ability to perceive and reproduce Polish words in that he repeated the sentences more thoroughly, repeated more words and repeated more words correctly after 8h00 of input than after 4h00. We also noticed that he showed signs of trying to understand sentences before he repeated them. In Chapter 7 we will present global results of our eight learners, analysing the sentence repetitions in terms of various factors that will further our understanding of the role of saliency in L2 perception.

The results of the oral translation tests reveal that Gilles had little to no problem processing simple SVO- and OVS-type sentences. The interpretation of these results, however, highlights the fact that future research requires more control over the choice of lexical items assigned to fill the function of subject and object in both the input and the corresponding tests. Data collected by means of tests in which word order and morphology cues compete with each other will provide the researcher with important information concerning learners' processing of these language properties. We also noticed from Gilles' data that a sentence with a verb in initial position was processed as a question, signalling a possible reliance on L1 for the processing of such a sentence. Gilles' data collected at Period 7h00 provide evidence for a better comprehension of sentences with an explicit subject as the focus element, such as *ja również* 'me too', than data collected earlier in the study.

Regarding grammatical analysis, Gilles showed a preference for SVO word order as of the first round of tests. This preference remained intact throughout the data collection period, although Gilles accepted non-SVO orders in grammaticality judgement tests. He produced a V-S word order in one instance, *przyjeżdża policja* 'arrive police'. This was the most frequent order in the input and the order preferred by 11 of our 12 native Polish speakers. This response may have been influenced by the frequency of this structure in the input, or by a certain sensitivity on the part of Gilles to the organisation of pragmatic information in Polish, or by both. What is clear is that his V-S response does not corroborate a hypothesis of L1 transfer, and this after only 7 hours of exposure to Polish.

Concerning the negator *nie*, Gilles placed the negator in pre-verbal position, the correct position in Polish, as of the first word order test and after only seven tokens of pre-verbal *nie* in the input. This choice was clearly not due to an influence of the L1 if one accepts the general consensus that the negator *nie* in Polish is equivalent to the negator *pas* in French (cf. 'Negation' in the third section of Chapter 3). We will return to this point in our analysis of Luc's data and in our group results (cf. second section of Chapter 9).

During the first word order test, Gilles placed the reflexive pronoun *się* in pre-verbal position, the required position in French. An analysis of the input reveals that the pronoun appeared as often in pre-verbal as in post-verbal position. The alternation hypothesis (Jansen *et al.*, 1981) predicts that when two alternatives are present in the input, learners will rely on their L1. Gilles' performance at Period 1h30 confirmed this hypothesis; however, this was not the case at Period 3h30. The order V-Refl became more frequent in the input, and Gilles began producing this order in his responses. He seemed to rely on his L1 at the beginning when the input showed equivalent frequencies for both positions, but as the input shifted to favouring one of the two orders, he followed the most frequent order, in this case the order *not* predicted by the alternation hypothesis.

Concerning verbal morphology, Gilles demonstrated a sensitivity to this phenomenon in Polish already after only 1h30 of input. During the various test periods, he regularly identified and corrected some but not all of the ungrammatical morphological markers. Analysis suggests a possible negative effect of semantic processing on Gilles' ability to find and correct errors of verbal morphology at this early stage of L2 acquisition.

Case Study 2: Luc

Like Gilles, Luc was born and raised as an only child in France by French-speaking parents. He was 27 years old at the time of the study, a year older than Gilles. His only second language was English, for which he gave himself the rating of 2 out of 5. An oral interview with a trained English instructor and evaluator revealed that his English was stronger than he had surmised, and he was rated similarly to Gilles with a 3.5.[2]

As English was the first foreign language choice of both Gilles and Luc in schools using the French national curriculum, we can assume that they followed a similar route in their acquisition of L2 English. Luc was also working towards a 'licence' (French equivalent to the Bachelor's) in FLE (French as a Foreign Language). In his journal entry following the first Polish session, Luc provides a frank explanation for his choice of Polish, that he needed to fulfil the requirement of the course entitled *Learning and Self-Observation*. He admits to choosing Polish for this reason, but adds that the experimental nature of the course intrigues him. He writes, 'Concerning my motivation, I sense that it was reinforced by this first class. Understanding the first lesson, even if simple, was on the whole quite gratifying'.

Although learners were unaware of the fact that our study involved an in-depth analysis of the Polish input, Luc seemed to have understood the importance of the constraints that such a study requires: 'The teacher asked us not to look through textbooks, not to seek out speakers of Polish, and not to use a dictionary. This is all part of a "contract" we have agreed to'.

Luc: Period 1h30

Luc describes his reactions to his first exposure with Polish on several levels. From the point of view of production, he remarks, 'I had to introduce myself and somehow managed to gabble that my name was Luc, that I spoke French and that I lived in Paris'. Referring to Polish grammar, he observes, 'The only thing I managed to figure out myself was that the subject complement agrees in gender with its subject'. We notice here Luc's metalinguistic work already in place with no prompting whatsoever on the part of the instructor (cf. 'The Polish instruction' in the second section of Chapter 4 for a description of constraints imposed on the Polish instructor).

Luc: Speech comprehension at Period 1h30

Luc seemed less sure of himself than Gilles during the first oral translation test. Of the eight sentences heard, he mistranslated or failed to translate four, whereas Gilles had trouble with only two. Of the sentences that posed a problem for Luc, one was SVO, one was VSO (here the problem was lexical – Luc translated *lubi* as 'habite' 'lives' rather than 'aime' 'likes') and two were of the PP/Adv-V-S-(Adv) type. The latter two appear below:

18) Sentence heard: *po polsku mówi ona dobrze*
                en polonais parle elle bien
                (in Polish speaks she well)
                PP/Adv V S Adv
    Luc's translation: parler (to speak)

(19) Sentence heard: *w Krakowie pracuje Jacek*
                à Cracovie travaille Jacques
                (in Krakow works James)
                PP/Adv V S

Luc provided no translation for this sentence.

Of the four sentences for which Luc provided correct translations, two were of the SVO type, one was C-V-S-Adv and one was V-S-C. It appears that word order was not the deciding factor for whether or not Luc comprehended the Polish sentence. His inability to translate certain sentences was more likely due to being unfamiliar with the Polish lexical items, compounded by the fact that these sentences were spoken out of context. As Bremer *et al.* (1996) point out, problems of the lexical type are often the least difficult. In a natural setting, if learners do not understand a given word, they can request a definition from their interlocutor. However, in a test situation such as this where sentences are void of context, Luc absconds.

Luc: Grammatical analysis at Period 1h30

Luc: Basic constituent word order at Period 1h30.   The first word order test of the study posed a variety of problems for Luc. He responded correctly to only 4 of the 10 sentences (Gilles responded correctly to 7), partially completed another 4 sentences and provided incorrect word orders in the remaining 2 sentences. His accurate responses show a preference for SVO word order, as did Gilles'. Of the four sentences to which he only partially responded, three of them required the placement of *nie*. Luc began a response for three of the four sentences, but after producing one word, he stopped. The following pair of sentences serves as an example:

20) Context sentence: *Tomek mieszka w Paryżu*
                Tomek habite à Paris (Tomek lives in Paris)
    Words to put in order: *nie – on – lubi – Paryża*
                pas-il-aime-Paris (not – he – likes – Paris)

Learners were instructed to put the words in the second sentence in order. In response to Sentence (20) above, Luc began with the word *on* (il 'he'), but went no further. In one of the sentences in which the person in question was a woman, he began with *ona* (elle 'she') and again stopped. Looking at the grammaticality judgement tests and their translations administered immediately after the word order test, we were able to evaluate Luc's comprehension of subject pronouns. In the grammaticality judgement test, he added the explicit pronoun *ona* in three of the sentences that were in fact correct in Polish as they were, with an implicit subject. He then translated this same pronoun with 'elle' (she), confirming that he understood the meaning of the pronoun *ona*.

If we return to the results of the word order test, it seems that Luc was searching for a subject to complete the sentence. He found the pronouns *on* and *ona*, neither of which posed a problem for him. In all cases, however, it was the predicate that caused difficulty. Having been instructed to use the negator *nie* (and this, with no information about *nie* in the first 1h30 of the Polish course), he took no risks.

During the grammaticality judgement test, Luc not only added explicit subjects, but also changed the order of the basic constituents of the two sentences with non-SVO word order to SVO. For example, the word order in Sentence (21) below was V-Refl-S-C. Luc replaced it with the order S-V-Refl-C:

21) Original sentence: *nazywa się ona Mary*
                          appelle se elle Mary (is called Refl she Mary)
    Luc's response: *ona nazywa się Mary*
                          elle appelle se Mary (she is called Refl Mary)
    Luc's translation: Elle se nomme Mary
                          (She herself names Mary' = She calls herself Mary')

In Sentence (22), the original order was V-S-PP/Adv. Luc changed it to S-V-PP/Adv.

22) Original sentence: **mieszkam ona w Chicago*
                          (je) habite elle à Chicago (live she in Chicago)
    Luc's response: *ona *mieszkam w Chicago*
                          elle *(je) habite à Chicago (she *[I] live in Chicago)
    Luc's translation: Elle habite à Chicago. (She lives in Chicago.)

Like Gilles, Luc showed a preference for SVO word order when formulating Polish sentences at Period 1h30. In addition, he seemed to have understood the pronouns *on* and *ona*, as well as their syntactic function, that of the subject.

Luc: Placing the negator nie *at Period 1h30.*   We pointed out earlier that the sentences in the word order test containing the negator *nie* posed problems for Luc. He provided incomplete responses for all sentences that required the placement of *nie*. We can only speculate that his inability to process the item was due to the fact that he had not yet received any information about it (only 7 tokens during Period 1h30). It appears, in fact, that Luc was unable to formulate a testable hypothesis about the placement of *nie*. The grammaticality judgement test included a case of the negator placed in pre-verbal position, the appropriate position in Polish. Luc modified nothing in this sentence; however, he also provided no translation for the sentence, leading us to believe that he was, for whatever reason, unable to process a sentence with *nie*. These results suggest that at this period of acquisition, the placement of the negator *nie* is a troubling phenomenon for Luc, to the extent that he was unable to accomplish the task at hand.

    Luc: Placing the reflexive pronoun się *at Period 1h30.*   In the word order test, Luc's word arrangements resulted in two sentences with Refl-V (the order in French and one of the orders in the input). During the grammaticality judgement test, he accepted a sentence with the order V-Refl. The input contained 51% tokens of *się* in Refl-V order and 49% V-Refl order. As the alternation hypothesis (Jansen *et al.*, 1981) predicts, when exposed to two alternatives in the input, learners will opt for that of their L1. It seems fair to say that Luc's responses fail to argue in favour of the alternation hypothesis. It seems, rather, that Luc is struggling between two hypotheses, a pre- and post-verbal placement of *się*, reflecting a possible effect of the input in that both are possible. We will return to Luc's placement of *się* later on in our analyses of data collected at Period 3h30.

Luc: Verbal morphology at Period 1h30

    Contrary to Gilles, who demonstrated a fairly strong sensitivity to the Polish inflexional system from the beginning, Luc showed no sign of this sensitivity. As can be seen in Table 6.6, of the three ungrammatical verb forms presented in the first grammaticality judgement test, Luc identified none.

    Input seems to have had no effect on Luc's ability to find and correct errors of verbal morphology at Period 1h30. His translations of two of the clauses in the test, however, suggest that his trouble finding ungrammatical forms did not affect his overall comprehension of the sentence. An explicit subject was present in only one of these two clauses, an essential cue for comprehension if a learner is unable to process morphological

Table 6.6 Gilles' and Luc's responses to grammaticality judgements and frequency of verb forms in the input at Period 1h30

Appropriate variant (not in test)	*Corrected (Gilles)*	*Corrected (Luc)*	*Inappropriate variant in test*	*Tokens in the input (1h30)*
pochodzi (3p sg)	Yes	No		**52**
			pochodzisz (2p sg)	16
mieszka (3p sg)	Yes	No		**41**
			mieszkam (1p sg)	19
zna (3p sg)	No	No		**11**
			znasz (2p sg)	17

information on the verb. The original clause with no overt subject appears below followed by Luc's response and translation:

23) Original clause: *i *pochodzisz ze Stanów Zjednoczonych*
             et *(tu) viens de Etats Unis
             (and *[you] come from United States)
    Luc's modification: *i ona *pochodzisz ze Stanów Zjednoczonych*
             et elle *(tu) viens de Etats Unis
             (and she *[you] come from United States)
    Luc's translation: 'et elle vient des USA'
             (and she comes from the USA)

The verb form in the original clause is inappropriately second person singular. Luc apparently used context from previous clauses and supplied an overt subject *ona* (elle 'she') indicating third person singular. He then translated the Polish verb (2p sg) with 'vient' (comes), third person singular in French. This is a case where context was provided, and Luc took advantage of it.

The clause with no overt subject posed a different type of problem for Luc:

24) Original clause: *i *znasz dobrze język hiszpański*
             et *(tu) connais bien langue espagnole
             (and *[you] know well language Spanish)

The context continued to require the third person singular form *zna* (connaît 'knows'). Luc began his translation with the conjunction 'et' (and), but failed to continue. He apparently found nothing to rely on; even the context clue provided by *ona* (she) failed him here. Luc's inability to translate the clause suggests that he had trouble processing individual lexical items. As a result, he was left unequipped and unable to accomplish the task.

Luc: Period 3h30

In his second journal entry, Luc comments on the strategies he used to manage the acquisition of his new foreign language. In terms of perception and comprehension, he writes the following: 'The strategies I use in class involve listening assiduously to everything said'. Concerning the processing of lexical items, he adds, 'As this language proves quite difficult for me, I limit the vocabulary to be learned to words that are absolutely necessary so that I can master them'. In essence, he claims to control his own intake in order to avoid overloading his cognitive system.

From the perspective of the student-learner-informant, the third Polish session proved challenging in that a large number of tests were administered during this session. Although Luc expressed frustration with his 'guinea pig' status, he wrote, 'Even if the tests were not designed specifically for our Polish course, they still help us evaluate our language development. Indeed, this series of tests seemed significantly easier than those taken during the first class session'.

Luc: Speech comprehension at Period 3h30

Luc's responses during the second oral translation test after 3h30 of input are difficult to interpret. Firstly, he failed to translate one sentence and only partially translated others, including those with words that had a high frequency count in the input. Let us take a look at two such sentences with non-SVO word order:

25) Sentence heard: *po polsku mówi ona dobrze* (PP/Adv-V-S)
                en polonais parle elle bien
                (in Polish speaks she well)

Luc provided no translation for this sentence, replying with a question mark only.

26) Sentence heard: *zupę zje Jacek* (O-V-S)
                soupe mangera Jacques (soup will eat James)
Luc's translation: Jacek est... (Jacek is . . .)

In contrast, Luc correctly translated several sentences that contained non-SVO word order, such as the following:

27) Sentence heard: *nie lubi Ewa Krakowa* (Neg-V-S-O)
                pas aime Eva Cracovie (not likes Eva Krakow)
Luc's translation: Ewa n'aime pas Cracovie
                (Eva doesn't like Krakow)

The one SVO sentence that posed a problem for him, as it did to a certain extent for Gilles as well, was a sentence with an explicit subject pronoun:

28) Sentence heard: *ja również zjem deser* (S-Adv-V-O)
                moi aussi mangerai dessert
                (me too will eat dessert)
Luc's translation:... mange un dessert (... eat a dessert)

We will analyse the learners' translations of this sentence in more detail in Chapter 8 in an attempt to understand what caused the difficulty in comprehending a simple SVO Polish sentence with an explicit subject pronoun.

When designing this test, we wrote certain test questions in such a way that the same elements appeared in two distinct sentences with two distinct word orders:

29) Sentence heard: *Anna lubi lody* (SVO)
                Anna aime les glaces (Anna likes ice cream)
30) Sentence heard: *lody lubi Anna* (OVS)
                les glaces aime Anna (ice cream likes Anna)

Luc translated both sentences as 'Anna aime Londres' (Anna likes London). Word order apparently had no effect on Luc's translations. The problem for Luc was the lexical item *lody*, which he misinterpreted in both sentences, regardless of word order. This may be another case where lack of context makes the task at hand nearly impossible, in spite of the fact that all words in the sentences heard had appeared quite frequently in the input. Does input count as 'context' for the learner? Bremer *et al.* (1996: 23) point out the importance of carefully defining the term 'context': '...it is important to take as the point of departure the participants' perspective on context'. Luc, in this case, had no immediate context to rely on. The sole context available was that suggested by the lexical items themselves, useful information if, and only if, Luc understood the items.

Luc: Grammatical analysis at Period 3h30

Luc: Basic constituent word order at Period 3h30.   Luc completed the second word order test at Period 3h30 more successfully than the first, as the comment in his journal predicted. He provided 7 out of 10 correct responses (compared to 4 out of 10 at Period 1h30) all with SVO word order. In the three remaining responses, Luc placed the reflexive pronoun *się* incorrectly, but his choice of basic constituent word order remained SVO, the predominant word order at Period 1h30. The second grammaticality judgement test presented only one occurrence of an order other than SVO. Luc modified it in favour of the order SVO, as did all of our Polish NS informants:

31) Original clause: *piwa   napije   się   on*
                          bière   boira   se   il (beer will drink Refl he)
     Luc's response: *on   napije   piwa   się*
                          il   boira   bière   se (he will drink beer Refl)
Luc's translation:'Il boit de la bière.' (He drinks beer.)

Luc's preference for SVO remains predictable: SVO is preponderant in the input and is the dominant word order of his L1. What interests us, however, is to know when, if ever, he will begin to understand the nuances Polish can express by means of a word order other than SVO.

Luc: Placing the negator nie *at Period 3h30.*   At Period 1h30, we were unable to comment on Luc's hypothesis concerning the placement of *nie*, if he had formulated one at all. Data collected at Period 3h30 reveal an important development concerning this phenomenon. In the four sentences with *nie* in the word order test, Luc placed the negator in preverbal position, the appropriate position in Polish. During the grammaticality judgement test, he accepted the sentence in which *nie* was correctly placed and modified the one in which it was incorrectly placed:

32) Original sentence: **Piotr   *lubię   nie deserów*
                             Pierre aime (1p sg) pas dessert
                             (Peter like not dessert)

Luc's response: *Piotr   nie   *lubię   deserów*
Pierre pas aime (1p sg) dessert
(Peter not like dessert)
Luc's translation: 'Piotr n'aime pas les desserts.'
(Piotr does not like desserts.)

Remember that *nie* was frequent in the input between Periods 1h30 and 3h30 (58 tokens). These results suggest that input played an important role in the development of Luc's interlanguage with regard to his placement of the negator *nie*.

Luc: Placing the reflexive pronoun się *at Period 3h30.*   In his journal entry following the fourth Polish class, Luc reflects on this enigma in Polish, *się*: 'I've been wondering about a sentence structure that appears from time to time, the particle *się*, because I do not understand its function. The instructor was unwilling to respond explicitly to my question about it as this would have required the explanation of a grammar rule. I have finally understood that this particle is somehow linked to specific verbs, but that it corresponds to nothing translatable in French.'

During the Period 1h30 series of tests, while Luc showed a preference for the order Refl-V (that of his L1) in his productions, he accepted the order V-Refl in the one sentence with *się* in the grammaticality judgement test. The results of the Period 3h30 series of tests verify that Luc is indeed bothered by this pronoun. As we mentioned in the preceding section on basic constituent word order, the three sentences that posed a problem for Luc were those containing the pronoun *się*. In the first sentence, he placed *się* in pre-verbal position (normally an appropriate position in Polish), but in this case, this placement resulted in *się* being in sentence-initial position, a position in which *się* is not permitted (cf. 'Reflexive verbs' in the third section of Chapter 3 for details about this phenomenon). In the two other sentences, he produced the order V-C-Refl, judged as ungrammatical by Polish NSs. In the one clause of the grammaticality judgement test in which *się* appeared, Luc replaced the original appropriate order O-V-Refl-S with the order S-V-O-Refl:

33) Original clause: *piwa napije się on*
                    bière boira se il (beer will drink Refl he)
      Luc's response: *on napije piwa się*
                    il boira bière se (he will drink beer Refl)
      Luc's translation: 'Il boit de la bière.' (He drinks beer.)

In spite of his inappropriate placements and his own expressed confusion about this phenomenon, Luc was in fact quite consistent in his placement of *się*, placing it in either sentence-initial or sentence-final position. What might be an explanation for the difficulty of this task? In the case of the verb *napić się* (boire 'to drink'), we could hypothesise that because it has a spoken French equivalent 'se boire' (Refl to drink), as in the sentence, 'On se boit rapidement une bière' (Let's quickly drink a beer), it should be easy. None of our learners, however, translated the various forms of *napić się* using a reflexive pronoun in French. In contrast, the reflexive verb *nazywać się* (s'appeler 'to be called'), introduced in the first Polish class, has a formal French equivalent, 's'appeler', comprised of a reflexive pronoun and a verb as in Polish, and our learners used the French pronoun in their translations. Luc seemed disturbed by both Polish verbs, whether a French equivalent exists or not. Comparing the choices Luc made about word order in similar sentences that appeared in both the word order test and the grammaticality judgement test, his confusion becomes even more evident. In the word order test, he produced the following structure:

34) Luc's response: *się napije piwa* (Refl-V-O)
                    se (il) boira bière (Refl [he] will drink beer)

In the subsequent grammaticality judgement test, however, he modified the word order of the original clause, resulting in the following:

35) Luc's response: *on napije piwa się* (S-V-O-Refl)
                    il boira bière se (he will drink beer Refl)

After 3h30 of Polish input, although Luc was well aware of the existence of *się* and expressed his desire to understand its function, he was unable to produce grammatical sentences with *się*. His strategy at this point seemed to be: place *się* on the sentence periphery until I figure out how to deal with it – in this way, it does not interfere with my comprehension or production of the major sentence elements.

Luc: Verbal morphology at Period 3h30

During the first period of the study, Luc found no ungrammatical forms in the grammaticality judgement test. This pattern continued during the Period 3h30 testing, suggesting that the Polish system of verbal inflexion was not a priority for Luc. He appeared to be focusing his attention on other areas of the language, such as lexical items. This logically follows an observation expressed in his journal: '...meaning has priority over form'. This said, the ungrammatical forms inserted in the test did not appear to interfere with Luc's comprehension of the sentences. He relied on other cues to translate the verbs, and as we already observed in Period 1h30, he did not rely on verbal morphology to obtain information about person and number. When asked to translate the sentences in the grammaticality judgement test, in some cases, Luc translated them into French not according to form, but rather, according to context. The first clause in the text at Period 3h30 establishes *Piotr* as the agent:

(36) Original clause: *Piotr jest w restauracji*
                      Pierre est à restaurant (Peter is at restaurant)

Luc's translation: 'Piotr est au restaurant.'
(Peter is at the restaurant.)

The fourth clause appears as follows:

(37) Original clause: *on również *chcą zieloną sałatę*
il aussi *(ils) veulent verte salade
(he also *[they] want green salad)
Luc's translation: il commande aussi de la salade verte
(he orders also some salad green)

Luc translated a Polish third person plural verb with a French third person singular verb. This implies a reliance on context (*Piotr* and/or *on* 'he') over formal verb endings.

Luc: Period 4h00

Luc: Speech perception/sentence repetitions at Period 4h00

Luc's reaction to the first sentence repetition test can be summed up in the following journal comment: 'It was a practically impossible task'.

Of 17 total sentences, Luc reproduced nothing in five of the sentences, and in four he repeated only one word. When Luc managed to repeat sentences, however, he repeated them well. The number of total words to be repeated was 113. The results of word repetitions are shown in Table 6.7.

Table 6.7 Results of Luc's sentence repetitions (measured in words) at Period 4h00

Total words repeated		Words repeated correctly	
Raw score (n = 113)	*Percentage*	*Raw score (n = 113)*	*Percentage*
33	29	27	24

Altogether, Luc repeated 27 words (24% of all the words) correctly. Learner style may have come into play here. Luc was prudent, even more so than Gilles, and took few risks. He repeated the minimum, but what he repeated was generally accurate. For a drastic comparison, we present the data of another learner from our study, Dalia, collected from this same test. Dalia repeated 65 of the 113 words (58%) accurately, compared to Luc's 24%. Even though Dalia and Luc were both monolingual native French speakers and were exposed to the same input, they responded very differently to the task at hand. This type of detailed analysis highlights how individuals differ in their processing of a foreign language. This observation, in addition to the differences observed between Gilles and Luc, serves as a confirmation that individual

variability must be taken into consideration in models of second
language acquisition.

Luc: Period 7h00

Luc continued his metalinguistic reflection in his journal, commenting
on how the titles/themes of the Polish lessons helped him understand
the structure of Polish: 'The titles of new lessons are always presented in
the target language. For example, in the last class, in order to introduce
us to the dialogue we were about to hear, the instructor presented us
with two titles, *Agnieszka opowiada film* and *Opowiadanie Agnieszki*, which
mean "Agnes recounts a film" and "The story of Agnes" respectively.
These titles offer two benefits: the learner is better able to understand the
meaning of the word "Story": it can be a verb or a common noun. The
learner can also understand that the word declines differently depending
on whether is it the subject or an adjective. The instructor provides us
with no clues. It is up to us, the learners, to figure it out.'

Luc: Speech comprehension at Period 7h00

Several of the sentences heard in the oral translation test posed
problems for Luc. Let us examine two sentences in the test (SVO and
OVS) that contain the same words and share the same semantic content
(they differ only from a pragmatic point of view):

38) Sentence heard: *Jacek zna restaurację* (SVO)
    Jacques connaît restaurant
    (James knows restaurant)
  Luc's translation: 'Jacek...'

39) Sentence heard: *restaurację zna Jacek* (OVS)
    restaurant connaît Jacques (restaurant knows
    James)
  Luc's translation: La même à l'envers (que la 5)
    (The same in reverse [as n° 5])

Luc apparently viewed the two sentences as carrying the same
meaning in spite of their different word orders; however, he appeared
not to understand the content of either sentence. This suggests a certain
sensitivity to the variability in TL constituent word order, independent of
the comprehension of individual lexical items.

Two other sentences merit a comparative analysis:

40) *Marek lubi zupę* (Marc aime soupe 'Mark likes soup'-SVO)
41) *zupę lubi Marek* (soupe aime Marc 'soup likes Mark'-OVS)

Luc translated both sentences with 'Marek aime la soupe' (Marek likes
soup), suggesting that word order had little to no effect on his
comprehension of a simple Polish sentence, at least when the subject
was animated and the direct object was not.

We saw that Gilles accurately translated the terms *ja również* (je/moi aussi 'I/me also') during the oral translation test after 7h00 of input. Luc's translation, however, was incomplete, as seen in the example below:

42) Sentence heard: *ja   również   napiję   się   piwa*
                moi   aussi   boirai   se   bière
                (me   too will drink beer)

Luc's translation: ...boit de la bière. (...drinks beer.)

In this translation, we witness the problem of comprehension linked most probably to a lack of knowledge about the system of verbal morphology and the implicit subject in Polish. Luc translated the verb with the form 'boit' (drinks – 3p sg), showing that for him, the referent is 'il' (he) or 'elle' (she). Even though the pronoun *ja* 'I/me' was frequent in the input, Luc appeared unable to extract the first person singular information to apply it to the verb. In the absence of knowledge about verbal morphology and in the absence of context, Luc was left with no reference points, making it impossible for him to complete the translation.

Luc: Grammatical analysis at Period 7h00

Luc: Basic constituent word order at Period 7h00.   In 12 of the 13 sentences in the word order test after 7h00 of input, Luc placed words in the correct order, and without exception, in SVO order. The remaining sentence was judged incorrect because of Luc's placement of the reflexive pronoun *się*, not because of the basic constituent word order he assigned, which was SVO as well. Results of the grammaticality judgement test, however, suggest a flexibility on his part with regard to word order in Polish in that Luc accepted the two non-SVO clauses in the test. We found this same phenomenon with Gilles, who usually produced sentences of SVO order on the word order test while also accepting non-SVO structures in the grammaticality judgement test. Our analyses of group results in Chapter 9 will provide us with further insight into this phenomenon.

Luc: Placing the negator nie *at Period 7h00.*   The learners were required to place the negator in five of the sentences of the word order test. As with Gilles at this period of exposure to Polish, Luc placed all occurrences of *nie* in the appropriate position, preceding the verb. In the grammaticality judgement test, however, Luc failed to correct the one occurrence of *nie* which appeared in post-verbal position.

Luc: Placing the reflexive pronoun się *at Period 7h00.*   As a reminder, we designed the three word order tests (administered after 1h30, 3h30 and 7h00 of input) in such a way that certain sentences occurred in all three tests. In this way, we could compare learners' responses over the three periods. The following provides an example of how Luc responded differently at each period.

43) Context sentence: *Jak się nazywasz?*

Comment se (tu) appelles?

(How Refl [you] are called?)

Luc's responses: Period 1h30

Barbara się nazywam (C-Refl-V)

Barbara se (je) appelle

(Barbara Refl [I] am called)

Period 3h30

*nazywam Barbara się (V-C-Refl)

(je) appelle Barbara se ([I]) am called Barbara Refl)

Period 7h00

nazywam się Barbara (V-Refl-C)

(je) appelle se Barbara ([I]) am called Refl Barbara)

His response at Period 3h30 is ungrammatical in Polish; the other two are correct. It seems that after 1h30 of input, Luc's first hypothesis about *się* was that it functioned in the same manner as reflexive pronouns in French and was therefore placed in pre-verbal position. In the two hours between Periods 1h30 and 3h30, however, this hypothesis was disturbed, most likely by an input effect, resulting in his placement of the pronoun at the end of the sentence, an inappropriate position in this sentence. Finally, after 7h00 of input, Luc placed *się* in post-verbal position, the most frequent position in the input.

Another example involves the reflexive verb *nazywa się* (s'appeler 'to be called'):

44) Context sentence: *Jak ona się nazywa?* (C-S-Refl-V)

Comment elle se appelle?

(How she Refl is called?)

Luc's responses: Period 1h30

Anka ona się nazywa (C-S-Refl-V)

Anka elle se appelle (Anka she Refl is called)

Period 3h30

ona nazywa Anka się (S-V-C-Refl)

elle appelle Anka se (she is called Anka Refl)

Period 7h00

ona się nazywa Anka (S-Refl-V-C)

elle se appelle Anka (she Refl is called Anka)

At Period 1h30, Luc placed the pronoun in the position required in French (pre-verbal), and at Period 3h30 at the end of the sentence, as he did with the previous sentence we analysed. His placements at Period 7h00 are not as consistent, however. In our analysis of Sentence (43) at Period 7h00, *nazywam się Barbara* ([je] appelle se Barbara 'am called Refl Barbara'), we speculated that Luc's response was due to the frequency of the order V-Refl in the input. Luc's response to Sentence (44) at Period

7h00, *ona się nazywa Anka* (elle se appelle Anka 'she Refl is called Anka'), fails to confirm this. The Refl-V word order he used is correct in Polish and exists in the input, but it is less frequent than the order V-Refl. It is worth noting that his response corresponds to the only possible order of the equivalent structure in French, Refl-V.

The third occurrence of *się* at Period 7h00 (Sentence (45) below) contains the verb *napije się* (boira 'will drink' – perfective). The same sentence appears in the tests at Periods 3h30 and 7h00:

45) Context sentence: *Jacek jest w restauracji i*

Jacques est à restaurant et

(James is at restaurant and)

Luc's responses: Period 3h30

*się napije piwa (Refl-V-O)

se (il) boira bière (Refl [he] will drink beer)

Period 7h00

*napije piwa się (V-O-Refl)

(il) boira bière se ([he] will drink beer Refl)

The order provided by Luc at Period 7h00, V-O-Refl, never appeared in the input. Did he resort to his Period 3h30 strategy of placing *się* at the sentence periphery? A more detailed analysis of the verb *napić się* leads us to question whether his confusion stems from the existence in the input of both the imperfective *pić* and the perfective forms *napić się* (cf. 'The verb' in the fourth section of Chapter 3 for a description of imperfective/perfective pairs in Polish). The verb *pić* (boire 'to drink') is not accompanied by *się*, whereas *napić* is. The learners often heard the phrase *pije piwo* '(he/she) drinks beer' for example. It would not be surprising if Luc thought this structure was viable for the verb *napije* as well, resulting in the structure *napije piwo* (although the correct form to be used with *napije się* is *piwa*-Gen). It could be that when Luc placed the verb, *napije*, he applied his knowledge of how the verb *pije* functions syntactically, the word *się* becoming superfluous in the process. If this analysis is correct, it reveals an important sensitivity on the part of Luc to certain aspects of the TL input, but not all (morphology, shown in previous examples, not being one of them). As he noted in his journal, he was ready to make an effort to learn words that were 'absolutely necessary'.

Luc: Verbal morphology at Period 7h00

In his journal entry following the fourth class session (Period 5h45), Luc made the remark that, 'Polish is a language with declensions, but I still find it impossible to use them'. As a reminder, in the first two grammaticality judgement tests (Periods 1h30 and 3h30), Luc found no ungrammatical morphological forms. During the third test, at Period 7h00, however, he found and corrected two such forms. He corrected the verb form *jestem* (1p sg) with the form *jest* (3p sg) and the verb *piją* (3p pl) with *pije* (3p sg). We conclude from this that Luc's sensitivity to verbal endings that mark number and person appeared sometime between 3h30 and 7h00 of exposure to the Polish language.

Luc: Period 8h00

In his journal entry after the sixth class session (Period 8h00), Luc comments on his overall experience in the Polish course: 'I was able to observe a certain development in my own learning. I was able to understand, to express myself, and to follow the evolution of the course without too much trouble, which obviously had a gratifying effect'.

Luc: Speech perception/sentence repetitions at Period 8h00

During the second repetition test administered to our learners at Period 8h00, Luc reproduced more Polish words than he had at Period 4h00. Table 6.8 allows for a comparison of his repetitions at Periods 4h00 and 8h00. We see from Table 6.8 that Luc's total repetitions increased from 29% of all words to be repeated to 41% between the two periods, and that his total correct repetitions increased as well, from 24% to 30%.

Table 6.8 Results of Luc's sentence repetitions (measured in words) at Periods 4h00 and 8h00

Period 4h00				*Period 8h00*			
Total words repeated		*Words repeated correctly*		*Total words repeated*		*Words repeated correctly*	
Raw score (n = 113)	%	*Raw score* (n = 113)	%	*Raw score* (n = 113)	%	*Raw score* (n = 113)	%
33	29	27	24	46	41	34	30

Table 6.9 shows both Gilles' and Luc's word repetition scores at the two periods. We see in Table 6.9 that both Gilles and Luc developed in their capacity to repeat the words of a Polish sentence between Periods 4h00 and 8h00. At both periods, Luc repeated fewer words than Gilles, and the gap between the number of words repeated correctly by Gilles and by Luc increased with time, Luc repeating fewer words than Gilles and with less accuracy (Luc's 30% to Gilles' 53%). We will not speculate on the reasons for this difference; once again, we merely point out that the difference exists. We point out as well that this difference is not only of a quantitative nature (Gilles repeats *more* than Luc), but of a qualitative nature as well. They repeat different words (sometimes Gilles repeats a word that Luc fails to repeat, and vice versa). In cases where they repeat

Table 6.9 Results of Gilles' and Luc's sentence repetitions (measured in words) at Periods 4h00 and 8h00

	Period 4h00				Period 8h00			
	Total words repeated		Words repeated correctly		Total words repeated		Words repeated correctly	
	Raw score (n =113)	%	Raw score (n =113)	%	Raw score (n =113)	%	Raw score (n =113)	%
Gilles	45	40	40	35	67	59	60	53
Luc	33	29	27	24	46	41	34	30

the same word, they often repeat it differently (one or the other or both producing an incorrect repetition). They are apparently 'taking in' differently. In Chapter 7, we will discuss correct word repetitions of our eight monolingual learners of Polish as a function of various factors in an attempt to identify the effect that these factors have on our learners' ability to perceive and reproduce a Polish word, thus contributing important information about saliency in L2 processing.

Luc: Summary of development – a comparison to Gilles' development

The results of the sentence repetition tests reveal a clear development in Luc's ability to perceive and reproduce certain elements of the Polish language. Both Gilles and Luc showed improvement over time. After 4h00 of input, Gilles correctly repeated 35% of the 113 Polish words and Luc 24%. After 8h00, Gilles correctly repeated 53% and Luc 30%.

In speech comprehension, Luc took few risks. During the oral translation tests over the three periods, he often responded with incomplete sentences. Luc had more difficulty translating lexical items than did Gilles and showed signs of being more affected by the lack of context. Unlike Gilles, even at Period 7h00, Luc did not grasp the meaning of the explicit subject in the statement *ja również* 'me too'. He seemed to have more trouble than Gilles in extracting grammatical information from the given structures. On the other hand, Luc and Gilles showed similarities in their processing of the various word orders. As with Gilles, basic constituent word order did not seem to have an effect on Luc's ability to process simple Polish sentences, at least the type presented in this study.

With respect to word order, Luc's data suggest a strong preference for the order SVO during all phases of the data collection period, as did

Gilles'. At Period 7h00, Luc's responses to all 13 sentences of the word order test were of the SVO type.

After 1h30 of exposure to Polish, Luc had apparently not yet formulated a hypothesis on the placement of the negator *nie*, providing incomplete sentences when the placement of *nie* was required. As of Period 3h30, however, this phenomenon posed little problem for him. During the second and third word order tests at Periods 3h30 and 7h00, he correctly placed the negator in pre-verbal position. Gilles had identified the correct position of the negator already at Period 1h30.

After 1h30 of input, Luc placed the reflexive pronoun *się*, as did Gilles, in pre-verbal position, the position required for equivalent French pronouns and one of the two orders present in the input. In the grammaticality judgement test, however, Luc accepted a sentence where the pronoun was placed after the verb. As a reminder, the two positions, pre- and post-verbal are correct in Polish and appeared in the first 1h30 of input with approximately the same rate of frequency. In subsequent input, however, the post-verbal position of *się* was more frequent. After 3h30 of input, Luc differed from Gilles in that this phenomenon began to trouble him. Whereas Gilles revised his hypothesis at Period 3h30 and placed all occurrences of *się* in post-verbal position from then on, Luc placed *się* differently in each sentence. He continued to do this when tested at Period 7h00 as well. Luc's difficulty could have been at least partly due to conflicting information between the rules of his L1 and the Polish to which he was exposed. After 3h30 of contact with Polish, and even more so after 7h00 of Polish, the order Refl-V (that found in French) was significantly less frequent in the input than was the order V-Refl, creating a conflict between the L1 structure and the most frequent structure in the input. This brings us back to the hypotheses raised in Chapter 3 concerning the learner's processing of the TL when faced with conflicting structures in the L1 and the TL input. We will return to this debate in our group results in Chapter 9.

Concerning verbal morphology, unlike Gilles, who paid attention to verbal morphology from the very beginning, Luc showed no sign of processing morphological markers in the first stages of the study. It was not until after 7h00 of input that he began to show signs of sensitivity to markers of number and person on the verb.

Discussion

In this chapter, we have followed the first 8 hours of the acquisition of Polish by two French native speakers, Gilles and Luc. We found similarities in their initial processing of Polish, but their processing was by no means identical. L1 clearly played an important role for both learners, but to different extents and for different periods of time. Luc seemed to rely on his L1 to a greater extent and for longer periods of time than did Gilles. Gilles seemed to scrutinise the input more effectively from the very beginning, formulating stable hypotheses about the TL earlier than Luc. In perception, Luc needed more exposure to Polish than Gilles in order to repeat correctly Polish words during the sentence repetition tests, and the words they repeated often differed. In comprehension, Gilles was able to translate the majority of Polish sentences correctly from the beginning. In contrast, Polish lexical items posed more of a problem for Luc than for Gilles. In grammatical analysis, Gilles formulated hypotheses that corresponded to the TL structure earlier than Luc. Gilles placed the Polish negator in the appropriate pre-verbal position at Period 1h30 (Luc at Period 3h30). Gilles placed the reflexive pronoun *się* in post-verbal position (the most frequent position in the input) at Period 3h30 (Luc never consistently placed *się* in post-verbal position). Gilles showed sensitivity to verbal morphology at Period 1h30 (Luc at Period 7h00). Why did our two learners with nearly identical profiles process certain elements of the Polish input so differently?

Learner differences are often attributed to distinctions in proficiency level or in the quantity or quality of previous input received (e.g. type of exposure, such as instructed versus natural, or immersion versus non-immersion). In this study, Gilles and Luc (same L1 and L2) began their acquisition of Polish at the same proficiency level of Polish (level 0) and received the same input. Proficiency level and input, often variables in SLA studies, were held constant. The differences in Gilles' and Luc's performances cannot, therefore, be explained by differences in proficiency level, in prior input received or in their L1 or L2s. Something else is happening here.

Considerable research has been conducted on learner strategies and motivation, specifically with regard to developing these strategies in the learner within an instructional setting (cf. Cohen & Dörnyei, 2002; Oxford, 2001). These studies, however, tend toward the atheoretical, focusing on practical guidelines for teachers rather than on theories or models to explain or predict these differences (cf. Dörnyei & Skehan, 2003 for an overview). As Dörnyei & Skehan (2003: 622) point out, '...the current formulations of learning strategies, while containing pedagogical promise, seem to lack a clear theoretical basis'.

From a cognitivist perspective, Robinson (2001: 379) indicates hypotheses in the SLA literature that argue the following: '...IDs [individual differences] in cognitive resources and abilities are fundamental to understanding SLA processes and the causes of variation in levels of adult language learning attainment'. In his article, Robinson outlines the Aptitude Complex/Ability Differentiation framework, which seeks to apply measures of aptitude complexes and ability factors to L2 processing. Aptitude complexes comprise aptitude for focusing on form or for incidental learning, for example. Ability factors include noticing the gap and memory of contingent speech. As a detailed account of cognitive aptitudes and abilities is beyond the scope of this book, we will not pursue this line of discussion. Our objective, rather, is to highlight the importance of including individual differences in our models and theories of SLA as these differences clearly play an important role in input processing, and consequently, in L2 acquisition.

Conclusion

This chapter has allowed us to formulate hypotheses based on an in-depth analysis of the data collected from two L2 learners at the early stages of L2 acquisition. The results presented here confirm Giacobbe's (1992a) conclusion that learners show considerable variation in their approaches to language activity. In the following three chapters, we propose a global analysis of the data of our eight French learners of Polish, testing hypotheses that we have formulated in this chapter and in Chapter 3 in order to better understand our learners' language activity during the first 8 hours of acquisition of a new target language.

Notes
1. The asterisk * at the beginning of a word indicates an incorrect morphological form.
2. The difference in how Gilles and Luc rated themselves in English suggests a distinction in learner style, reflecting a difference not on the linguistic level, but rather, on the psychological level. A detailed study of psychological factors such as confidence, attitude and motivation falls outside the scope of this study. See the conclusion to this chapter for further comments.

Chapter 7
Speech Perception

In an overview of theories in psychology, linguistics and language pedagogy, Gaonac'h (1991) calls our attention to one of the principal themes
treated by Gestalt-Psychology: the perception and resolution of problems. He cites the work of Koffka (1935), for whom the determiners of
acquisition cannot be reduced to an informant's physical environment.
A certain number of internal factors must be taken into consideration as
well, such as the individual's attitudes, needs and abilities. Gaonac'h
concludes that the learning problem becomes secondary with respect to
the problem of perception. In other words, perception is a prerequisite
for learning; one cannot learn something that has not been or cannot be
perceived. Therefore, the difficulty of a learning problem is first and
foremost a perception problem. Following this approach, we consider
'perception' as the fundamental language activity necessary for comprehension and grammatical analysis, to be discussed in subsequent
chapters.

Sentence Repetition Test

Applying this notion of a 'perception problem' to the acquisition of a
second language, we devote this chapter to an analysis of data collected
to investigate the perceptual activity of our French learners of Polish.[1]
To expand upon the Zwitserlood *et al.* (2000) psycholinguistic study in
which native Dutch speakers were exposed to 15 minutes of Chinese
input, we used a sentence repetition test with two participant groups,
namely, one group of 'first exposure' informants and our group of
8 monolingual French learners of Polish. In their study, Zwitserlood *et al.*
found that learners were able to recognise certain regularities in Chinese
even after only 15 minutes of exposure. Along the same lines, we were
interested in discovering what elements of Polish could be perceived and
repeated by our informants upon absolute first contact with the language
and at specific intervals of exposure thereafter.

Slobin (1985: 1164) points out for child language acquisition that, 'On
the most basic level, accessibility of linguistic material can be defined in
terms of PERCEPTIBILITY. That is to say, the only linguistic material that
can figure in language-making are stretches of speech that attract the
child's ATTENTION to a sufficient degree to be noticed and held in
memory'. We envisage a similar scenario in adult language acquisition.
The problem for the researcher lies, therefore, in discovering a means to
identify those elements that constitute the data that the learner perceives

and stores in memory. Following Slobin (1985) and Peters' (1985) work in L1 acquisition, we apply certain objective measures of what we think 'saliency' is to our learners' performance in order to see whether these measures have an effect on this performance. We assume that what we think of as 'saliency' will aid learners' perceptual activity when exposed to TL input. In this chapter, we examine the factors that render an item in the input 'salient' for our 'first exposure' French native speaker informants and for our French learners of Polish.

For L1 acquisition, Slobin (1985: 1251) proposes the following Operating Principle (OP) regarding attention to speech:

> OP: ATTENTION: SOUNDS. Store any perceptually salient stretches of speech.

He points out that this OP requires specification of 'perceptually salient' and refers his readers to Peters (1985). The main question of interest here is: What do learners extract from the language data received and how do they it? Peters (1985: 1030) defines Extraction as the process of recognising and remembering chunks of speech. For child language acquisition, Peters (1985: 1030) claims that a set of 'saliency factors' directs the child's attention to which sorts of information to notice first:

> It is clear that children do not extract everything they hear said around and to them. Rather they pick and choose what to pay attention to and what to try to remember, and these choices will be affected by factors involving both linguistic and psycholinguistic salience: factors which should be reflected in the Operating Principles (OP) that guide Extraction.

She describes 'salient' stretches of speech as those that are reasonable candidates for extraction, namely, recognising and remembering.

Klein (1986: 71) recognises the difficulty in testing the perceptual ability of learners: 'There is no easy way of knowing what the learner actually understands of an utterance in the target language: we cannot see inside his head'. A possible technique for exploring and measuring how a learner manages to detect important regularities of the unknown language is the sentence repetition task proposed in the Heidelberger Forschungsprojekt 'Pidgin-Deutsch' (HPD, 1979, summarised in Klein, 1986: 71–74). The task has been used as a way to determine how a learner perceives and memorises, in the short term, an expression in the TL. To understand how this task can provide useful data for our study, we present the reader with two example sentences of comparable intellectual content in French and Polish, the source and target languages of our study:

French: Pierre habite à Cracovie et étudie l'informatique
Polish: *Piotr mieszka w Krakowie i studiuje informatykę*
'Peter lives in Krakow and studies computer processing.'

We can be confident that French speakers with no knowledge of Polish will repeat the French version more successfully than the Polish version because they know French, but not Polish: they know the meaning of the French words and the rules of combination, and they have had plenty of practice speaking French. We also assume that after being actively exposed to Polish, they will be better able to segment a Polish sentence into its component parts, better able to assign meaning to the inter-relating component parts, and, perhaps, better at the articulatory gymnastics involved (for a French speaker) in speaking Polish.

As outlined in Chapter 2, the problem is that only a handful of studies have systematically tested *how much* exposure is needed to significantly improve the performance of an adult language learner. We know very little about how incomprehensible noise becomes processable sounds, or how a mental lexicon is built up from the start, that is, how form-meaning associations are established and attributed combinatorial properties. Hardly any research has in fact systematically tested the first minutes or hours of exposure to see what type of capacity can be brought to bear on totally new linguistic material in order to start to segment out units. Even Perdue (1996: 138), after a stirring 'Far too little empirical attention has been paid to the very beginnings of the acquisition process', merely presupposes some ability to segment the speech stream and assign meaning to its component parts.

Krashen (1985) simply posits 'understanding', which implies 'comprehensible input', without addressing the process by which a learner makes the input comprehensible. In Krashen's wake, VanPatten (2000) proposes an on-line input processing model that addresses this process; however, he applies his model to the investigation of comprehension strategies, while presupposing perceptual strategies. Slobin (1985: 1161), on the other hand, breaks this 'understanding' up into two tasks, one of converting the speech stream into units which can be processed in working memory (a perceptual task), and hence the other, organising these units into a mental lexicon. In short, what is perceived is then available for further processing. The perceptual task is helped by something called 'saliency', and it is this that we attempt to characterise in this chapter. More precisely, we are interested in how the speech stream is processed, that is, perceived, stored in short-term memory and reproduced, in relation to certain absolute and variable properties often associated with 'saliency'. These properties are presented in the 'hypotheses' section below. We then see how 4 hours of exposure to Polish, followed by 4 more hours of exposure, affects processing in relation to these particular properties. This is why, amongst all the tasks our informants were called upon to perform, the sentence repetition test seems an appropriate tool for measuring the evolution of certain aspects of the informants' perceptual performance during the first hours of exposure. Furthermore, repeating an interlocutor's words is probably among the most used strategies of naturalistically acquiring learners (Bremer *et al.*, 1996) in, as they put it, 'achieving understanding'.

Hypotheses

In our analysis of the sentence repetitions, we examined the relevance of certain factors to participants' ability to correctly repeat a word, on the assumption that these factors rendered certain elements of the input more 'salient' in Peters' sense of the word. We first looked at the effect of global input, i.e. the hours of exposure to the TL. We then examined the following lexical factors: the length of the word measured in number of syllables, word stress, phonemic distance (from French) and the transparency of the word in light of the results of a transparency test to be described below. Two contextually determined factors were observed as well: the position of the word in the sentence and the frequency of the word in the input, after 4 hours and after 8 hours of exposure to Polish. We propose a specific hypothesis associated with each of these seven factors in what follows.

(1) *Hours of instruction.* We hypothesised an effect of the number of hours of input on participants' ability to repeat Polish words during the sentence repetition test, that is, that learners at Period 4h00 would outperform those at Period 0h00, and that learners at Period 8h00 would outperform those at Periods 0h00 and 4h00.

(2) *Word length.* Word length was measured in number of syllables. Words were grouped into three categories: prepositions such as *w* 'in' and *we* 'in' were placed in the 0–1-syllable group; *ale* 'but' and *bardzo* 'very' were placed in the 2-syllable group; and words such as *studentem* 'student' and *uniwersytecie* 'university' fell into a 3–6-syllable group. We hypothesised that informants at all periods would be better able to repeat 2-syllable words, given that 0/1-syllable words may present problems of perception in certain contexts (cf. Dommergues & Segui, 1989), and that 3–6-syllable words may present problems for correct repetitions due to factors such as pronounceability and short-term memory limitations.

(3) *Word stress.* Words the participants heard were categorised as either stressed or unstressed by a native speaker of Polish. Slobin (1985: 1251) proposes the following Operating Principle for L1 acquisition which converts speech input into stored data:

> OP: ATTENTION: STRESS. Pay attention to stressed syllables in extracted speech units. Store such syllables separately and also in relation to the units with which they occur.

Following Slobin and applying his principle to L2 acquisition, we hypothesised that informants at all periods would pay attention to stress and would better repeat Polish words with stress than those without stress (cf. 'Prosody' in the second section of Chapter 3 for a discussion of stress in Polish and French).

(4) *Phonemic distance.* Phonemic distance was measured by means of a contrastive analysis of the French and Polish phonemic systems. A word was considered 'distant' if it fulfilled one of the two following criteria: (1) contained a consonant that does not exist in the system of standard Parisian French,[2] such as *cz* or *ci*, both approximately realised with a /tš/ in the word *nauczyciel* 'teacher'; (2) contained a consonant cluster that does not exist in French, such as 'wł' /vw/ in *włoszką* 'Italian'. Words that did not meet either of the above criteria were categorised as phonemically 'close'. The hypothesis was that words with sounds that were familiar to French speakers would be better repeated than words with sounds that were unfamiliar, with an increased success rate of unfamiliar words with more hours of input (cf. the second section of Chapter 3 for a contrastive analysis of Polish and French phonemic systems).

(5) *Transparency.* To identify criteria for 'transparency', we used the results of the oral word translation test presented in Chapter 5 in which an independent group of 15 'first exposure' French monolinguals who had had no contact with Polish were asked to listen to a list of Polish words and translate what they thought they understood into French. Generally, the criteria in Chapter 5 will be relevant here as well, although in this chapter we will be discussing lexical items that were presented in the context of a sentence. An example of the transparency measure is given in Table 7.1, which shows how the informants responded to the spoken word *studentem* 'student'.

As we said in Chapter 5, translations that were semantically related to the given word were accepted as correct translations regardless of their grammatical composition. In the example shown in Table 7.1, the first three translations (*étudiant*, *étude* and *étudient*) were accepted as correct. Summing their percentages, *studentem* was assigned a transparency rating of 60%. Words were then placed into three categories: 'opaque' (rating of 0% correct translations), 'fairly transparent' (rating of 1–50%) and 'very transparent' (rating of 51–100%). The hypothesis was that informants with no exposure to Polish would rely heavily on transparency to repeat the Polish

Table 7.1 Translation of *studentem* 'student' by a 'first exposure' group ($n = 15$)

Informants' French translations	English translations	% Responses
étudiant(s)	student(s)	47
étude	study (noun)	6.7
étudient	(they) study	6.7
stupéfait/stupéfiant	stunned/stunning	13
soudain	sudden	6.7
No response		20

words, while informants at Periods 4h00 and 8h00 would rely on transparency as well, but to a lesser degree as they would have other sources of information at their disposal.

(6) *Word position.* Cross-linguistic data suggest that final and initial syllables are perceptually salient (Slobin, 1985). Proposed by Slobin (1985: 1166) for L1 acquisition, the following Operating Principles concerning position in a speech unit are based on this assumption:

> OP: ATTENTION: END OF UNIT. Pay attention to the last syllable of an extracted speech unit. Store it separately and also in relation to the unit with which it occurs.
> OP: ATTENTION: BEGINNING OF UNIT. Pay attention to the first syllable of an extracted speech unit. Store it separately and also in relation to the unit with which it occurs.

As described in Chapter 1, VanPatten (1996, 2000) has proposed, for L2 acquisition, parallel principles with respect to word position in his model of on-line input processing. He cites findings that support the following generalisations:

> P4. Learners first process elements in sentence/utterance initial position.
> P4a. Learners process elements in final position before elements in medial position. (VanPatten, 2000: 300)

In line with Slobin and VanPatten, the present study investigates learners' perception of the recorded Polish words in distinct sentence positions: initial, middle, and final. In our analysis of 17 sentence repetitions (113 words) for each participant, 'initial' position comprises the first word in the 17 sentences, hence 17 words in all. Likewise, 'final' position includes the last word in each sentence, hence 17 words. Finally, 'middle' position includes the remaining words in each sentence (79 words). As Slobin's principles are language-independent, we expect them to apply right from Period 0h00. Whether there is a saliency hierarchy between initial and final position, as VanPatten's results suggest, remains to be seen.

(7)　*Word frequency.* In order to measure the frequency of a word in the input, all input provided as Polish language instruction to the learners was transcribed using the CHILDES format (MacWhinney, 2000) and analysed using its programming tools. This analysis resulted in frequency scores for each word in the input. In addition, we counted the number of occurrences of each word spoken more than once during the sentence repetition test, as these occurrences were viewed as input to our informants as well. (The conjunction *ale* 'but', for example, was only presented once, whereas the verb form *zna* 'knows' was heard eight times.) Taking heed of Goldschneider and DeKeyser's (2001: 30) comment that 'Finding a good operatio-nalized measure of input frequency is not easy', the following categories for frequency of a word in the input were adopted (cf. also Ellis, 2002; Hintzman, 1988; Trueswell, 1996): 'absent' (0 tokens), 'rare' (1–20 tokens), 'frequent' (21–600 tokens). Given that the actual words heard during the sentence repetition test were counted as input, at Period 0h00 the first occurrence of a repeated word was listed as 'absent' in the input, whereas the second occurrence was categorised as 'rare' (1–20 tokens) in the input, in that one occurrence had already preceded it. As a result, the two categories for words repeated at Period 0h00 were 'absent' (words being heard for the first time) and 'rare' (words that were heard in a preceding sentence). No words during Period 0h00 testing were repeated often enough to reach the category of 'frequent'. The contrary was true with frequency scores at Period 4h00 and Period 8h00 when taking into account the overall input received during the first 4 and 8 hours respectively. For learners to respond to the effects of 'frequency', a certain degree of *storage* on their part is required, as pointed out by Slobin (1985: 1251–1252). We anticipated that learners would be sensitive to a 'frequency effect', namely that the percentage of correct repetitions of a word would increase when the frequency of occurrences of that same word in the L2 data increased.

Each factor was examined relative to the number of correct repetitions by learners at each level. Two criteria were used to identify a 'correct repetition':

(1)   The number of syllables in the repeated word had to be the same as the number of syllables found in the original word to be repeated.[3]

(2)   Only one phoneme per syllable could be repeated incorrectly.

If a repetition did not meet these two criteria, as determined by a native Polish speaker, it was not counted as a 'correct repetition'.

Results

In the case of the current study, our dependent variable was 'correct repetitions'. Participants heard 20 Polish sentences, only 17 of which were analysed (a set of 113 experimental words), and were asked to repeat them (see Appendix 2 for test items). Time of exposure was considered as a repeated factor: it implied three periods of instruction (no instruction, 4 hours of instruction and 8 hours of instruction). Such lexical characteristics as word length, word stress, phonemic distance (between Polish and French), lexical transparency and word position served as main factors in the statistical analyses.

Hours of instruction

Given the lack of research conducted on first contact with a TL, it was important to ask the following question: do hours of L2 exposure (measured at Periods 0h00, 4h00 and 8h00) have any significant effect on the learners' ability to produce correct repetitions of Polish words in sentences? Figure 7.1 shows that, indeed, the period factor had an

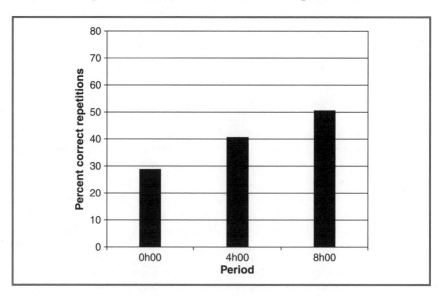

Figure 7.1 Global effect of L2 exposure on correct repetitions

important effect on the correct repetition of the 113 Polish words in the test.

A global one-way ANOVA with repeated measures showed that the period factor, i.e. L2 exposure, had a significant effect on word repetitions, F (2,224) = 46.966, $p < 0.01$. We can therefore conclude that there was a global effect of the input on learner performance. Now the task remains of identifying more precisely the factors and conditions that led to this development.

Word length

We then looked at the effect of word length measured in number of syllables. Our questions were the following: do hours of instruction have a significant effect on the repetitions of words of a particular length? And does word length play a role in the learners' ability to correctly repeat the word at Period 0h00, 4h00 or 8h00? Figure 7.2 shows the distribution of correct repetitions of words of three different length groups (0–1, 2 and 3–6 syllables) as a function of period (0h00, 4h00, 8h00).

Overall input, that is hours of instruction, appears to have had a decisive impact on correct repetition. A two-way ANOVA (with word length as an intergroup factor and periods as repeated measures) confirmed a main effect of period on the correct repetition of all words regardless of the number of syllables, F (2,220) = 40.9, $p < 0.01$, but the ANOVA did not reveal any effect of word length, F (2,110) = 0.496, n.s. In other words, the length of the word as measured in syllables did not appear to play a significant role in the ability of the learner at any of the three periods to correctly repeat the word. Finally, and logically, the ANOVA did not show any interaction between period and word length,

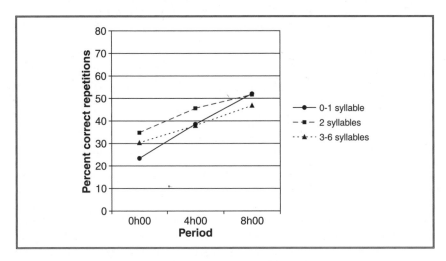

Figure 7.2 Correct repetitions relative to word length

F (4,220) = 1.825, n.s. Indeed, word length does not appear to have been a crucial factor in determining the successful repetition of a word.

Word stress

The overall effect of word stress (two stress values: stressed or unstressed) is shown in Figure 7.3. A two-way ANOVA (with word stress as an intergroup factor and periods as repeated measures) confirmed a significant effect of period on the correct repetition of stressed and unstressed words, F (2,222) = 51.083, $p < 0.01$. Results showed a main effect of stress on correct repetitions at the three periods, F (1,111) = 10.835, $p < 0.01$. Most importantly, there was also a significant interaction between period and word stress, F (2,222) = 8.307, $p < 0.01$. This interaction (as can be seen in Figure 7.3) was due to a relative weakening of effect of word stress in relation to increased hours of Polish instruction. At Period 0h00, the difference between stressed and unstressed words was the greatest, but this difference regularly weakened through Periods 4h00 and 8h00. These results also suggest that the informants who had not been exposed to Polish before testing *did* perceive Polish stress and spontaneously made the most of it from the very beginning.

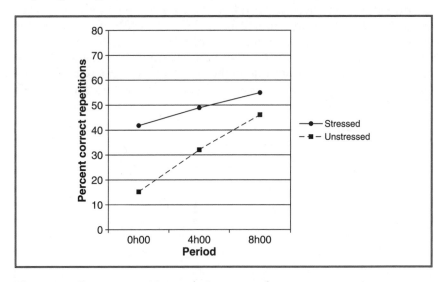

Figure 7.3 Correct repetitions relative to word stress

Phonemic distance

Figure 7.4 shows the percentage at the three periods of correct repetitions of Polish words considered as 'close' or 'distant' with respect to the French phonemic system. The results of a two-way ANOVA (with phonemic distance as an intergroup factor and periods as repeated

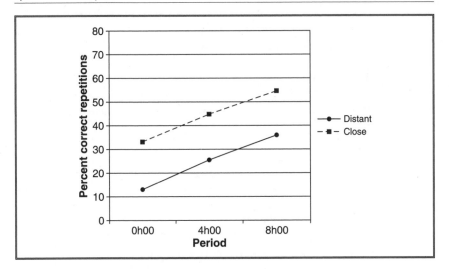

Figure 7.4 Correct repetitions relative to phonemic distance

measures) confirmed a main effect of period for all words whether categorised as 'close' or 'distant', F (2,222) = 32.343, $p < 0.01$. We also found a main effect for phonemic distance across periods, F (1,111) = 8.813, $p < 0.01$. These results show that even though the global effect of input was strong for words that were considered both distant and close, the words with familiar sounds were consistently better repeated than those with unfamiliar sounds at all three levels. This suggests that learners relied on phonemic familiarity to repeat Polish words, but that this familiarity did not impede them from making progress in the repetition of words with sounds that were unfamiliar, and therefore potentially more difficult to perceive and to pronounce.[4] Lastly, there was no significant interaction between period and phonemic distance, F (2,222) = 0.034, n.s., which suggests that the significant advantage of 'close' words was kept constant over the three periods involved.

Transparency

Figure 7.5 shows the effect of lexical transparency (three degrees of transparency: opaque, fairly transparent and very transparent) at the different levels. A two-way ANOVA (with transparency as an intergroup factor and periods as repeated measures) confirmed a global significant effect of period on the correct repetition of words, F (2,220) = 33.496, $p < 0.01$. A PLSD Fisher comparison showed that this main effect was due to a significant difference between 'opaque' and 'fairly transparent' ($p < 0.01$) and between 'opaque' and 'very transparent' ($p < 0.01$), as seen in Figure 7.5. In other words, increased exposure to Polish had a stronger

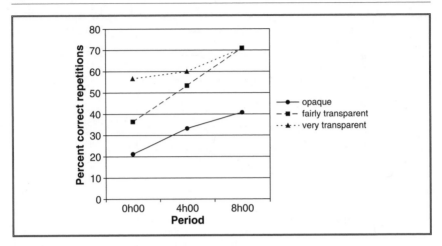

Figure 7.5 Correct repetitions relative to transparency

influence on the repetitions of opaque and fairly transparent words, with little to no influence on very transparent ones.

There was a main effect of transparency across periods, $F\ (2,110) = 11.643$, $p < 0.01$, as well as a light interaction between period and transparency, $F\ (4,220) = 2.48$, $p < 0.05$; this interaction was obviously due to the converging lines of 'very transparent' and 'fairly transparent' at Period 8h00. These results, taken as a whole, provide evidence that transparency played an important role in the ability of our participants at all levels to repeat Polish words, and that it is a very important factor for learners on first exposure to Polish.

Word position

As mentioned above, we will report here on three possible word positions in a sentence: initial (I), middle (M) and final (F). Figure 7.6 shows the percentage of correct repetitions of words in the three positions by participants at the three periods.

The results of a two-way ANOVA (with position as an intergroup factor and periods as repeated measures) confirmed a clear overall effect of period, $F\ (2,220) = 17,31$, $p < 0.01$. The two-way ANOVA with repeated measures revealed a main effect of position, $F\ (2,110) = 9.814$, $p < 0.01$. PLSD Fisher comparisons revealed that this effect was not due to a difference between I and F (n.s.), but rather to differences between both I and M, and M and F ($p < 0.05$ in both cases). The percentage of correct repetitions was higher for words in initial position than for those in final position; however, this particular difference was not statistically significant in our data. There was no significant interaction between period and position. Obviously, as with other factors discussed here, a

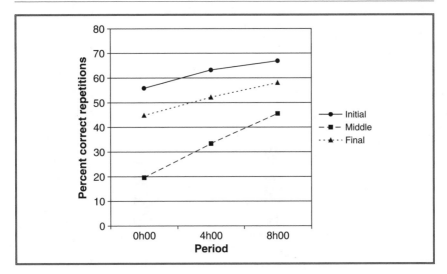

Figure 7.6 Correct repetitions relative to position in sentence

better understanding of the way learners exploit the position factor would require further analysis (after 12 hours of input, 15 hours of input, etc.) in future research.

Word frequency

Correct repetitions as a function of frequency were examined independently at Periods 0h00, 4h00 and 8h00. Figure 7.7 presents correct repetitions of words that appeared during the sentence repetition test at Period 0h00. Some words were heard for the first time and categorised as 'absent', whereas others were heard several times ('rare').

As expected, a one-way ANOVA did not show any effect of frequency on correct repetitions at Period 0h00, the two modalities being 'absent' and 'rare', $F (1,111) = 0.834$, n.s.

Similar results were found when measuring the effect of word frequency in the input (three modalities: absent, rare and frequent) after 4 hours of Polish instruction and the ability of learners at Period 4h00 to repeat the words correctly. Figure 7.8 represents repetitions at Period 4h00.

Results showed no significant effect of frequency on correct repetitions at Period 4h00, $F (2,110) = 0.712$, n.s.

It was only at Period 8h00 that we found a significant main effect of frequency (three modalities as above), $F (2,110) = 7.348$, $p < 0.01$ (as seen in Figure 7.9).

These results suggest, along the same lines as Slobin (1985), that frequency, being cumulative, needs time to get going. The more overall input learners received, the more they relied on a familiarisation with the so-called 'frequent' words to correctly reproduce what they had heard in

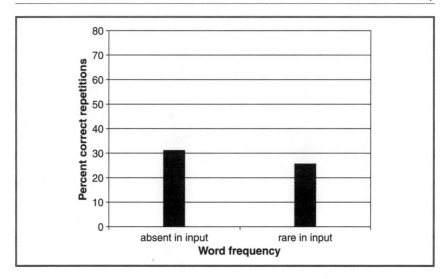

Figure 7.7 Correct repetitions relative to frequency of word in the input at Period 0h00

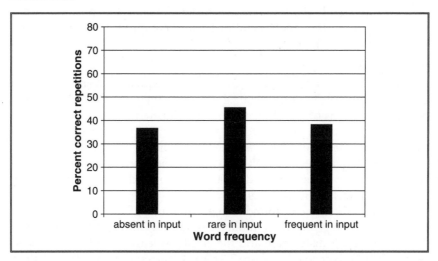

Figure 7.8 Correct repetitions relative to frequency of word in the input at Period 4h00

the TL. That this phenomenon, as well as several others described in this chapter, became obvious after a mere 8 hours of exposure to the L2 is certainly worth noting.

Interactions between independent variables

Three-way ANOVAs with repeated measures (periods) were conducted to investigate the effect of different combinations of independent

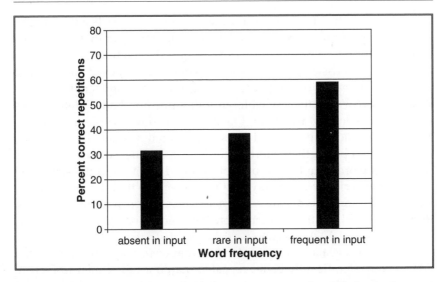

Figure 7.9 Correct repetitions relative to frequency of words in the input at Period 8h00

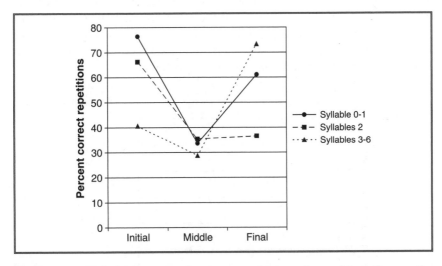

Figure 7.10 Global interaction between position and word length over the 3 periods

factors. We performed analyses on all the possible two-way combinations of these factors (not all combinations were possible). It was found that word length and position were significantly related, $F_{(4,104)} = 2.571$, $p < 0.05$, as is shown in Figure 7.10.

Concerning the effect of position, we pointed out earlier that results showed a significant effect of position at all periods, and that informants had most trouble reproducing words in middle position. As shown in Figure 7.10, words in middle position consistently posed the greatest difficulty for repetition, regardless of period and word length. Nevertheless, short words (0–1 syllable) in initial position had a high success rate, whereas longer words (3–6 syllables) in initial position suffered. This phenomenon did not hold for words in final position: longer words were repeated better than shorter words. Apparently, correct repetitions depend on word length as a function of word position in the sentence.

A further series of three-way ANOVAs revealed that the independent variable of phonemic distance interacted most often with other factors. Results showed a strong interaction between phonemic distance and word stress, F $(1,109) = 14.469$, $p < 0.01$, as illustrated in Figure 7.11.

Figure 7.11 reveals that stressed words that were phonemically close to French were significantly better repeated than ones dissimilar to French. In Figure 7.11, although it may seem like 'distant' words that were not stressed seemed to be better repeated than 'distant' words that were stressed, an analysis of the contrasts involved revealed that the difference was not significant, $F = 1,51$, n.s. All the other contrasts were significant ($p < 0.05$). We hypothesise that other factors, such as position, may have had a stronger effect than stress on the reproduction of words with phonemes that are unfamiliar to French speakers.

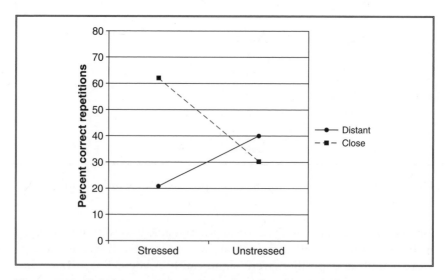

Figure 7.11 Global interaction between word stress and phonemic distance over the 3 periods

We therefore investigated a possible interaction between phonemic distance and position. As shown in Figure 7.12, a significant interaction was found between these two factors, F (2,107) = 5.707, $p < 0.01$. It appears that repetitions of Polish words that share phonemes with the French phonemic system were aided by the position in the sentence: words that were categorised as 'close' had a high success rate of reproduction when found in initial and final positions. Words categorised as 'distant' were unaffected by their position in the sentence and globally led to few correct repetitions (around 20% on average).

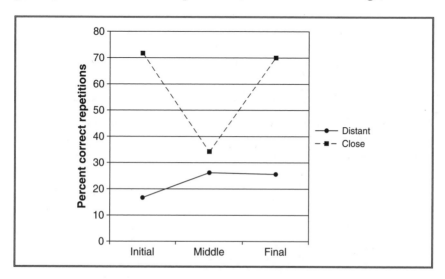

Figure 7.12 Global interaction between position and phonemic distance over the 3 periods

Analyses were performed to investigate possible interactions between phonemic distance and the frequency of words in the input at each period. A two-way ANOVA was conducted for each period, taking into account only the repetitions at the period in question in order to obtain interpretable results. For instance, when investigating the interaction between frequency at Period 0h00 and phonemic distance, only repetitions at Period 0h00 were considered, and so on. Figures 7.13, 7.14 and 7.15 show the results of combinations of phonemic distance and frequency at Periods 0h00, 4h00 and 8h00.

Results revealed no significant interaction between phonemic distance and frequency at Period 0h00 or at Period 4h00. A significant interaction was found at Period 8h00, F (2,107) = 3.960, $p < 0.05$. As expected, words that had not appeared in the input and that were categorised as 'distant' were the most difficult for participants to reproduce at all periods. We

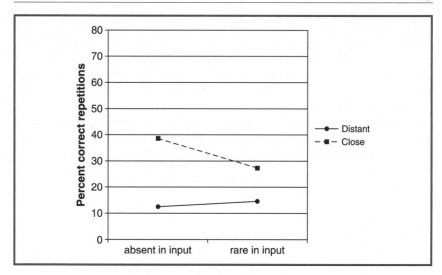

Figure 7.13 Interaction between frequency of words in the input and phonemic distance at Period 0h00

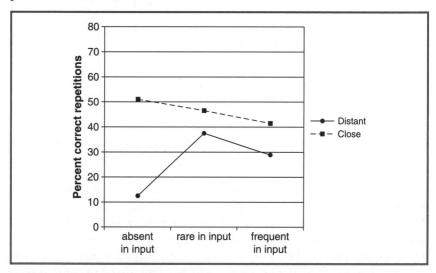

Figure 7.14 Interaction between frequency of words in the input and phonemic distance at Period 4h00

observed a significant improvement in the repetition of 'distant' words that appeared only rarely (1–20 tokens) in the input before Period 8h00. This points to a global influence of the input. Words with sounds that were unfamiliar to a French speaker at Period 0h00 had a low rate of reproduction. After only 8 hours of input, these words with unfamiliar sounds appear to have posed less of a problem for our learners.

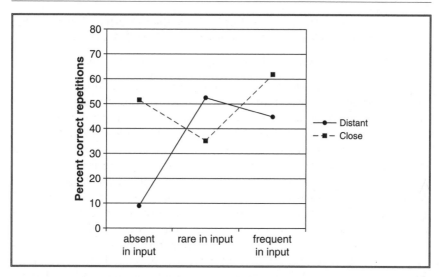

Figure 7.15 Interaction between frequency of words in the input and phonemic distance at Period 8h00

Discussion

The data presented here suggest that the more time learners spent with the L2, the better they repeated the Polish words, even over such a short time span. When investigating the independent variables individually or in pairs, overall input, generally speaking, had an effect on most of the factors taken into consideration. The only ones on which it had little to no effect were those words that were categorised as 'very transparent', and words that were in initial position, presumably because these words did not pose problems for informants who had not received any Polish instruction. In addition, our results did not confirm our hypothesis that 2-syllable words would be better repeated at all periods than words of 0–1 or 3–6 syllables. In fact, analyses showed no effect for word length across periods.

Participants who had not received Polish instruction were helped more by word stress than were participants who received instruction, and the effect of stress diminished with the increasing hours of instruction. Returning to Slobin's OP (1985: 1251), 'Pay attention to stressed syllables in extracted speech units...', we point out that Slobin refers to 'extracted speech units'. Peters' (1985: 1066) adaptation of this OP for perception appears under the heading 'SEGMENTATION':

> SG: STRESS. Segment off a stressed syllable of an Extracted unit and store it separately.

She too refers to the 'Extracted unit'. If we then return to Peters' (1985: 1065) initial discussion of Extraction, we find the OP EXTRACT:

EX: EXTRACT. Extract whatever salient chunks of speech you can.

What we have tried to do here is determine the exact nature of 'salient chunks of speech'. Our results suggest that word stress makes a segment salient when learners are exposed to the TL for the first time, that is at Period 0h00, and even at Period 4h00, although to a lesser extent. Word stress did not have a significant effect on correct repetitions at Period 8h00. We can note here that although native French speakers may not be accustomed to systematically looking for distinctive lexical stress while decoding French words (as French does not have such stress), they seem nonetheless to spontaneously pay attention to word stress in Polish, at least upon first contact with the language. Indeed, even though stress can be taken here as a salient feature (i.e. 'enhanced input' – if an item is stressed, it is louder, and if it is louder, we are more likely to perceive it), this does not imply that learners have started building a phonological system yet. Further empirical work would be appropriate here.

As hypothesised, phonemic distance played an important role in our informants' ability to repeat TL words. However, we predicted an increased success rate of unfamiliar words corresponding to the increase in hours of L2 exposure. This prediction was not confirmed: no interaction was found between period and phonemic distance. In other words, at all periods, the words with 'close' sounds were consistently and proportionately reproduced at a more successful rate than words with 'distant' sounds. Overall exposure to the L2 was shown to aid learners in their repetitions of words in both categories. Interactions were found between phonemic distance and respectively word stress, position and frequency of the word after 8 hours of input, which highlights the crucial role that phonemic characteristics played in the task at hand.

We hypothesised that transparency would play an important role in participants' ability to repeat Polish words correctly at all periods, but especially at Period 0h00. Results confirmed a main effect for the transparency variable across periods. Thus, transparency was a factor in the sentence repetition test, as it was in the word translation test (cf. Chapter 5). Transparency helps make a form-meaning association, and *therefore*, helps in segmenting the speech stream. The decontextualised results presented in Chapter 5 have relevance for perception and repetition of the speech stream.

In addition, we found that increased exposure to Polish had a stronger influence on the repetitions of non-transparent words than fairly transparent ones. Little to no influence of global input was found on repetitions of very transparent words. These results confirm our hypothesis, while also adding precision about the effects of different degrees of transparency. Our data, however, did not allow us to investigate interactions between transparency and other variables.

As mentioned earlier, previous research has assumed a high saliency rating for initial and final positions. Our results confirm that the position of a word in the sentence is a strong cue for learners at this early stage of acquisition, while also suggesting they may rely less and less on this cue as acquisition progresses. We found VanPatten's principles P4 and P4a (that learners first process elements in sentence/utterance initial position and those in final position before elements in medial position) to partially operate with our learners: at all periods, words in initial and final position were better repeated than those in medial position. As we surmised, Slobin's Operating Principles of position (BEGINNING and END OF UNIT) do indeed operate in the first stages of L2 acquisition. We did not, however, find a statistically significant difference between repetitions of words in initial position and those in final position. We would like to point out here that we are not going as far as to say that position aids acquisition. We are merely saying that certain positions are more salient than others and that saliency (i.e. certain positions in this case) aids perception, which, we all seem to agree, is necessary for input processing.

The frequency of a word in the input played an insignificant role in the repetitions of participants at Periods 0h00 and 4h00. Frequency only became a significant factor after 8 hours of Polish instruction. Slobin (1985: 1251) highlights the importance of frequency in his OPs grouped as 'Entering and Tagging Information in Storage':

> Keep track of the frequency of occurrence of every unit and pattern that you store [...] Determine whether a newly extracted stretch of speech seems to be the same as or different from anything you have already stored. If it is different, store it separately; if it is the same, take note of this sameness by increasing its frequency count by one.

Determining whether or not Slobin's OPs of frequency operate in SLA may be a problem, once again, of the researchers' understanding of the process of 'extraction'. Have our participants truly 'extracted' the word – or a 'stable' lexical item – when they repeat it? Are they able, with such limited input, to take note of 'sameness' and increase the frequency count? Our results suggest that, with some time (in our case, 8 hours of exposure to the L2), they are, perhaps remarkably, able to do this.

Conclusion

The objective of this chapter was to investigate the perceptual activity of our 'first exposure' informants at Period 0h00 and of our learners at subsequent periods after exposure to Polish. We now have a better idea of which of the *a priori* criteria that researchers propose to define saliency are relevant for learners. Results of the sentence repetition test suggest the following: (1) even as little as 8 hours of exposure improves performance on a sentence repetition task and allows the researcher to measure such progress; (2) the influence of global input can be made more precise by certain factors, such as those studied here: word length, word stress, phonemic distance with regard to the learners' L1, transparency, position of the item in the sentence and frequency of the item in the input; (3) the role these factors play evolves over time, and this evolution can be understood and predicted. The current study is limited to the first 8 hours of exposition to Polish by native French speakers. Further research in a controlled setting over longer periods of time is needed to provide more information on questions raised in this study, such as: (1) at what point do correct repetitions of phonemically 'distant' words begin to converge with those of 'close' words, and (2) at what point do words in middle position pose less of a problem for perception and reproduction relative to those in initial and final positions? The results presented here reveal that, upon first contact with an unknown language, French informants, whose L1 does not have lexical stress, relied on this property when reproducing words in Polish. Continued investigation into the effect of word stress on perception relative to other factors and to other source and target language combinations would prove fruitful. Indeed, future work in an input-controlled environment should profitably extend this type of analysis to longer periods of time, to other language combinations and to other ways of tapping the learner's perceptual activity. What has been presented here is a first step in resolving the 'perception problem' alluded to earlier by characterising what helps and what does not help the learner's perceptual activity at the very beginning of the second language acquisition process. We now continue the discussion of our learners' language activity in the following chapter by returning to a question already discussed in Chapter 5: what helps or does not help the learner's comprehension of a new target language? In Chapter 5 we discussed the comprehension (or lack thereof) of an isolated lexical item; in Chapter 8, we extend this to the comprehension of sequences of words combined into sentences.

Notes

1. The first version of these results appeared in an article co-authored with Jean-Yves Dommergues in 2003 (Rast & Dommergues, 2003). Results are reprinted here with the permission of John Benjamins.
2. It may, however, exist in foreign words used in French; vowels were excluded as they are virtually similar in French and Polish. The vowel that

may pose a problem for French speakers of Polish is 'y' realised as [ɨ] as in *uniwersytecie* 'university'. We did not take this into account due to problems hearing the difference between the two sounds in the reproductions of our participants.

3. We have used the unit 'word' as a unit of measurement for correct repetitions. It is important to note that we make no assumptions here about the segmentation of speech into meaningful units. We are concerned with the perception, memorisation and repetition of acoustic-phonetic properties of the data.

4. To investigate whether the effect of phonemic distance was due to difficulty in *producing* (i.e. repeating) distant phonemes or *perceiving* them or both would require discrete phonemic analyses along the lines of Best and Strange (1992) and Flege (1992). Such an investigation merits reflection.

Chapter 8
Speech Comprehension

In Chapter 4, we touched on some of the current trends in L2 comprehension research, one of which hypothesises that the automatisation of certain operations of cognitive activity facilitates comprehension (Gaonac'h, 1991). We can also invert this concept and propose that in the absence of this automatisation, the execution of a comprehension task in the TL becomes costly in terms of cognition. In our analysis of the data collected by means of an oral sentence translation test, we will attempt to identify not only strategies used by our learners to accomplish the task at hand, but also constraints that prevent them from succeeding.

In Chapter 3 (cf. 3.3.1), our contrastive analysis of French and Polish predicted that the difference between the two systems of basic constituent word order would probably pose more problems for our learners in perception and comprehension than in production. If in the language being acquired the word order alone provides insufficient information to identify the semantic role relations within an utterance, then knowledge of the TL morphological system becomes crucial for the learner. We can imagine the reverse as well, that French learners who have not yet acquired Polish morphology will resort to the word order strategies of their NL to understand a Polish utterance.

Oral Sentence Translation Test

To test a learner's comprehension of TL sentences, Klein (1986) conducted an oral translation test (Heidelberger Forschungsprojekt 'Pidgin-Deutsch' [HPD], 1979; cf. also Klein, 1986) during which learners heard sentences in their TL and translated them immediately into their NL. This task is considered to be a way to gather evidence about how learners '... analyse utterances as input to the language processor' (Klein, 1986: 74). We adapted HPD's translation test for our own purposes and administered distinct versions of the test to our learners at three different periods: 1h30, 3h30 and 7h00 (see test items in Appendix 3). Each test consisted of 8–10 Polish utterances. The instructions were to listen to each utterance twice and then translate it into written French on the response sheet provided. When reporting learners' translations in this chapter, we have maintained their exact translations, respecting their spelling, capitalisation and punctuation.

Klein (1986) makes two important observations pertaining to his results of the oral translation test. Firstly, he observes that his learners differ in terms of risk taking and deducing. He cites the responses of two learners at the same level. One translated close to nothing, whereas the other provided detailed translations, even if most were incorrect. Secondly, Klein shows how the perception of a one-syllable lexical item can lead to a misinterpretation of the entire sentence. He provides an example in German L2. Four Spanish learners of German used 'hijo' (son) or 'niño' (child) in their translations of a German sentence even though the sentence in question made no reference to a son or child. A phonological analysis revealed that the root of the problem lay in the processing of the adverb 'sonst' (otherwise), likely to be confused with the noun 'Sohn' (son). Klein (1986: 77) concludes with the following: 'The two points made above make it clear that we must be very cautious in our assumptions about what the learner actually 'hears' and how he interprets what he has (or seems to have) heard'.

In this chapter, we propose to contribute to Klein's observations about the oral translation of the TL in two ways. Firstly, we are able investigate the strategies L2 learners use to comprehend an unfamiliar language because our learners had received such little Polish input at the time of testing. Secondly, having controlled the Polish input, we can compare the learners' translations with the type and quantity of input received. In this study, 'input' is a constant in that it does not vary from one learner to the next.

Data analyses were conducted from two angles: (1) comparing the translations of several sentence types in terms of basic constituent word order at the same period; (2) comparing translations of sentences that were kept constant over the three test periods. The former comparison will provide information about the role of word order in L2 sentence processing, whereas the latter will allow us to follow the evolution of our learners' performance relative to the Polish input they received. In both comparison types, we analyse the influence of the following four factors (our independent variables in mathematical terms) on our learners' translations: (1) word order; (2) word frequency; (3) word transparency; (4) sentence length.[1] We hypothesise that in the case of our French learners of Polish the following will aid them in their comprehension of Polish sentences: (1) SVO order; (2) a high score of word frequency; (3) a high rating of word transparency; and (4) short sentence length.

For the purpose of comparison between translations of different sentence types and at different periods, we established the category 'correct translations' as our dependent variable. This category reflects French translations of entire Polish sentences and not of individual words (as was the case in the analysis of sentence repetitions in Chapter 7). This said, when pertinent, we analyse individual lexical items in terms of their frequency in the input and their transparency as these are hypothesised to be influential factors in a learner's L2 sentence processing. The term 'correct translations' refers to French translations that express the same semantic and grammatical information as that of the original Polish sentence. In cases in which two or more words could be used to express a similar meaning, such as *znać* 'to know' and *mowić* 'to speak' for 'She speaks Polish' and 'She knows Polish', we accepted all possibilities that conveyed a clear comprehension of the Polish lexical item within the given context. Whether or not a learner correctly translated aspectual information (i.e. perfective versus imperfective) or pragmatic information, such as emphasis or contrast, was not taken into consideration when judging the correctness of sentences. We could not expect learners to translate pragmatic information, defined here as relating signs to their users and interpreters within a particular context, because no context was provided in this exercise. For this reason, in cases where context was required to accurately translate the sentence, we accepted translations based only on semantic and grammatical information. For example, a translation in which the aspect of a given Polish verb was not properly translated was still considered a 'correct translation' if all other required information was expressed. In the data analyses, an asterisk precedes all translations considered 'incorrect'. Note that translations resulting in incorrect French formulations were not considered 'correct' even if all sentence components had been accurately translated. Criteria for our four independent variables are outlined as follows:

Word order. Our discussion of word order is limited to the basic constituents of a sentence, that is, verb-argument structure. In this chapter, we make use of the traditional SVO, OVS and VSO word order categories. The 'O' space, however, may be occupied by a structure such as an adverbial prepositional phrase (PP/Adv) or a complement (C), hence our usage of the expression 'SVO-type', 'OVS-type' or 'VSO-type' sentence.

Word frequency. To measure the frequency of a word in the input, we followed the criteria established in the preceding chapter (cf. 'Hypotheses' in the first section of Chapter 7): 'absent in the input' (0 tokens); 'rare' (1–20 tokens); 'frequent' (21–650 tokens). We note separately the frequency of the exact form of the word in the input and the frequency of its grammatical variants (e.g. *język* 'language-Nom/Acc' versus *języka* 'language – Gen').

Transparency. To establish the rate of word transparency we used the results of the transparency test described in the preceding chapter (cf. 'Hypotheses' in the first section of Chapter 7): 'opaque' (rating of 0% correct translations); 'fairly transparent' (1–50%); 'very transparent' (51–100%). The transparency rating is based on the exact form of the word in the Polish sentence, not on its grammatical variants.

Sentence length. We measure sentence length in number of syllables. The sentences that appeared in the oral translation test ranged from 5 to 13 syllables. For facility of discussion, we grouped sentences into four categories: 'short' (5–6 syllables); 'fairly short' (7–8); 'fairly long' (9–10); 'long' (11–13).

Speech comprehension at Period 1h30

In what follows, we present our analyses of the data collected from the oral translation test after 1h30 of Polish input.

Processing SVO-type sentences (Period 1h30)

The first set of analyses concerns the SVO-type sentences in the test:
1) *Ona pochodzi z Francji.*
   elle vient de France (she comes from France)
2) *Ona się nazywa Anna.*
   elle se appelle Anna (she Refl is called Anna)
3) *Ines nie zna dobrze języka polskiego.*
   Ines pas connaît bien langue polonaise
   (Ines not know well language Polish)
Our learners translated the first sentence as follows:

1) Sentence heard:	*Ona pochodzi z Francji.*
	[Pron-Nom, f, sg] [V 3p sg] [Prep] [N-Loc]
	elle vient de France (she comes from France)
Dalia:	Elle vient de France
Emma:	elle vient de France.
Gilles:	Elle vient de France.
Julie:	elle vient de France.
Luc:	Elle vient de France
Nadine:	Elle est d'origine française / Elle provient de France
	'She is of French origin / She comes from France'
Sabine:	*Elle parle français 'She speaks French'
Sandra:	Elle vient de France.

(* denotes an incorrect translation)

The results clearly show that, with the exception of Sabine, our learners translated the sentence correctly. Sabine found the subject of the sentence, but misinterpreted the predicate. To explain this success after only 1h30 of exposure to the TL, we examined word frequency (in the first 1h30 of input) and the transparency of the four words in the sentence (see Table 8.1).

According to our criteria established for frequency, all the words in Sentence (1) were frequent in the input (21 or more tokens). *Francji* was rated as 'fairly transparent', whereas the others were rated as 'opaque'. These results suggest an effect of word frequency (already at Period 1h30) on the ability of learners to translate a Polish sentence. Results discussed in Chapter 7 (cf. 'Results' in the first section) suggested that the effect of frequency on correct repetitions did not kick in until Period 8h00

Table 8.1 Sentence 1: Word frequency in the input at Period 1h30 and word transparency

Correct translations	Sentence 1 (S-V-PP/Adv) – 4 words, 7 syllables (fairly short) 7 (out of 8)			
	ona *(she)*	**pochodzi** *(comes)*	**z** *(from)*	**Francji** *(France)*
Freq[a] (exact form)	30	52	83	34
Freq (variants)[b]	18	50	12	1
Transparency[c]	0%	0%	0%	70%

[a]Freq, frequency in the input (0 = absent; 1–20 = rare; >20 = frequent)
[b]Variant, grammatical variants (inflections) of the Polish word in question
[c]Transparency (0% = opaque; 1–50% = fairly transparent; >50% = very transparent)

(after 8 hours of input), at least when measured as the sole independent variable. As a reminder, the nature of the data was such that we were unable to test the interaction of all of our independent variables. It is possible that an effect of frequency on correct translations in an oral translation test may be due to interacting factors, such as frequency, word order and/or sentence length. Further research in this area would be worthwhile.

Let us now take a look at a second SVO-type sentence. As with Sentence (1), Sentence (2) posed few problems for our learners:

2) Sentence heard: *Ona się nazywa Anna.*
  [Pron-Nom, f, sg] [Refl] [V 3p sg] [N-Nom]
  elle se appelle Anna (she Refl is called Anna)
Dalia: Elle s'appelle Ana
Emma: Elle s'appelle Ana.
Gilles: Elle s'appelle Anna.
Julie: elle s'appelle Anna.
Luc: Elle s'appelle Anna.
Nadine: Elle s'appelle Ana.
Sabine: Elle s'appelle Anna
Sandra: *Elle... 'She...'

Of eight learners, seven translated the sentence correctly. Sandra found the subject, but she failed to translate the predicate.

Table 8.2 shows a detailed analysis of Sentence (2). Like Sentence (1), Sentence (2) is 'fairly short'. With regard to frequency in the input, three of the four words in (2) were frequent in the input, but not transparent. The infrequent word, the first name *Anna*, appeared only three times in

Table 8.2 Sentence 2: Word frequency in the input at Period 1h30 and word transparency

Correct translations	Sentence 2 (S-V-C) – 4 words, 8 syllables (fairly short) 7 (out of 8)			
	ona *(she)*	się *(Refl)*	nazywa *(call)*	Anna *(Anna)*
Freq[a] (exact form)	30	72	26	3
Freq (variants)[b]	18	–	44	–
Transparency[c]	0%	0%	0%	53%

[a]Freq, frequency in the input (0 = absent; 1–20 = rare; >20 = frequent)
[b]Variant = grammatical variants (inflections) of the Polish word in question
[c]Transparency (0% = opaque; 1–50% = fairly transparent; >50% = very transparent)

the input; however, it was categorised as 'very transparent'. Results presented in Chapters 5 and 7 point to a strong effect of transparency in both perception and comprehension. Based on analyses of (1) and (2), we hypothesise that when all words in a sentence carry a high score of word frequency and/or a high rate of word transparency, the learners' comprehension of the Polish sentence is facilitated.

Our learners' translations of Sentence (3) reveal problems of comprehension not observed in the previous two sentences:

3) Sentence heard: *Ines nie zna dobrze języka polskiego.*
   [N-Nom] [Neg] [V 3p sg] [Adv] [N-Gen, sg] [Adj-Gen, sg]
   Ines pas connaît bien langue polonaise
   (Ines not knows well language Polish)
   (= Ines does not know the Polish language well.)

Dalia: *(no response)
Emma: *Ines n'est pas Polonaise. 'Ines is not Polish.'
Gilles: Ines ne parle pas bien polonais.
            'Ines does not speak Polish well.'
Julie: *Ines (?)
Luc: *(no response)
Nadine: *Ines parle polonais. 'Ines speaks Polish.'
Sabine: *(no response)
Sandra: *Ines ne connait pas la Pologne.
            'Ines does not know Poland.'

Gilles is the only learner who grasped the essence of this sentence. Three learners supplied no response. Sandra processed *polskiego* as 'Pologne' (Poland) and Emma as 'Polonaise' (Polish nationality – feminine). What could be the cause of this difficulty?

As with the two previous sentence analyses, let us examine the sentence in detail, beginning with word frequency and transparency (see Table 8.3).

Several observations can be made about Sentence (3). First, regarding word frequency, the first name *Ines* was not produced by the instructor in the first 1h30 of the Polish course. Nor was it included in our transparency test. It is a fairly common first name in France, however, which may explain why five of our learners managed to translate it. Secondly, in addition to *Ines*, neither the exact form *języka* 'language' (N-Gen) nor the form *polskiego* 'Polish'' (Adj-Gen) appeared in the input, although both share the same stem with forms that did appear: *język* (Nom) for the former and *polska* (Nom), *polski* (Gen) and *po polsku* (PP/Adv) for the latter. The verb *zna* 'knows' scored a 'rare' in the input but has several grammatical variants that also appeared. The negator *nie*, however, was 'rare' in the input with no variants and rated as 'fairly transparent'. Interestingly enough, the one form that was produced frequently by the Polish instructor, the adverb *dobrze* 'well' (104 tokens), was only translated by one learner. In summary, Sentence (3) comprises few exact forms that appeared in the input, and no words fit the category of 'very transparent'.

Let us take a look at the two other factors hypothesised to have an effect on correct translations: sentence length and word order. Concerning sentence length, Sentence (3) (6 words, 13 syllables) is longer than Sentences (1) and (2) (4 words, 7 and 8 syllables respectively), therefore increasing the demand on memory. With regard to word order, we

Table 8.3 Sentence 3: Word frequency in the input at Period 1h30 and word transparency

Correct translations	Sentence 3 (S-V-O) – 6 words, 13 syllables (long) 1 (out of 8)					
	Ines *(Ines)*	**nie** *(not)*	**zna** *(knows)*	**dobrze** *(well)*	**języka** *(language)*	**polskiego** *(Polish)*
Freq[a] (exact form)	0	15	11	104	0	0
Freq (variants)[b]	0	0	31	–	17	47
Transparency[c]	NA[d]	47%	0%	0%	0%	NA

[a]Freq, frequency in the input (0 = absent; 1–20 = rare; >20 = frequent)
[b]Variant, grammatical variants (inflections) of the Polish word in question
[c]Transparency (0% = opaque; 1–50% = fairly transparent; >50% = very transparent)
[d]NA, not available

predicted that the basic constituent word order SVO would help our learners in this sentence comprehension task. It appears, however, that other factors overrode the benefits of the SVO word order. Indeed, in Sentence (3), the exact components of the sentence were absent or rare in the input, transparency was weak, and the sentence was longer than the two analysed previously.

We can perhaps pursue our explanation of the difficulty in comprehending this sentence by considering research conducted within the Competition Model on cue cost (Bates & MacWhinney, 1987; Kail, 1990, 2000). There are certain cases in which the saliency of a word can be increased or decreased depending on the cost of processing a given structure. This notion is divided into two concepts: perceivability and assignability. The perceivability of cues refers to the degree of difficulty encountered by the listener in detecting a cue that could be of help during sentence processing. If we consider, for example, the verbal inflexional system in French from the point of view of subject–verb agreement compared to that of English, we notice the following contrasts:

(a)   Elle mange   She eats
(b)   Elles mangent   They (feminine) eat
(Bates & MacWhinney, 1987: 179)

In written French, the contrast in subject–verb agreement is marked, but it is not perceivable in spoken French ('mange' and 'mangent' are pronounced identically). In both written and spoken English the third person singular final -s can be perceived, which gives English a higher rating for perceivability with respect to this phenomenon. Results presented in Chapter 7 led us to claim that a rating for perceivability (or saliency) must also take into consideration factors such as frequency and transparency. This would then partly explain why learners had difficulty translating Sentence (3).

The assignability of cues refers to the facility with which a given cue can be seen as assigning a role. Certain cues are considered 'local', that is the cue can be categorised and assigned a role immediately, such as with casual suffixes in Turkish. In this case, the assignability is optimal. Other cues, however, referred to as 'topological' or 'global', require the hearer to wait for additional information in the sentence before assigning a role to the cue in question. These cues have a weak assignability. Bates and MacWhinney (1987: 180) point out that, 'If the processing system is under stress and/or if the processor has limited auditory storage, global cues may become so costly to handle that they are abandoned despite their information value'.

With respect to our learners, we can assume that their ability to benefit from local cues, such as morphological markers in Polish, was limited given that they had only been exposed to Polish for 1h30. This said, Sentences (1) and (3) were SVO, which, according to a full L1 transfer hypothesis, should have helped our French learners in the absence of knowledge about Polish word endings. Again, other factors appear to have overridden SVO order, however, such as sentence length (long), low transparency ratings and minimal input.

Processing OVS-type sentences (Period 1h30)

Our next analysis consisted of comparing the translations of SVO-type sentences to those of the OVS type:

4) *Po polsku mówi ona dobrze.*
   en polonais parle elle bien (in Polish speaks she well)
5) *W Krakowie pracuje Jacek.*
   à Cracovie travaille Jacques (in Krakow works James)

The first sentence posed problems for most of the learners:
4) Sentence heard: *Po polsku mówi ona dobrze.*
                      [PP/Adv] [V 3p sg] [Pron-Nom, f, sg] [Adv]
                      en polonais parle elle bien
                      (in Polish speaks she well)
                      (= Elle parle bien le polonais.
                      ' = She speaks Polish well.')

Learners' translations:
Dalia: *ona = elle 'ona = she'
Emma: *elle parle le polonais. 'she speaks Polish.'
Gilles: Elle parle bien polonais. 'She speaks Polish well.'
Julie: *Polonais est la langue que je parle. 'Polish is the language that I speak.'
Luc: *parler 'to speak'
Nadine: *La Pologne, elle parle 'Poland, she speaks'
Sabine: *je parle polonais 'I speak Polish'
Sandra: Elle parle bien le polonais. 'She speaks Polish well.'

As a reminder, our eight learners have similar linguistic profiles; they are all monolingual native French speakers with knowledge of other L2s (not Slavic) exposed to the same Polish input for the first time. Despite this common ground, no two learners translated Sentence (4) identically, providing evidence for interlearner variation. Sandra and Gilles, who translated the sentence correctly, came the closest, diverging only in their use of a definite article. Emma apparently understood the general meaning of the sentence, failing only to translate the adverb *dobrze*. As we observed in the translations of (3), in spite of the high rate of frequency of *dobrze* in the input (104 tokens), few learners translated it.

The explicit pronoun *ona* 'she' posed problems for Sabine and Julie in (4) as witnessed by their translation 'je' (I); this was not the case in (1) and (2), providing evidence of *intra*learner variation. Julie and Nadine's translations are worth looking at closely. They both noticed the non-SVO word order and adapted the syntax of their translations accordingly. Nadine even seems to have noticed *po*, translating it with the French article 'La' (the). Note that Dalia and Luc translated only one word of the sentence. We have examples here of both inter- and intralearner variation. All responses taken together are inconsistent across learners, and the responses of each learner are, in some cases, inconsistent across sentences. In Chapter 6, we argued the importance of incorporating learner variation into our models and theories of SLA. The data collected from the oral translation test confirm this line of thought and argue for the incorporation of both inter- and intralearner variation.

Let us take a look now at what factors render Sentence (4) more or less difficult to comprehend by examining the four independent variables. Table 8.4 shows that our learners were frequently exposed to all five words in (4) and that transparency ratings were low. The sentence is longer (5 words, 9 syllables) than (1) and (2) (4 words, 7 and 8 syllables respectively), but shorter than (3) (6 words, 13 syllables). Given that word frequency was high and the sentence was not much longer than sentences (1) and (2), we could have expected better results than only two correct translations. This suggests that the non-SVO word order may have had a negative effect on the learners' processing of this sentence or that frequency and transparency do not necessarily compensate for one another.

Table 8.4 Sentence 4: Word frequency in the input at Period 1h30 and word transparency

Correct translations	Sentence 4 (PP/Adv-V-S) – 5 words, 9 syllables (fairly long) 2 (out of 8)				
	po (in)	polsku (Polish)	mówi (speaks)	ona (she)	dobrze (well)
Freq[a] (exact form)	139	24	31	30	104
Freq (variants)[b]	–	23	41	18	–
Transparency[c]	0%	13%	0%	0%	0%

[a]Freq, frequency in the input (0 = absent; 1–20 = rare; >20 = frequent)
[b]Variant = grammatical variants (inflections) of the Polish word in question
[c]Transparency (0% = opaque; 1–50% = fairly transparent; >50% = very transparent)

Let us take a look at another OVS-type sentence:
Learners translated (5) as follows:

5) Sentence heard: *W Krakowie pracuje Jacek.*
                      [Prep] [N-Loc] [V 3p sg] [N-Nom]
                      à Cracovie travaille Jacques
                      (in Krakow works James)
                      (= Jacques travaille à Cracovie. '= James
                      works in Krakow.')

Dalia: Yatzek travaille à Cracovie
Emma: Jacek travaille à Cracovie / le Cracove. 'Jacek works in
          Krakow.'
Gilles: Jazek travaille à Krakovie.
Julie: *Kracovie, Yatse cconnait. 'Krakow, Yatsec knows.'
Luc: *(no response)
Nadine: Yatsek travaille en Krakovie
Sabine: *Elle vient de Cracovie 'She comes from Krakow'
Sandra: Jazek travaille à Cracovie.

We are not concerned here with the spelling of the proper names
Krakowie and *Jacek*. What is important is that the learner has understood
that *Jacek* is a person (who works) and *Kraków* is a place, the latter
revealed by the correct usage of a preceding preposition. Given this
information, five learners grasped the essence of the sentence. Of those
who did not, we observe that Julie placed 'Kracovie' at the beginning of
her French translation, using the same strategy as with the previous
sentence. She appears to have again noticed the non-SVO word order,
finds the SV ('Yatsec knows') and parses the pre-posed adverb as the
direct object. This does not imply, however, that she maintained the
identical word order of the Polish sentence. The original sentence is
PP/Adv-V-S; her translation is O-S-V.

Luc also had trouble translating this non-SVO sentence, as with (4),
providing no translation whatsoever this time. In Chapter 6 we observed a
strong preference for the order SVO on the part of Luc. Could it be that an
order other than SVO posed an obstacle to Luc's ability to translate these
sentences? Table 8.5 provides a detailed analysis of the sentence items.

The information presented in Table 8.5 reveals that *Krakowie* was rare
in the input and fairly transparent. As students/learners of Polish, most
managed to respond with a form that at least resembled 'Cracovie' on the
test, very likely due to their own encyclopaedic knowledge. Of the
French informants taking the transparency test (translating words heard
in Polish into French), 33% identified *Krakowie* as 'Cracovie', and this
without knowing that Polish was the language of the test. *Jacek* was
inexistent in the input and a transparency rating is unavailable. The verb
pracuje 'works' was frequent in the input, which clearly aided learners

Table 8.5 Sentence 5: Word frequency in the input at Period 1h30 and word transparency

Correct translations	Sentence 5 (PP/Adv-V-S) – 4 words, 8 syllables (fairly short) 5 (out of 8)			
	w *(in)*	**Krakowie** *(Krakow)*	**pracuje** *(works)*	**Jacek** *(James)*
Freq[a] (exact form)	61	1	31	0
Freq (variants)[b]	16	4	12	0
Transparency[c]	0%	33%	0%	NA[d]

[a]Freq, frequency in the input (0 = absent; 1–20 = rare; >20 = frequent)
[b]Variant, grammatical variants (inflections) of the Polish word in question
[c]Transparency (0% = opaque; 1–50% = fairly transparent; >50% = very transparent)
[d]NA, not available

from the point of view of lexical processing, five of whom found the correct translation. Sentence length is similar to that of (1) and (2), fairly short. Returning to the question of why Luc had such difficulty with this sentence, it appears that several factors may have played a role: non-SVO word order, low word frequency and low transparency ratings for two of the four words. From these data, we cannot conclude that it was word order alone that hampered Luc's comprehension.

To sum up the results obtained from Sentences (1)–(5), Sentences (1) and (2) had the highest rate of correct translations (7 learners translated both of them correctly). Both are of the SVO type, both are fairly short sentences (4 words, 7 and 8 syllables), and the vast majority of their elements were frequent in the input. The one word that appeared rarely in the input, *Anna*, received a high transparency rating. We predict that the factors of item 'frequency' and 'transparency' can compensate for one another during sentence processing. In other words, a lexical item may be easily processed if it is *frequent* in the input but *not transparent* because it can be memorised and reused; likewise, a lexical item may be easily processed if it is *transparent* but *not frequent*, in this case, because it can be recognised. The latter prediction was shown to be true in Chapters 5 and 7 under certain conditions. The former, however, is not yet clear.

Sentence (5) had the next level of success, translated correctly by five learners. This sentence is PP/Adv-V-S, it is fairly short, and two of the items, both rated as 'opaque', were frequent in the input. One of the infrequent words carried a 'fairly transparent' rating. Sentences (1), (2) and (5) are all fairly short, therefore ruling out sentence length as a variable in our comparison of these three sentences. If in fact 'frequency' and 'transparency' balance each other out, then we could conclude that the non-SVO word order had a negative effect on the translations of our three learners who translated (5) incorrectly. The absence of a transparency rating for *Jacek*, however, prevents us from definitively concluding as such. We will continue to investigate this point during our analyses of OSV-type sentences.

Concerning Sentence (4), only two learners translated it in its entirety. Its components were all frequent in the input, but not transparent (one word was 'fairly transparent'). The sentence is non-SVO and fairly long (9 syllables).

Finally, it is Sentence (3) that resulted in the least number of correct translations (only 1). This is not surprising given the following: (1) the sentence is long (6 words, 13 syllables); (2) only one word was frequent in the input, 2 were rare and 3 were absent; (3) one word was categorised as 'fairly transparent', 3 were 'opaque' and 2 were not rated for transparency. The basic constituent word order, however, is SVO. This analysis suggests that SVO word order was not the strongest indicator of potential sentence comprehension. It seems that the cost of processing cues played a role here. Perceivability and assignability being weak, the result was difficulty in processing the sentence. This analysis highlights the complexity of the interacting factors involved in sentence comprehension, at least within the first hours of TL exposure.

Processing VSO-type sentences (Period 1h30)

To gather more information on the role of word order in sentence comprehension, we also analysed two VSO-type sentences from the same oral translation test:

6) *Nie lubi Ewa Krakowa.*
    pas aime Eva Cracovie (not likes Eva Krakow)
7) *Nazywa się on Marek.*
    appelle se il Marc (is called Refl he Mark)

Sentence (6) was translated in the following way:

6) Sentence heard: *Nie lubi Ewa Krakowa.*
                    [Neg] [V 3p sg] [N-Nom] [N-Gen]
                    pas aime Eva Cracovie
                    (not likes Eva Krakow)
                    (= Eva n'aime pas Cracovie.
                    ' = Eva doesn't like Krakow.')

Learners' translations:

Dalia:	Eva n'aime pas Cracovie
Emma:	Eva n'aime pas Cracovie. 'Eva doesn't like Krakow.'
Gilles:	Eva n'aime pas Krakowa. 'Eva doesn't like Krakowa.'
Julie:	*elle n'habite Krakovie. 'she not lives Krakow.'

Luc: *Eva n'habite pas Kracovie. (?) 'Eva doesn't live Krakow. (?)'

Nadine: *Niela Krakova n'est pas là. 'Niela Krakova is not there.'

Sabine: *elle n'aime pas Cracovie 'she doesn't like Krakow'

Sandra: Eva n'aime pas Cracovie.

Unlike in (5), where we could verify the learners' comprehension of a 'place' via the presence or absence of a preposition ('à Cracovie' 'in Krakow'), this was not possible in (6). We opted to count Gilles' response ending in 'Krakowa' as correct because of his use of a capital letter to indicate a proper noun and his correct translation of 'à Krakovie' in Sentence (5). In sum, four learners translated the sentence correctly. Table 8.6 shows the sentence elements in detail.

Sentence (6) is short (4 words, 8 syllables) and two of the words were rated as fairly or very transparent. None of the words, however, were very frequent in the input and the word order was VSO. In short, in (6), according to our hypotheses, the factors in favour of correct translations are shortness in sentence length and a fairly high transparency rating of two of the four words. The positive effects of these factors, however, did not entirely outweigh the apparent negative effects of low frequency and VSO word order.

Table 8.6 Sentence 6: Word frequency in the input at Period 1h30 and word transparency

Correct translations	Sentence 6 (V-S-O) – 4 words, 8 syllables (fairly short) 4 (out of 8)			
	nie (not)	lubi (likes)	Ewa (Ewa)	Krakowa (Krakow)
Freq[a] (exact form)	15	13	2	3
Freq (variants)[b]	–	6	–	2
Transparency[c]	47%	0%	69%	NA[d]

[a]Freq, frequency in the input (0 = absent; 1–20 = rare; >20 = frequent)
[b]Variant, grammatical variants (inflections) of the Polish word in question
[c]Transparency (0% = opaque; 1–50% = fairly transparent; >50% = very transparent)
[d]NA, not available

The other sentence was translated as follows:

7) Sentence heard: *Nazywa się on Marek.*
                       [V 3p sg] [Refl] [Pron-Nom, m, sg] [N-Nom]
                       appelle se il Marc
                       (is called Refl he Mark)
                       (= Il s'appelle Marc. ' = His name is Mark.')

Learners' translations:

Dalia: *(no response)
Emma: Il s'appelle Marek. 'His name is Marek.'
Gilles: *Comment s'appelle Marek? 'What is Marek's name?'
Julie: il s'appelle Marek.
Luc: Il s'appelle Marek.
Nadine: Il s'appelle Marek.
Sabine: Il s'appelle Marek
Sandra: *Que connait Marek? 'What knows Marek?'

We accepted the Polish version of 'Mark', *Marek*, in the translations. Five learners translated the sentence correctly. Of the three who did not, two responded with a question and one provided no translation.

As can be seen in Table 8.7, on the one hand, Sentence (7) is 'fairly short' (4 words, 7 syllables) and three of the four words appeared frequently in the input. On the other hand, all words are 'opaque' and the word order is non-SVO. The relative shortness of the sentence in addition to the high score of frequency apparently aided many of the learners. Two learners were clearly influenced by non-SVO word order, which led them to comprehend the declarative sentence as an interrogative. Again, we are observing learners with similar profiles processing *differently*.

Table 8.7 Sentence 7: Word frequency in the input at Period 1h30 and word transparency

Correct translations	Sentence 7 (V-S-C) – 4 words, 7 syllables (fairly short) 5 (out of 8)			
	nazywa *(calls)*	się *(Refl)*	on *(he)*	Marek *(Mark)*
Freq[a] (exact form)	26	72	18	1
Freq (variant)[b]	44	–	30	–
Transparency[c]	0%	0%	0%	0%

[a]Freq, frequency in the input (0 = absent; 1–20 = rare; >20 = frequent)
[b]Variant, grammatical variants (inflections) of the Polish word in question
[c]Transparency (0% = opaque; 1–50% = fairly transparent; >50% = very transparent)

The comparison of two sentences in the test composed of similar elements in variant word orders (Sentences 2 and 7 shown above) proves interesting:

Sentences heard (2):   *Ona się nazywa Anna.*
                        [Pron-Nom, f, sg] [Refl] [V 3p sg] [N-Nom]
                        elle se appelle Anna
                        (she Refl is called Anna)
                        (= Elle s'appelle Anna. ' = Her name is Anna.')

(7):   *Nazywa się on Marek.*
      [V 3p sg] [Refl] [Pron-Nom, m, sg] [N-Nom]
      appelle se il Marc
      (is called Refl he Mark)
      (= Il s'appelle Marc. ' = His name is Mark.')

Table 8.8 Processing SV and VS sentences: A comparison at Period 1h30

Learners	Sentence 2 (S-V-C)	Sentence 7 (V-S-C)
Dalia	Elle s'appelle Ana	*(no response)
Emma	Elle s'appelle Ana.	Il s'appelle Marek.
Gilles	Elle s'appelle Anna.	*Comment s'appelle Marek?
Julie	elle s'appelle Anna.	il s'appelle Marek.
Luc	Elle s'appelle Anna.	Il s'appelle Marek.
Nadine	Elle s'appelle Ana.	Il s'appelle Marek.
Sabine	Elle s'appelle Anna	Il s'appelle Marek.
Sandra	*Elle...	*Que connait Marek?
Total correct	7	5

Looking at Table 8.8, we note that more learners correctly translated Sentence (2) than Sentence (7) (7 correct translations compared to 5). We note as well that two learners, Gilles and Sandra, translated Sentence (7) with the interrogative form, suggesting that they recognised a sentence-initial verb, which, for a French native speaker, could reasonably trigger the interrogative form. We suspect an influence of the native language here in the form of a structure such as 'S'appelle-t-il Marc?' (Is called he Mark? = Is his name Mark?).

Another area that needs attention when comparing sentences such as these is analysis of individual lexical items. The pronouns *on* and *ona* had similar ratings in terms of frequency and transparency. The first names, *Anna* and *Marek*, had similarly low word frequency scores (3 tokens versus 1 token), but differed significantly in their transparency rating. *Anna* rated 'very transparent' (53%) and *Marek* 'opaque' (0%). This difference in transparency ratings poses a problem for the comparative analysis of these sentences. The fewer correct translations of (7) compared to (2) could be due to the difference of word order or to the low transparency rating of *Marek*. We will return to this problem in our analyses of speech comprehension at Periods 3h30 and 7h00.

Speech comprehension at Period 3h30

After 3h30 of Polish instruction, we administered a second oral translation test in the same format as the first. We will not present the results of this test in the same quantitative manner as those of Period 1h30, in part because the Polish input to which the learners were exposed after Period 1h30 was not analysed in such detail. Rather, what is of interest to us here are two distinct comparisons. The first is the comparison of sentences composed of identical components that differ in word order to observe the influence of word order on learners' ability to process the sentences. The second is the comparison of identical sentences during the two periods, 1h30 and 3h30, to observe the effect of hours of instruction on sentence translations.

We will begin with the first comparison. During the test administered at 3h30, the learners heard the SVO sentence first, followed by six other sentences and finally the OVS sentence. As a result of problems comparing two sentences at Period 1h30 composed of different lexical items (*Anna* versus *Marek*), we kept all items constant in the two comparison sentences at 3h30, as can be seen below:

8) *Anna lubi lody.* (SVO)
[N-Nom] [V 3p sg] [N-Acc, pl]
Anna aime glaces
(Anna likes ice cream)
(= Anna aime les glaces. ' = Anna likes ice cream.')
9) *Lody lubi Anna.* (OVS)
[N-Acc, pl] [V 3p sg] [N-Nom]
glaces aime Anna
(ice cream likes Anna)
(= Anna aime les glaces. ' = Anna likes ice cream.')

Table 8.9 presents the learners' translations, revealing that the same three learners correctly translated both sentences. As both sentences resulted in the same number of correct translations, our hypothesis that Polish OVS sentences are more difficult for a French NS to process than Polish SVO sentences does not hold in this case. Several observations can be made, however. Firstly, we notice that Dalia was unable to translate the OVS sentence. In the SVO version, she translated *lody* as 'Londres' (London) and *lubi* as 'habite' (lives) and seemed to understand that *Anna* referred to a person. Given Dalia's misunderstanding of the semantic content of *lody* and *lubi*, it is understandable that she would have trouble with the concept 'London lives Anna', the consequence of the OVS order. Luc and Emma, on the other hand, also provided no translation or an inaccurate translation for the lexical item *lody*, but word order *per se* did not seem to affect their ability to translate in that they responded

Table 8.9 Processing SVO and OVS sentences: A comparison at Period 3h30

Learners	Sentence 8 (S-V-O)	Sentence 9 (O-V-S)
Dalia	*Ana habite Londres	*?
Emma	*Ana aime	*Anna aime
Gilles	Anna aime les glaces.	Anna aime les glaces.
Julie	*Anna aime 'lode'.	*aime Anna.
Luc	*Anna aime Londres.	*Anna aime Londres.
Nadine	Anana aime les glaces.	Anana aime les glaces.
Sabine	*Anna aime lode	*Lode aime Anna
Sandra	Anna aime les crèmes glacées.	Anna aime les crèmes glacées.
Total correct	3	3

identically for both sentences. Julie and Sabine translated the sentences in the order in which they heard them, an observation made already at Period 1h30 for these two learners. They both placed *Anna* in final position in the OVS sentence.

The second type of comparison was designed to test the development of our learners' speech comprehension. We maintained three sentences constant during the two testing periods (1h30 and 3h30), two VSO types and one OVS. The two VSO-type sentences are the following:

Sentences heard (6): *Nie lubi Ewa Krakowa.*

[Neg] [V 3p sg] [N-Nom] [N-Gen]
pas aime Eva Cracovie
(not like Eva Krakow)
(= Eva n'aime pas Cracovie.
' = Eva doesn't like Krakow.')

(7): *Nazywa się on Marek.*
[V 3p sg] [Refl] [Pron-Nom, m, sg] [N-Nom]
appelle se il Marc
(is called Refl he Mark)
(= Il s'appelle Marc. ' = His name is Mark.')

The translations appear in Tables 8.10 and 8.11. When combining the total number of correct translations in the two sentences presented in Tables 8.10 and 8.11, we observe a slight improvement between Periods 1h30 and 3h30 with 9 out of 16 correct translations at Period 1h30 (Sentences 6 and 7 combined) and 11 out of 16 at Period 3h30. Note that

Table 8.10 Processing a V-S-PP/Adv sentence at Periods 1h30 and 3h30 (Sentence 6)

Learners	Period 1h30	Period 3h30
Dalia	Eva n'aime pas Cracovie	*Ewa n'habite pas à Cracovie
Emma	Eva n'aime pas Cracovie.	Ewa n'aime pas Cracovie.
Gilles	Eva n'aime pas Krakowa.	Ewa n'aime pas Cracovie.
Julie	*elle n'habite Krakovie.	*n'aime pas Eva Cracovie.
Luc	*Eva n'habite pas Kracovie. (?)	Ewa n'aime pas Cracovie.
Nadine	*Niela Krakova n'est pas là.	*Ewa n'aime pas les 'Krakowa'.
Sabine	*elle n'aime pas Cracovie	Eva n'aime pas Cracovie
Sandra	Eva n'aime pas Cracovie.	Ewa n'aime pas Cracovie.
Total correct	4	5

Table 8.11 Processing a V-S-C sentence at Periods 1h30 and 3h30 (Sentence 7)

Learners	Period 1h30	Period 3h30
Dalia	*(pas de réponse)	*D'où vient Marek?
Emma	Il s'appelle Marek	Il s'appelle Marek.
Gilles	*Comment s'appelle Marek?	Il s'appelle Marek.
Julie	il s'appelle Marek.	*s'appelle Marek.
Luc	Il s'appelle Marek.	Il s'appelle Marek.
Nadine	Il s'appelle Marek.	Il s'appelle Marek.
Sabine	Il s'appelle Marek	Il s'appelle Marek
Sandra	*Que connait Marek?	Il s'appelle Marek.
Total correct	5	6

in her translation of Sentence (6), Julie continued to produce a French sentence using incorrect word order, confirming some kind of effect of word order on her sentence translations. In her translation of (7), she positioned the verb as the initial basic constituent, as in the original Polish sentence. Interestingly enough, she translated the overt subject pronoun *on* at Period 1h30, but not at 3h30. Notice as well that no learners at either period translated (6) as a question, whereas they did

Table 8.12 Processing an PP/Adv-V-S sentence at Periods 1h30 and 3h30 (Sentence 4)

Learners	Period 1h30	Period 3h30
Dalia	*ona = elle	*?
Emma	*elle parle le polonais.	Elle parle très bien le polonais.
Gilles	Elle parle bien polonais.	Elle parle bien polonais.
Julie	*Polonais est la langue que je parle.	*polonais parle elle...
Luc	*parler	*?
Nadine	*La Pologne, elle parle	Elle parle polonais correctement.
Sabine	*je parle polonais	Elle parle très bien le polonais
Sandra	Elle parle bien le polonais.	Elle parle très bien le polonais.
Total correct	2	5

with (7). Could this be due to the sentence initial verb in (7)? We observe that Dalia was unable to respond at Period 1h30 and responded with a question form at Period 3h30. The two learners who produced questions at Period 1h30 produced accurate translations in the form of a declarative sentence at Period 3h30.

The final comparison sentence between Periods 1h30 and 3h30 was the following:

Sentence heard (4):   *Po polsku mówi ona dobrze.*
[PP/Adv] [V 3p sg] [Pron-Nom, f, sg] [Adv]
en polonais parle elle bien
(in Polish speaks she well)
(= Elle parle bien le polonais.
' = She speaks Polish well.')

Although the precise translation for *dobrze* in French is 'bien' (good), we accepted 'très bien' (very good) as a correct translation as well. Notice again that Julie's translation at 3h30, as observed at 1h30, betrays French word order. She responded with the same order as the Polish sentence she heard, placing the argument of the verb in initial position. Table 8.12 also shows some improvement in our learners' ability to correctly translate Polish sentences over time. More learners translated (4) at Period 3h30 (5 correct translations) than at Period 1h30 (2 correct translations). 8.13 shows the combined results of data presented in Tables 8.10, 8.11 and 8.12.

Table 8.13 Correct sentence translations-combined results of Tables 8.10, 8.11 and 8.12

	Total correct responses	
	Period 1h30 (raw scores) n =8 for each sentence	Period 3h30 (raw scores) n =8 for each sentence
Sentence 6	4	5
Sentence 7	5	6
Sentence 4	2	5
Total	11	16

As can be seen in Table 8.13, 11 of the possible 24 translations (8 learners x 3 sentences) were correct at Period 1h30 (46%), whereas 16 were correct at Period 3h30 (67%). In Chapter 7, our results showed a positive effect of hours of instruction (4 and 8 hours) on our learners' ability to *repeat* Polish sentences. The results discussed here suggest a similar positive effect of time of exposure, even as few as 2 hours, on our learners' ability to *comprehend* Polish sentences.

Speech comprehension at Period 7h00

Our learners took the oral translation test for the third time after 7h00 of exposure to Polish. Our focus again was a comparison of sentences with different word orders composed of identical elements. The first comparison we made involves analysis of the translations of an SVO and an OVS sentence. The sentences are presented below:

Sentences heard: (10) *Marek lubi zupę.* (SVO)
  [N-Nom] [V 3p sg] [N-Acc]
  Marc aime soupe
  (Mark likes soup)
  (= Marc aime soupe. ' = Mark likes soup.')
(11) *Zupe lubi Marek.* (OVS)
  [N-Acc] [V 3p sg] [N-Nom]
  soupe aime Marc
  (soup likes Mark)
  (= Marc aime soupe. ' = Mark likes soup.')

As shown in Table 8.14, although Emma translated (11) with an SVO structure 'Marek aime la soupe' (Mark likes soup), she indicated an OVS order with the arrow she drew from 'la soupe' to 'Marek'. We remind the reader that the instructions for the oral translation test were 'Translate the sentences you hear'. Although we accepted her translation as

Table 8.14 Processing SVO and OVS sentences at Period 7h00 (Sentences 10 and 11)

Learners	Sentence 10 (S-V-O)	Sentence 11 (O-V-S)
Dalia	Marek aime la soupe	Marek aime la soupe
Emma	Marek aime la soupe.	Marek aime la soupe. (with arrow)
Gilles	Marek aime la soupe	Marek aime la soupe
Julie	Marek aime la soupe.	*Soupe aime Marek.
Luc	Marek aime la soupe	Marek aime la soupe
Nadine	Marek aime la soupe.	Marek aime la soupe.
Sabine	Marek aime la soupe	Marek aime la soupe
Sandra	Marek aime la soupe	Marek aime la soupe
Total correct	8	7

'correct', the arrow implies, it seems, a doubt on the part of Emma as to whether or not she translated this sentence correctly or performed the task properly. Julie again began the OVS sentence with the word heard in Polish and completed the French translation using OVS word order. It seems clear that Emma and Julie were somehow disturbed by the OVS word order, and whether they actually understood the sentences as whole units is not entirely clear.

A final comparison of another pair of SVO and OVS sentences present in the test at Period 7h00 confirms previous results.

Sentences heard (12): *Jacek zna restaurację.* (SVO)
                [N-Nom] [V 3p sg] [N-Acc]
                Jacques connaît restaurant
                (James knows restaurant)
                (= Jacques connaît le restaurant.
                ' = James knows the restaurant.')
       (13): *restaurację zna Jacek.* (OVS)
                [N-Acc] [V 3p sg] [N-Nom]
                restaurant connaît Jacques
                (restaurant knows James)
                (= Jacques connaît le restaurant.
                ' = James knows the restaurant.')

As can be seen in Table 8.15, word order had no effect on correct translations of Sentences (12) and (13) (3 for each). Emma and Julie continued to place the direct object in initial position in their translations

Table 8.15 Processing SVO and OVS sentences at Period 7h00 (Sentences 12 and 13)

Learners	Sentence 12 (S-V-O)	Sentence 13 (O-V-S)
Dalia	*Jacek connaît la restauration.	*Jacek connaît le restauration.
Emma	*Jacek?	*Le restaurant Jacek.
Gilles	Jacek connaît le restaurant	Jacek connaît le restaurant.
Julie	*Yacek au restaurant	*Restaurant est Jacek
Luc	*Jacek...	*La même à l'envers (que la 5)
Nadine	Jacek connaît le restaurant.	Jacek connaît le restaurant.
Sabine	Jacek connaît le restaurant	Jacek connaît le restaurant
Sandra	*Jacek mange au restaurant	*Jacek mange au restaurant
Total correct	3	3

of the Polish OVS sentence. Julie's translation culminated in a French OVS sentence; Emma's is less clear as she failed to translate the verb *zna* 'knows'. As mentioned earlier, with translations such as these, it is difficult to know whether or not Emma and Julie 'comprehended' the verb-argument structure of the sentence. Luc identified the resemblance in our two sentences and had difficulty translating both orders. The remaining learners seemed undisturbed by the difference in word order.

Discussion

This chapter investigated four factors that were hypothesised as having an effect on a beginning learner's ability to correctly translate a Polish sentence into French: basic constituent word order, word frequency, word transparency and sentence length.

Our hypothesis about word order was that the order SVO would aid French learners' aural comprehension of a Polish sentence in the absence of knowledge about Polish morphology. Generally speaking, the order SVO appeared to have helped some of our learners, but basic constituent word order was not as strong a cue in the case of isolated sentence translation as our original hypothesis predicted. The results imply that the success of a sentence translation was due, not to one factor alone, but to an interaction between two or more factors.

To learn more about the role of basic constituent word order in sentence processing at the early stages of L2 acquisition, TL lexical items must be carefully chosen. In L1 acquisition, Pléh (1990) demonstrates how children acquiring Hungarian as their first language, a highly inflected language with flexible word order like Polish, use canonical SVO word order as a cue to interpret the sentence when inflexion is absent or difficult to perceive. In L2 acquisition, Bates and MacWhinney (1981, 1987) predict that learners will rely on word order as well. For native speakers of an SVO language, for example, the first noun, by default, is the subject. Further testing of their hypothesis with learners at the initial stages of L2 acquisition would be worthwhile. The challenge, once again, is to establish which forms must appear in the input *prior* to instruction and testing so that lexemes (or forms) can be properly combined to create the testing situation outlined here. Polish poses a methodological problem in that many of its nominative and accusative forms are identical, highlighting yet another reason why lexical items must be carefully selected.

On the lexical level, our data show that a word had a greater chance of being understood if it was transparent and/or frequent in the input (with the exception of *dobrze* 'well'). As a general rule, if the word did not carry one of these qualities, learners had trouble translating it. This said, our data also suggest that the successful translation of lexical items that were frequent in the input or categorised as 'transparent' depended on other factors as well, such as sentence length. Another interesting result is that frequency had an effect on the comprehension of some words (e.g. *pochodzi* 'comes from') but not others (e.g. *dobrze* 'well'). We noted in Chapter 7 that an effect of frequency on sentence repetitions was not found until Period 8h00; the data presented in this chapter reveal as well that a frequency effect is not a given. Whether or not we observe an effect seems to depend on both the quantity and quality of the input provided to the learners. Word frequency as a factor is then relative: its role in L2 speech comprehension and acquisition is likely dependent on other factors.

Sentence length appears to have played a role in the learners' capacity to comprehend and translate the elements of the sentence. At Period 1h30, 'fairly short' sentences were translated correctly by more learners than were 'fairly long' or 'long' sentences. This is not surprising as processing load increases with the accumulation of items that the learner must store in short-term memory.

Future research must continue to identify appropriate data collection techniques that will allow us to test our hypotheses about this early stage of acquisition. We propose, for example, an adaptation of the oral translation test in which our control over the variables is more stringent to avoid confounding factors. As mentioned earlier, tests are needed in which all but one variable is kept constant, for instance, a test in which sentences of variant lengths contain only words that are frequent in the input. This would allow for a clear analysis of the effect of sentence length on correct translations with word frequency being held constant. One could also compare sentences of the same length in which a given number of words were frequent or infrequent in the input. This should result in a clearer picture of the role word frequency plays in the ability to correctly translate sentences in an unfamiliar language.

Data from this chapter also complement observations made in Chapter 6 about inter- and intralearner variability. In examining individual learner translations, we found that although correct translations showed little variability, incorrect translations provided abundant information about how our learners attempted to process a TL sentence after such little exposure. Numerous researchers have discussed the role that learner style plays in comprehension (cf. Klein, 1986; Lambert, 1994b). Luc, for example, took fewer risks than the other learners, often translating nothing or only one word. Julie maintained TL word order in her NL translations, and after 7h00, Emma showed signs of this tendency as well. Once again, we emphasis the need to consider these learner differences.

We also need to be aware of not only what is comprehended, but also what is *noticed*. It was often reported in this chapter that learners incorrectly translated a Polish form that they at least noticed. An example is Nadine's translation of the Polish preposition *po* with the French definite article. A short word in initial position preceding a lexical item *Polsku*, with which she was somewhat familiar, *po* is a good candidate for determiner status if seen from a French native speaker's perspective. Future work needs to investigate when and under what conditions learners *notice* (i.e. *perceive*), but fail to comprehend. Findings from such research should provide us with invaluable information about how 'input' becomes 'intake' at one level (perception) but not at another (comprehension).

The data presented in this chapter complement those presented in Chapter 7 in that they also provide evidence of improved learner performance over time. Comparable sentences were shown to be correctly translated by more learners at Period 1h30 than at 3h30 and again at 7h00. As pointed out in Chapter 7, the fact that learners improve and that we as researchers are able to observe this improvement after such little exposure requires our serious attention.

One final comment concerns a point made by Lambert (1990) regarding TL comprehension. We need a better understanding of the role of memory in language comprehension, namely an understanding of what constitutes short-term and long-term memory, as well as the processes of lexical and semantic storage. From an inverse perspective, it may well be that research on how learners comprehend a novel non-native language may in return inform us about these memory processes.

Conclusion

The results presented in this chapter constitute a first step in our attempt to understand the processes involved in comprehending sentences in a new TL at the initial stages of L2 acquisition. Continued research is needed to further explain these processes, but our hope is that the analysis of not only our data, but also our methodology, will lead to more precise data collection procedures in the future, ultimately allowing us to explain how adult learners comprehend elements of a novel language and make predictions about these processes. The following chapter pursues this discussion with an investigation into our learners' ability to grammatically analyse Polish input.

Note

1. Note that in Chapter 7 we measured the effect of *word* length on correct word repetitions. In this chapter we measure the effect of *sentence* length on correct sentence translations.

Chapter 9
Grammatical Analysis

In Chapter 5, we established that grammatical analysis on word classes and inflexion is already at work upon first exposure to a new target language. In this chapter we pursue our examination of grammatical analysis – word order and verbal morphology in particular – by studying the data collected from our eight monolingual French native speakers over the first 8 hours of exposure to Polish, as well as data collected from all of our learners present during the first 1h30 of Polish instruction ($n = 19$).

We used three written tests to collect data on our learners' processing of grammatical information: a word order test, a grammaticality judgement test and a written translation of the grammaticality judgement test (see appendixes for test items). Different versions of the three test-types were administered at Periods 1h30, 3h30 and 7h00. During the word order tests, learners were given a context sentence in Polish followed by a sentence in which the Polish words were scrambled. They were asked to put the words in the appropriate order. The word order tests were designed to investigate our learners' processing of the following phenomena:

1. the order of basic sentence constituents (SVO, OVS, etc.);
2. the position of the Polish negator *nie* relative to its verb; and
3. the position of the Polish reflexive pronoun *się* relative to its verb.

The grammaticality judgement tests consist of short written texts containing a variety of basic constituent word orders in which errors of verbal morphology appear. We asked learners to read the text and make corrections if necessary. Results of these tests will be discussed in the sections on basic constituent word order and verbal morphology. After completing the grammaticality judgement tests, the learners were immediately asked to translate the short text into French. This allowed us to verify their comprehension of both lexical and morphological items present in the written text. In addition to reporting on our learners' performance during these tests, we also provide information about the oral and written Polish input to which our learners were exposed, where relevant, in order to identify potential correlations between the frequency of a specific word order or morphological form in the input and the learners' responses (cf. the second section of Chapter 4 for more information about the oral and written input provided to our learners).

Basic Constituent Word Order

As suggested in Chapter 3, a contrastive analysis between Polish and French predicts that the order of basic sentence constituents will pose more problems in perception and comprehension than in production. Data presented in Chapter 8 suggested that non-SVO sentences posed slightly more problems for the comprehension of some learners under certain conditions than did SVO sentences. In production, according to the alternation hypothesis (Jansen *et al.*, 1981; Lalleman, 1999), faced with a language in which two different orders exist, learners will choose the one that also exists in their L1. If this is true, we would expect our French learners of Polish to produce SVO sentences in Polish – regardless of the fact that Polish shows other orders – simply because SVO is the dominant word order in French. More radically, the Full Transfer/Full Access hypothesis (Schwartz & Sprouse, 1996) assumes a full transfer of the L1 in L2 acquisition. It would also predict that our French learners' acquiring Polish would begin by producing SVO sentences in Polish.

During our pilot study, also devoted to the acquisition of Polish by native French speakers at the beginning of L2 acquisition (Rast, 1998), we found that SVO was the preferred order of the study's learners. The dominant order in French, SVO, it turned out, was also the preponderant order in the input. This presented methodological problems for the study in that we were unable to test hypotheses concerning the role of the input compared to the role of the L1 in learners' productions: both concurred. In the current study, we attempted to vary the basic sentence constituents in order to expose the learners to possible Polish word orders other than SVO. The transcription of the input of the first Polish course (Period 1h30) allowed us to calculate the frequency of different word orders found in the input. The results showed that, in spite of the instructor's courageous attempt to use a variety of word orders in her first Polish class session, 92% of the declarative utterances were of the SVO-type. Other orders, that is VSO, OSV, VOS and SOV, represented the remaining 8%. This high percentage of SVO-type utterances once again imposes limits on our analyses and interpretations of the data. We cannot, for example, test hypotheses juxtaposing the influence of the input and that of the L1 on learners' performance because SVO is the dominant order in both the input and the L1. We can, however, comment on the patterns and trends observed in the choices that learners make when it comes to the word order of a Polish sentence. We can also assume that, given the preponderance of SVO in the input and the learners' L1, SVO will dominate in the learners' responses. Given this assumption, it follows that if learners' data show occurrences of *non*-SVO order, we may be able to learn something from this.

In our analyses of the data collected via the word order test, we refer to 'correct responses', that is, responses in which the learner used all the words present in the test and placed them in an order that was judged acceptable by a native Polish speaker. These results extend beyond basic constituent word order in that they include the correct placement of *nie* and *się* as well. For instance, a learner may have correctly placed the basic constituents (S, V, O) of a given sentence, but the sentence may have been judged 'incorrect' if either *nie* or *się* was placed incorrectly. This type of analysis allowed us to investigate the influence of hours of instruction (global input) on our learners' ability to place Polish words in appropriate sentence order over the three periods. We then analysed our learners' responses in terms of word order type, calculating the percentage of SVO-type responses on the word order tests at the different periods. As mentioned already in Chapter 8, we use the expression 'SVO/OVS/VSO-type' to designate sentences in which the object 'O' position may be occupied by a structure other than a direct object, such as C or PP/Adv.

Basic constituent word order at Period 1h30

The first test administered after 1h30 of exposure to Polish was a written word order test. Table 9.1 shows the global performance of learners in terms of their ability to correctly place words in a Polish sentence during the word order test. A total of 55% of the responses were judged 'correct' as seen in Table 9.1.

We then examined SVO-type responses. The results presented in Table 9.2 show that 81% of learners' responses were of the SVO type.

Table 9.1 Percentage of correct responses on the word order test at Period 1h30

Learners	Correct responses	max*	%
Dalia	5	8	63
Emma	2	8	25
Gilles	7	8	88
Julie	5	8	63
Luc	3	8	38
Nadine	5	8	63
Sabine	3	8	38
Sandra	5	8	63
Total	35	64	**55**

*'max' refers to the maximum number of possible written responses

Table 9.2 Percentage of SVO-type responses on the word order test at Period 1h30

Learners	SVO	max*	%
Dalia	8	8	100
Emma	7	8	88
Gilles	8	8	100
Julie	5	8	63
Luc	3	8	38
Nadine	8	8	100
Sabine	6	8	75
Sandra	7	8	88
Total	52	64	**81**

*'max' refers to the maximum number of possible written responses

What intrigues us about these results is the remaining 19% of responses that were *non*-SVO. What leads a learner to respond with a non-SVO word order when the input contains mostly SVO sentences and their L1 is an SVO language? We analysed one of the sentences in which four learners responded with non-SVO word order. The remaining learners responded with SVO as did all the informants of our Polish NS control group. The sentence in question is shown below:

1) Context sentence: *Jak ona się nazywa?*
                    Comment elle se appelle?
                    (What she Refl is called? = What's her name?)

Words to put in order: *ona-Anka – się – nazywa*
                             elle – Anka – se – appelle
                             (she – Anka – Refl – is called)

The responses of the 4 learners were as follows:
Julie: *Anka ona nazywa się*
    Anka elle appelle se
    (Anka she is called Refl) (C-S-V-Refl)
Luc: *Anka ona się nazywa*
    Anka elle se appelle
    (Anka she Refl is called) (C-S-Refl-V)
Emma and Sabine: *nazywa się ona Anka*
                  appelle se elle Anka
                  (is called Refl she Anka) (V-Refl-S-C)

We verified the learners' comprehension of all the sentence elements by comparing them to results of the follow-up translation test. Their comprehension was confirmed, with the exception of the first name *Anka*, which did not appear in the translation test. How can we explain these non-SVO productions? It may be that Julie and Luc, who both responded with an C-S order, made use of a pragmatic strategy whereby they responded immediately (initial position) to the context question 'What's her name?' with the focus expression 'Anka', that is, if they understood 'Anka' to be a name. The explanation for Emma and Sabine's responses (V-S-C), on the other hand, can possibly be found in the nature of the input. The V-S-C structure appeared in the written text distributed to the learners during a communicative activity in which they were asked to introduce themselves to their neighbour. Emma and Sabine may have chosen to 'practise' this order in their introductions, reinforcing the VSO word order, an observation that pleads for future research within an interactionist framework on initial processing in controlled input conditions.

Results of the grammaticality judgement test confirm the learners' preference for the order SVO. In the Period 1h30 test, three of the eight clauses were composed of a non-SVO order, as shown below (*indicates an error in verbal morphology):

2) Original clause: *nazywa się ona Mary* (V-Refl-S-C)
                    appelle se elle Mary (is called Refl she Mary)

Four of the eight learners modified (2) to show the order S-V-C. The second non-SVO proposition was the following:

3) Original clause: *mieszkam ona w Chicago* (V-S-PP/Adv)
                    *(je) habite elle à Chicago *([I] live she in Chicago)

Three of our eight learners changed the order to S-V-PP/Adv. The final non-SVO occurrence was as follows:

4) Original clause: *architektką jest* (C-Cop)
                    architecte (elle) est (architect [she] is)

Six of our eight learners reversed the original order to obtain Cop-C. In addition, Luc rendered the subject explicit in these three clauses, all of which originally had implicit subjects. In each case, he placed the subject in pre-verbal position.

Basic constituent word order at Period 3h30

Table 9.3 shows the percentage of correct responses on the word order tests after 1h30 and 3h30 of exposure to Polish.

A repeated measures ANOVA of the results presented in Table 9.3 showed that $F_{(1,7)} = 13.3; p < 0.01$. The percentage of correct responses on the word order test was significantly greater at Period 3h30 than at

Table 9.3 Percentage of correct responses on word order tests at Periods 1h30 and 3h30

Learners	Period 1h30			Period 3h30		
	Correct responses	max*	%	Correct responses	max*	%
Dalia	5	8	63	7	10	70
Emma	2	8	25	10	10	100
Gilles	7	8	88	10	10	100
Julie	5	8	63	9	10	90
Luc	3	8	38	7	10	70
Nadine	5	8	63	7	10	70
Sabine	3	8	38	7	10	70
Sandra	5	8	63	10	10	100
Total	35	64	**55**	67	80	**84**

*'max' refers to the maximum number of possible written responses

Table 9.4 Percentage of SVO responses on word order tests at Periods 1h30 and 3h30

Learners	Period 1h30			Period 3h30		
	SVO	max*	%	SVO	max*	%
Dalia	8	8	100	7	10	70
Emma	7	8	88	10	10	100
Gilles	8	8	100	10	10	100
Julie	5	8	63	10	10	100
Luc	3	8	38	10	10	100
Nadine	8	8	100	7	10	70
Sabine	6	8	75	10	10	100
Sandra	7	8	88	10	10	100
Total	52	64	**81**	74	80	**93**

*'max' refers to the maximum number of possible written responses

Period 1h30, confirming a positive effect of hours of instruction on correct responses. Table 9.4 reveals the percentage of SVO responses at the two periods.

Table 9.4 reveals an increase percentage-wise between Periods 1h30 and 3h30 in favour of SVO-type responses: 81% of the learners' responses were SVO at Period 1h30 and 93% at Period 3h30. A repeated measures ANOVA, however, shows this difference to be insignificant ($F_{(1,7)} = 0.97$; n.s.), probably because of a ceiling effect. The additional two hours of Polish input in which SVO remained the dominant word order had no significant effect on learners' choice of basic constituent word order, most likely because SVO was their preferred order from the beginning. From the viewpoint of the learner, if additional input has reinforced the existence of SVO word order in Polish, why then take the risk of responding with an order other than SVO? We will return to this question in the following section.

The grammaticality judgement test at Period 3h30 contained only one proposition with a word order other than SVO, as shown below:

5) Original clause: *piwa napije się on* (O-V-Refl-S)
     bière boira se on (beer will drink Refl he)
     (= Il prendra une bière. ' = He'll have a beer.')

All the learners, with the exception of Dalia and Gilles, modified the order in favour of SVO.

Basic constituent word order at Period 7h00

The word order test administered after 7h00 of input showed an 88% correct response rate. Table 9.5 shows the correct responses over the three periods: 1h30, 3h30 and 7h00. A repeated measures ANOVA of data presented in Table 9.5 showed that $F_{(2,14)} = 11.46$; $p < 0.01$. Clearly, there was a strong effect of hours of instruction on the percentage of correct responses on the word order test, which explains the gradual improvement we observe in our learners' ability to correctly put the words of a Polish sentence in order.

As can be seen in Table 9.6, after 7h00 of exposure to Polish, 95% of the learners' responses were of the order SVO. A repeated measures ANOVA revealed that the difference in responses at the three periods was not significant ($F_{(2,14)} = 1.27$; n.s.). We cannot claim an increase of SVO-type responses over the three periods because of the same ceiling effect as above; however, we can claim a stability with regard to their choice of SVO word order. These results corroborate the alternation hypothesis (Jansen *et al.*, 1981) that learners will be guided by their L1. We extend this hypothesis in the following way: it appears that the more learners are exposed to TL input that confirms an L1 phenomenon, the more they will rely on their L1 when faced with the equivalent structure in their TL.

Table 9.5 Percentage of correct responses on word order tests at Periods 1h30, 3h30 and 7h00

Learners	Period 1h30			Period 3h30			Period 7h00		
	Correct responses	max*	%	Correct responses	max*	%	Correct responses	max*	%
Dalia	5	8	63	7	10	70	10	14	71
Emma	2	8	25	10	10	100	11	14	79
Gilles	7	8	88	10	10	100	12	14	86
Julie	5	8	63	9	10	90	14	14	100
Luc	3	8	38	7	10	70	13	14	93
Nadine	5	8	63	7	10	70	13	14	93
Sabine	3	8	38	7	10	70	13	14	93
Sandra	5	8	63	10	10	100	12	14	86
Total	35	64	**55**	67	80	**84**	98	112	**88**

*'max' refers to the maximum number of possible written responses

Table 9.6 Percentage of SVO responses on word order tests at Periods 1h30, 3h30 and 7h00

Learners	Period 1h30			Period 3h30			Period 7h00		
	SVO	max*	%	SVO	max*	%	SVO	max*	%
Dalia	8	8	100	7	10	70	13	14	93
Emma	7	8	88	10	10	100	12	14	86
Gilles	8	8	100	10	10	100	12	14	86
Julie	5	8	63	10	10	100	14	14	100
Luc	3	8	38	10	10	100	14	14	100
Nadine	8	8	100	7	10	70	14	14	100
Sabine	6	8	75	10	10	100	13	14	93
Sandra	7	8	88	10	10	100	14	14	100
Total	52	64	**81**	74	80	**93**	106	112	**95**

*'max' refers to the maximum number of possible written responses

We predict this will be the case until learners become familiar with how other word orders may be used to convey pragmatic information such as emphasis or contrast in the TL. At what point in a learner's acquisitional process does this shift begin to take place? A detailed analysis of learners' non-SVO responses at Period 7h00 may provide a partial response to this question.

The first non-SVO structure to be analysed at period 7h00 appeared in the word order test. The context sentence and words to put in order are shown below:

> 6) Context sentence: *Charlot nie płaci w restauracji.*
>
>   Charlie pas paie au restaurant
>   (Charlie not pays at restaurant)
>
> Words to put in order:
>
>   *policja – i – zabiera – Charlot – przyjeżdża – do więzienia*
>   police – et – amène – Charlie – arrive – en prison
>   (police – and – take away – Charlie – arrive – to prison)

All but one of the informants in our Polish NS control group responded with the following sentence:

> *przyjeżdża policja i zabiera Charlot do więzienia*
> 'arrive police and take away Charlie to prison'

The remaining NS informant responded with SV 'police arrive'. This suggests that in Polish this particular context favours a VS order in the response, but other orders are possible.

Our learners' responses are presented below. A subsequent translation test revealed that all of them understood the phrase *do więzienia* and that only Luc had trouble with the verb *zabiera* 'take away', taking it to mean 'retourne' (returns). The expression *przyjeżdża policja* 'arrive police', however, posed problems for many of the learners. For this reason, in cases where a learner's French translation of one of the lexical items in the Polish sentence is incorrect, we provide a word-for-word hypothetical English translation (in brackets) based on the learners' translations of these words in the translation test. This will provide insight into the learners' internal word orders given their idiosyncratic comprehension of the sentence elements.

Dalia: *Charlot zabiera i policja przyjeżdża do więzienia*
  'Charlie take away and police <u>arrive</u> to prison'
  [Charlie take away and police <u>take him</u> (le prend) to prison]
Emma: *zabiera policja i przyjeżdża Charlot do więzienia*
  'take away police and arrive Charlie to prison'
Gilles: *przyjeżdża policja i Charlot zabiera do więzienia*
  'arrive police and Charlie take away to prison'
Julie: *policja zabiera Charlot i przyjeżdża do więzienia*
  'police take away Charlie and <u>arrive</u> to prison'
  [police take away Charlie and <u>arrest him</u> (*l'arrête*) to prison]
Luc: *policja zabiera Charlot i przyjeżdża do więzienia*
  'police <u>take away</u> Charlie and <u>arrive</u> to prison'
  [police <u>returns</u> Charlie and <u>arrest him</u> (*l'arrête*) to prison]
Nadine: *policja zabiera Charlot do więzienia* (*przyjeżdża* is missing)
  'police take away Charlie to prison'
Sabine: *policja zabiera Charlot i przyjeżdża do więzienia*
  'police take away Charlie and arrive to prison'
Sandra: *policja zabiera i przyjeżdża Charlot do więzienia*
  'police take away and arrive Charlie to prison'
  [police take away and ___ Charlie to prison] (*przyjeżdża* not translated)

Despite the obvious difficulty of the task after only 7h00 of input, we still observe a stable tendency for SVO word order. This said, two of our learners, Emma and Gilles, used VS word order in the first clause. Although Emma apparently confused the meaning of the two verbs, producing a unintelligible sentence, this had no effect on basic constituent word order. A look at the cumulative input provided to the learners before Period 7h00 testing reveals that the VS order *przyjeżdża policja* 'arrive police' appeared 14 times and the SV order *policja przyjeżdża* 'police arrive' 4 times. The former also appeared in the written input, whereas the latter did not. We venture to say, therefore, that Emma and Gilles may have been sensitive to non-SVO word order already after only 7h00, and this sensitivity was most probably due to the frequency of occurrence of this particular VS structure in the input.

The Period 7h00 grammaticality judgement test comprised two propositions with non-SVO order. The first is presented below:

7) Original clause: *przyjeżdża policja* (V-S)
               'arrive police'

Only one learner, Julie, reversed the order of the subject and verb, formulating an S-V structure 'police arrive'. The remaining seven learners modified nothing. This was the first sentence where such a large percentage of learners maintained a non-SVO order. However, as mentioned above, the subsequent translation test revealed that five learners misinterpreted the verb *przyjeżdża*, assigning it transitive status by translating it as 'prend' (take) or 'arrête' (arrest), or not translating it at all. This lexical confusion prevents us from commenting on learners' sensitivity to non-SVO word orders and points to the methodological challenge of lexicon building in early L2 acquisition.

The other non-SVO clause in the test appears below:

8) Original clause: *obiad je* (O-V)
               déjeuner (il) mange (lunch [he] eats)

Three of our eight learners reversed the order to form the V-O structure *je obiad* '(he) eats lunch'. The remaining five made no modification. Analysis of the input reveals 10 occurrences of V-O *je obiad* '(he) eats lunch' and 4 occurrences of O-V *obiad je* 'lunch (he) eats'. The translations of this clause reveal that all the learners understood the general sense that Charlie 'eats'. The problem in translation, however, is that in French *je obiad* or *obiad je* can be translated with a mere verb: 'déjeune' (eats lunch). Sabine did just that for her translation of *obiad je*, and four other learners translated it with 'mange' (eats) or 'il mange' (he eats). We were, therefore, unable to make interpretations about word order based on these translations.

Taken together, the results of the word order test and the grammaticality test at Period 7h00 reveal a clear preference for SVO word order, and one that was strengthened by increased exposure to Polish between Periods 1h30 and 3h30. The subsequent hours of exposure had no effect.

To conclude this section, the results presented here demonstrate a gradual amelioration in our learners' capacity to put Polish words in accurate sentence order. In addition, they confirm a strong preference on the part of our learners for SVO word order. The increase in percentage of responses of the SVO type during the word order test administered at

Period 3h30 suggests that the order SVO, which preponderates over other orders in both the Polish input and the learners' L1, is preferred in spite of the fact that other orders exist in the input and in French. Results of the word order test at Period 7h00 indicate that two learners may have shown a slight sensitivity to non-SVO word orders in Polish, but that this 'sensitivity' may merely have been the memorisation of a particular expression in the input. This needs further investigation. In response to the questions as to how much exposure is necessary for learners to begin to understand and use varying word orders in Polish, future research is needed in which the L2 acquisition of a group of learners is studied from the beginning and for a longer period of time.

Placing the Negator Particle *Nie*

In this section, we will analyse the data collected from not only our eight monolingual French learners of Polish, but also the other learners who attended the first Polish class and were therefore exposed to the first 1h30 of Polish input. This includes other French monolinguals, bilinguals and learners with knowledge of Russian. What follows is a brief description of the negation systems of Russian and of the other L1s known by our bilingual learners, namely Berber, Moroccan Arabic, Spanish and Portuguese.

Negation in learners' other L1s and Russian

We begin by examining negation in Berber. Chaker (1996: 9) provides us with the pattern of negation in a verbal utterance:

Neg1 + Verbe [possibly specific theme] + **(Neg2).**

He claims a common and obligatory pre-verbal element, of which the base form is *wer*[1] and remarks that numerous dialects of Berber completely ignore the second element of negation, *ara*. In these dialects the pre-verbal negator suffices to negate the utterance. It follows that in our analyses, we consider Berber as having a dominant pre-verbal negator.

Negation in Moroccan Arabic is similar to Berber in that it shows pre- and post-verbal elements as well. Caubet (1996: 79–80) explains that two possibilities for negation exist in Moroccan Arabic: either two discontinuous elements, *ma* and *š* (or *ši/šay*), which surround the predicate, or the continuous marker *ma ši*, which generally precedes the element over which it has scope. The latter is most often used in non-verbal predicates, as shown in the following example:

l-wəld **ma-ši** hna
the-boy ma-ši here
The boy is not here. (taken from Benmamoun 1997: 264)

According to Caubet, the second element, *š*, serves to reinforce the negation and can be replaced by other particles, such as *walu* 'nothing'. This second element only becomes obligatory under certain conditions and in certain dialects. Benmamoun (1997: 269) remarks that the element *š* does not appear in contexts that show negative polarity, such as in the following example where (b) represents the ungrammatical construction:

a) **ma**-qrit fiətta ktab
   neg-read.1S even book
   I didn't read any book.

b) ***ma**-qrit-š fiətta ktab
   neg-read.1S even book
   I didn't read any book.

In agreement with Caubet, Benmamoun points out that in certain Arabic dialects, negation of verbal predicates are expressed solely using the element *ma*. The above analyses point to the morpheme *ma* as the 'strong' negator in Moroccan Arabic, leading us to conclude that the dominant position of the negator in the Arabic dialect of our learners (Moroccan in this case) is pre-verbal.[2]

The particles *no* in Spanish and *não* in Portuguese precede the verb. Bosque (1980) confirms that the negation of the Spanish predicate is stable. The negator *no* is positioned in front of the finite verb with no other modifications, as seen in the following example:

No conozco a Juan
pas (je) connais à Juan (not [I] know at Juan = 'I don't know Juan')

In sum, in the languages investigated above (the other L1s of our bilingual informants), the 'strong' negator is found in pre-verbal position. Thus, our bilingual informants know that the negator can either precede or follow the finite verb in natural languages: French has post-verbal negation[3] and their other L1, be it Berber, Moroccan Arabic, Spanish or Portuguese, has pre-verbal negation.To add to this, several of our learners had studied a year of Russian before the onset of our project. Clausal negation functions almost identically in Russian and Polish. The negator precedes the verb as in the following example:

Rita ne pišet statej
Rita NEG writes articles
(= Rita doesn't write articles.) (adapted from Brown, 1999: 3)

Hypotheses on the placement of the negator *nie*

Using our data on the placement of *nie* in a Polish sentence, we propose to test three distinct hypotheses: (1) full L1 transfer; (2) psychotypology; and (3) information structure.

Full L1 transfer

Implicit in the previous section is that one of the principal hypotheses concerning the placement of *nie* relates to transfer. If we take as our starting point a hypothesis of full transfer from L1 to L2 (cf. Schwartz & Sprouse, 1996), the expectation is that beginning learners will apply their knowledge of French negation to Polish negation. As we saw in Chapter 3 (cf. 'Negation' in the third section of Chapter 3), researchers disagree on syntactic analysis of clausal French negation *ne... pas*. Although we view French negation as post-verbal, the lack of consensus on this issue leads us to propose two variations of a full transfer hypothesis. Those who would most likely argue that French *ne* is equivalent to Polish *nie* (Pollock, 1989; Rowlett, 1993; Rule & Marsden, 2006; Schwartz & Sprouse, 1996) would expect our monolingual French learners of Polish to place *nie* in pre-verbal position. Those who would argue, on the other hand, that French *pas* corresponds to Polish *nie* (Eubank, 1994; Gaatone, 1971; Zanuttini, 1997) would expect our monolingual French learners to place *nie* in post-verbal position.

Psychotypology

Our bilingual learners who have both French and either Berber, Moroccan Arabic, Spanish or Portuguese (all pre-verbal negation) as their two native languages are possibly faced with a conflict between cues in their L1 and cues in the input. If we extend Kellerman's (1983) framework of psychotypology to L3 acquisition (cf. Chapter 5), we can imagine a scenario in which learners evaluate the differences and similarities between their numerous prior language systems, that is their two L1 systems, their other L2 systems, and the TL system. Such a 'psychotypology hypothesis' predicts that our monolingual and bilingual learners with knowledge of other L2s will rely on the L1 or L2 structure that they perceive as being more similar to the TL structure in question. As mentioned earlier, several of our learners had some knowledge of Russian, a language that shares pre-verbal negation with Polish. If these learners place the negator in pre-verbal position during a Polish task, we can suppose a positive transfer of L2 Russian towards L3 Polish.

Information structure (Neg + X)

An altogether different hypothesis proposes an alternative to transfer as an explanation for learners' performance. This hypothesis predicts a role for information structure (cf. Dimroth & Starren, 2003; Klein & Perdue, 1992) as described by Bernini (2000: 403): 'In the functional approach, the syntactic behaviour of negation is considered to be a combined result of the strategies employed by the learners to organize the utterance depending on the means available to them and the need to signal the scope domain of negation within the utterance'. A series of studies have identified a strategy in early L2 adult acquisition that responds to cognitively based operating principles, often referred to as the NEG + X strategy (cf. Clahsen *et al.*, 1983; Hyltenstam, 1977; Meisel, 1997), whereby the negator precedes the element to be negated. As a result of this and other findings, Bernini (2000: 403) claims that, 'Preposition of negation with respect to the element to be negated serves to mark the scope domain of negation, whereby the semantic structure is directly mapped onto the surface structure, avoiding any discontinuity of interdependent elements'. In support of Bernini's claim, Giuliano (2004) found that beginning learners place the negative marker in front of that which it negates. Silberstein (2001) found the same phenomenon in her Italian learners of English. In a comparison of her data to those of Dietrich and Grommes (1998) on the acquisition of German by Italian native speakers, Silberstein confirms the application of a 'scope to the right' principle of negation at the initial stages of L2 acquisition. She concludes that it is conceptual and pragmatic knowledge that determines the organisational structure of pre-basic and basic varieties. Following this hypothesis, we would expect our learners, regardless of their language backgrounds (L1s and L2s), to place the Polish negator in front of that which it negates.

Analysis of the negator *nie* in the input

One of the outcomes of our pilot study on the processing of Polish by French native speakers (Rast, 1998) was the development of an exploratory experiment designed to test our learners' preferences with regard to the position of the negator in a Polish sentence *before* being exposed to it. In the word order test, learners were told that the word *nie* appeared in certain sentences and that it serves as a negator. We asked them to put *nie* where they felt it seemed appropriate. All the other words in the test had been frequent in the input, enabling the learners to accomplish the exercise despite limited exposure to Polish negation.

Before examining the results of the word order test, however, it is important to examine the input of the first Polish class relative to the phenomenon of Polish negation. As described in Chapter 4, several constraints were placed on the Polish instructor with respect to the input provided to the learners. One of the constraints included avoiding the use of *nie* in the first Polish class, that is, in the first 1h30 of input. In a discussion with the Polish instructor following the first class, she expressed her frustration with this constraint. Admittedly, in most natural communicative situations, the absence of negation during a period of 1h30 is highly unlikely. Added to this, the instructor attempted to create as natural a setting as possible in the classroom, making it that much more difficult to avoid the negator. As a result, *nie* was used minimally (as opposed to not at all), that is, 15 times within the 1h30 of first exposure to Polish, only 7 of which were instances of clausal negation (the phenomenon that concerns us here). Using our criteria for 'word frequency' (cf. 'Hypotheses' in the first section of Chapter 7), *nie* is classified as 'rare' in the input. In this section, we will therefore speak of *nie* as being *limited* in the input as opposed to *absent*. We classified the 15 tokens of *nie* in three groups below:

1. The negator *nie* occurred seven times in its function of responding in the negative to a previous utterance (the equivalent of 'non' in French), as for example in the utterance ***nie**, po angielsku mówi* '**no**, in English (she) speaks' (=No, she speaks English).
2. In one case, *nie* negated a sentence constituent other than the verb: *Tak, **nie** 'kim jest'* 'Yes, **not** "who (he) is"' (=Yes, *not* 'kim jest', but something else...).[4]
3. In seven cases, the *nie* carried the role of negating the verbal predicate (the equivalent of 'pas' in French), such as in, *ty **nie** znasz* 'you **not** know' (=You don't know). We refer to this as *clausal negation* or *sentence internal negation*.

It is the third classification that interests us here. The sentences in which *nie* appeared in pre-verbal position are reproduced below:

a. *Nie, **nie** mieszka w Ameryce.*
   'No, *not* (she) lives in America.'
b. *Ktoś, kto nic **nie** mówi?*
   'Somebody, who nothing *not* speaks?' (= Somebody who has said nothing?)
c. *Kto nic **nie** mówi?*
   'Who never *not* speaks?' (= Who never speaks?)
d. *ty **nie** znasz.*
   'You *not* know.'
e. *ty **nie** wiesz nic.*
   'You *not* know nothing.'
f. *a nie, a, **nie** wiedzieliśmy.*
   'And no, and, *not* (we) know.' (= And no, we don't know.)
g. *Tom **nie** jest Portugalką.*[5]
   'Tom *not* is Portuguese.'

In all, 15 tokens of *nie* appeared in the first 1h30 of input, 7 of which were clausal negators (Neg-V). Between Periods 1h30 and 3h30, we counted 58 tokens of *nie*, 48 of which negated the predicate (Neg-V), and between Periods 3h30 and 7h00, 178 tokens of *nie* were found. No syntactic analysis of *nie* in the input was conducted after Period 3h30.

Placing the negator *nie* at Period 1h30

Data from the word order test at Period 1h30 provide interesting results about our learners' analysis of Polish negation. We begin by analysing the responses of our eight French monolinguals. Three sentences in the word order test required learners to place the negator *nie*. They are presented below:

9) Context sentence: *Tomek mieszka w Paryżu.*
                           Tomek habite à Paris
                           (Tomek lives in Paris)

Words to put in order: *nie – on – lubi – Paryża*
                           pas – il – aime – Paris
                           (not – he – likes – Paris)

10) Context sentence: *Angelika jest sekretarką.*
                           Angelika est secrétaire
                           (Angelika is secretary)

Words to put in order: *pracuje – nie – ona – na – uniwersytecie*
                           travaille – pas – elle – à – université
                           (works – not – she – at – university)

11) Context sentence: *Język rosyjski Monika zna dobrze, ale*
                           langue russe Monika connaît bien, mais
                           (language Russian Monika knows well, but)

Words to put in order: *nie – rosyjskiego – lubi*
                           pas – russe – aime
                           (not – Russian – likes)

Our first observation is that all learners responded in the same way to the three sentences; that is, if they placed *nie* in pre-verbal position, they consistently did this for all three sentences. This suggests that each learner formulated a hypothesis on negation in Polish and applied it whenever *nie* appeared. We identified four distinct hypotheses formulated by our learners regarding the particle *nie* in Polish:

1. The negator belongs in pre-verbal position (the correct position in Polish). Three learners (Dalia, Gilles and Julie) adopted this hypothesis.
2. The negator belongs in post-verbal position (ungrammatical in Polish). Two learners (Sabine and Sandra) applied this hypothesis.
3. The negator belongs in sentence initial position (possible in both Polish and French to negate a previous statement). One learner (Nadine) formulated this hypothesis, separating the negator from the rest of the sentence with a comma (in 2 of the 3 cases).
4. The negator belongs in sentence final position (ungrammatical in both French and Polish). One learner (Emma) opted for this position.

The remaining learner, Luc, never placed *nie*. He began the first two sentences with the pronouns *on* and *ona*, but went no further. He provided no response for the third sentence. A χ^2 test conducted on the responses of our eight learners indicates that the distribution (1 initial, 2 pre-verbal, 2 post-verbal, 1 final, 1 no response) does not differ from chance distribution (1.6 all positions) (χ^2 (4) = 2.0, n.s.). We conclude, therefore, that no position was statistically salient.

These results fail to confirm either of the two full transfer hypotheses proposing that, with an infrequent exposure to *nie*, learners would rely on their L1 (French) and place the negator in either pre- or post-verbal position. As we have observed, three of our eight monolingual learners chose pre-verbal position and only two chose the post-verbal position. Generativists who view French negation as post-verbal (cf. *supra* and 'Negation' in the third section of Chapter 3) could argue that the three learners who chose the pre-verbal position had already noticed the discrepancy between their source and target languages with respect to this phenomenon (minimal input is input after all) and had already reset the parameter. To avoid this possibility in the future, we need to fine-tune our methodology to insure that zero tokens of the phenomenon under observation appear in the input before testing. To confuse matters further, Schwartz and Sprouse (1996), authors of the Full Transfer/Full Access Hypothesis, view French negation as pre-verbal. If this were the case, why then would two of our learners place *nie* in post-verbal position? This clearly merits further investigation.

In addition to the eight monolinguals of our study, we also analysed the responses of four other monolingual French learners, four bilingual learners and three learners with knowledge of Russian, all of whom were present for the first Polish class (1h30 of input) and the first series of tests. This allowed us to observe possible differences in learner responses due to an influence of other native languages (our bilingual informants) and of another Slavic language (Russian in this case).

Figure 9.1 presents the responses of our 19 learners relative to their linguistic profiles.

Group M (French monolinguals) includes our eight monolingual learners, as well as four other French monolinguals who participated in the first Polish class but were absent during subsequent classes. Of these four learners, three responded to all three sentences in the same way, as did our group of eight learners. Sonia placed the negator in post-verbal position, Romain in pre-verbal and Alice in sentence initial position. Carole responded differently for the three sentences, placing the negator in post-verbal position in the first two sentences and in pre-verbal position in the third sentence. An examination of these learners' other L2s as a function of their responses with *nie* showed no effect of L2 on their placement of the Polish L3 negator.

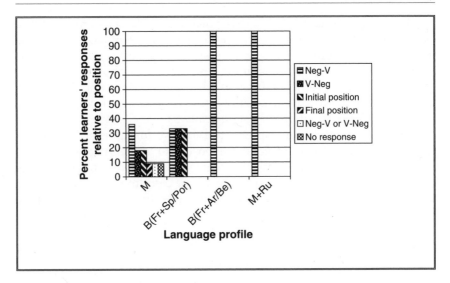

Figure 9.1 Placement of Polish negative particle *nie* at Period 1h30 relative to language profiles

Concerning our bilingual informants (B), Figure 9.1 shows that the two bilingual French/Arabic or Berber (Fr+Ar/Be) speakers placed the negator in pre-verbal position. As for the three bilingual French/Spanish or Portuguese (Fr+Sp/Por), their results were not so homogenous. One informant preferred pre-verbal, another preferred post-verbal and the third placed the negator in sentence initial position.

We predicted that our three informants who knew Russian (Ru), another Slavic language in which the negator appears in pre-verbal position as in Polish, would follow the rules of Russian when placing the Polish negator. Our predictions were borne out, confirming the positive influence of an L2 structure on the syntactic analysis of an L3 within the first 1h30 of exposure to a new target language.

To sum up, none of the analyses discussed so far attest to a full transfer of L1 clausal negation systems in monolinguals or bilinguals to the TL. Something else must be happening.

Looking now at the data from a pragmatic principles perspective, we can expect to find, at this early stage of acquisition, a right scope phenomenon. That is, rather than applying a syntactic analysis of Neg-V, we apply the organisational principle whereby the negator precedes that which it negates, in this case the predicate. To determine the nature of the strategy for those who placed the negator in post-verbal position (2 of our 8 learners in addition to 2 of the other monolingual learners), let us look again at Sentence (9) presented earlier.

Context sentence:	*Tomek mieszka w Paryżu.*
	Tomek habite à Paris
	(Tomek lives in Paris)
Words to put in order:	*nie – on – lubi – Paryża*
	pas – il – aime – Paris
	(not – he – likes – Paris)
Response V-Neg:	*on lubi nie Paryża*
	il aime pas Paris
	(he likes not Paris)

Even if this word order is ungrammatical in Polish, it is nevertheless logical from the point of view of the learner's sentence organisation if the learner wishes to express, 'not *Paris*, but somewhere else (*Kraków* for example)'. In this case, *nie* has scope over *Paryża*, hence its position in front of *Paryża*. The same can be said for Sentence (10):

Context sentence:	*Angelika jest sekretarką*
	Angela est secretaire
	(Angela is secretary)
Words to put in order:	*pracuje – nie – ona – na – uniwersytecie*
	travaille – pas – elle – à – université
	(works – not – she – at – university)
V-Neg response:	*ona pracuje nie na uniwersytecie*
	elle travaille pas à université
	(she works not at university)

Here again, if the learner wishes to express, 'not *at the university* but somewhere else' (*at the public library*, for example), we could interpret this response as *nie* having scope over *na uniwersytecie*. Those who placed the negator in pre-verbal position may have been influenced by the few tokens of pre-verbal *nie* in the input, or they may have used a pragmatic strategy as proposed here for those responding with post-verbal negation. In the case of pre-verbal negation, however, they placed *nie* in front of the verb, the verb being the element to be negated.

Transfer in fact may have little to do with learners' responses or may only play a partial role. It may be *one* of the many strategies learners use to accomplish a task in the TL. These results argue for a model of L2 grammatical analysis in which learners make use of the following strategies: 'transfer' from L1 and from other L2s (whether these are similar to the TL or not); psychotypology (learners look for similarities between linguistic systems they already know and their TL); information structure (learners structure their utterances 'logically' relative to pragmatic principles). If their grammatical, perceptual and informational strategies do not conflict, there should be no problem. But what if they do? Our models need to predict and explain what learners do then.

The results presented in this section serve to demonstrate the various types of analyses that can be conducted from a syntactic or pragmatic point of view in order to better understand the strategies applied by adult learners of a new TL, while also reminding us of the methodological challenge of collecting informative data at the early stages of acquisition. Clearly a pragmatic analysis requires more context than our word order test was able to provide, a point that deserves continued reflection.

Placing the negator *nie* at Period 3h30

In the data collected from the word order test at Period 3h30, we analysed four sentences containing *nie*, two of which were identical to sentences found in the Period 1h30 test and two of which were introduced for the first time in the Period 3h30 test. It is important to mention here that tests were corrected and returned to our learners only after the full observation period (after 8 hours of instruction). In this way, they received no explicit feedback concerning their performance. Seven of our eight French monolingual learners responded in the same way to each of the four sentences and their responses were all of the order Neg-V (the correct order in Polish), revealing a strong tendency for learners to correctly place the Polish negator *nie*. A plausible explanation for this progress is that the group as a whole has now noticed (or possibly even 'taken in') the Neg-V structure of the input.

The remaining learner, Sabine, responded with Neg-V in two of the sentences, but with Neg-S-V in the two others. It turns out that when Sabine's response is Neg-S-V, S represents a subject pronoun, whereas when her response is S-Neg-V, S represents a lexical subject. The translation test confirms that she understood the meaning of the pronouns *on* (he) and *ona* (she). At Period 1h30, Sabine consistently placed the negator in post-verbal position. The input between Periods 1h30 and 3h30 led her to reformulate her hypothesis in the direction of pre-verbal negation, but not to the extent that the negator is always positioned directly in front of the verb. We will see in the next section whether or not she pursues a reformulation of her hypothesis.

Placing the negator *nie* at Period 7h00

Although the frequency of the order Neg-V in the input after Period 3h30 was not calculated, we can account for 178 occurrences of *nie* in the input between Periods 3h30 and 7h00, most of these being clausal negations, hence Neg-V.

The word order test administered at Period 7h00 contained five sentences in which learners were asked to place *nie*. Two of the sentences were identical to those in the word order tests at Periods 1h30 and 3h30, two were identical to two sentences introduced for the first time in the Period 3h30 test and one sentence appeared for the first time in the Period 7h00 test.

Figure 9.2 shows the development of the use of *nie* as a clausal negator in the interlanguage of our eight learners at the three periods: 1h30, 3h30 and 7h00. As can be seen in Figure 9.2, the results of the word order test at 7h00 show that our eight French monolinguals responded with the correct Polish word order, Neg-V, in 100% of the sentences. This shows an effect of the number of hours of instruction on our learners' ability to correctly place the clausal negator *nie* in a Polish sentence. This effect is already clear at Period 3h30 but is maximal at Period 7h00. We notice as well that Sabine apparently reformulated her hypothesis on the placement of *nie*. Even in sentences with a subject pronoun as opposed to a lexical subject, she placed *nie* in pre-verbal position.

In this section, we observed the strategies used by our learners to find the appropriate position of *nie* in a Polish sentence. With limited tokens of *nie* in the input at the moment of the first word order test, learners individually formulated hypotheses that led them to place *nie* in a regular position in all of their responses, with the exception of Luc, who was apparently unable to formulate a hypothesis and failed to construct sentences that required the use of *nie*. We identified four working hypotheses with respect to the position of *nie* at period 1h30: pre-verbal, post-verbal, sentence initial and sentence final. After two additional hours of exposure to Polish, seven of our eight monolingual learners had

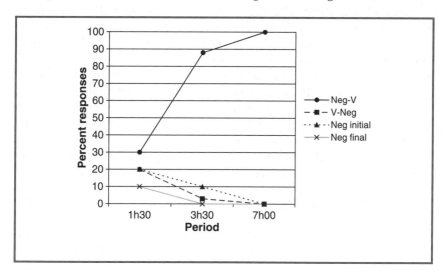

Figure 9.2 Negation: The evolution of response types from Period 1h30 to 7h00

reformulated their hypotheses and placed *nie* in the correct position, pre-verbal. After 7 total hours of Polish input, all learners were able to correctly place the Polish negator in the word order test. With regard to the three research hypotheses we proposed at the beginning of this section, we conclude that these results, taken as a whole, confirm that the task of placing the clausal negator in an unknown or little known language is much more complex than a simple transfer from the L1. Even an analysis of transfer from other L1s and L2s does not explain our learners' perfor-mance. Our results suggest, rather, that a hypothesis based on pragmatic principles may best explain our learners' responses. We say this because a pragmatically plausible interpretation of negator placement is always possible, but we do not have access to the way our learners completed the context for the test sentence. To better understand this phenomenon, future research at the very beginning of L2 acquisition is needed, research in which the placement of scope particles, including negators, is tested *before* the item appears in the input and with a larger group of learners.

Placing the Reflexive Pronoun *Się*

In Chapter 3 (cf. 'Reflexive verbs' in the third section), we provided a detailed description of the Polish reflexive pronoun *się* and its equiva-lents in French (*me, te, se*, etc.). In terms of syntax, Polish *się* can appear in pre- or post-verbal position. The analogous French pronoun, however, is always pre-verbal. The question we pose in this section is the following: faced with two orders, pre- and post-verbal, both of which appear in the input, but only one of which reflects the order in the L1, will the learners rely on their L1? Before delving into our analysis, we will first examine the Polish input to see if in fact both orders were represented equally. At Period 1h30, we found that both orders appeared to an almost equal extent, 51% for the pre-verbal position and 49% for the post-verbal, constituting an excellent condition for testing the alternation hypothesis (Jansen *et al.*, 1981; Lalleman, 1999). The results of our pilot study (Rast, 1998, 1999) in which we examined the placement of *się* by our French learners of Polish did not confirm the alternation hypothesis. While French requires the order Refl-V, the learners preferred the order V-Refl. One aspect of the input that we had not discussed during our pilot study was the nature of the sentences or the context in which the orders Refl-V or V-Refl occurred. A closer look at the tokens of *się* in the input of the current study at 1h30 revealed that 35 of the 37 sentences containing the order Refl-V were interrogative; in contrast, only 2 of the 35 sentences with the order V-Refl were interrogative. In other words, the Polish instructor generally used Refl-V in questions and V-Refl in statements. This trend continued throughout the data collection period. We will take this information into consideration in our discussion of the data.

We also investigated the nature of the verbs that *się* accompanied. We found throughout the Polish instruction that in the vast majority of cases Polish *się* appeared with inflexional variants of two verbs: *nazywać się* (s'appeler 'to be called') and *napić się* (boire 'to drink'). An analysis of the use of these verbs by the Polish instructor shows an even distribution of their use in Refl-V versus V-Refl type sentences and in interrogatives versus declaratives at all periods. It is important to note here as well that, whereas *nazywać się* (s'appeler) is translated into French using a reflexive pronoun, *napić się* (boire) is generally not. The form 'se boire' (to drink) exists in spoken French, but it is rare. Take for example the following proposition, which appeared in the translation test at Period 3h30:

Piwa napije się on
bière boira se il (beer will drink Refl he)

The majority of learners translated this as 'Il boit de la bière' 'He drinks beer'; no learner used the spoken form with the reflexive pronoun 'se boire' (Refl to drink) in the sentence translations. It follows that the reflexive verb *się napić* (se boire) poses a different problem for French speakers than does the reflexive verb *się nazywać* (s'appeler). As the reflexive pronoun is linked to the verb 'appeler' in French as *się* is linked to *nazywać* in Polish, we would not be surprised to see French speakers notice this L1-equivalent pattern. The French equivalent for *się napić*, however, requires no reflexive pronoun. It is possible, therefore, that *się* was processed differently in sentences with the verb *się napić* than in those containing the verb *się nazywać*. We will investigate this in our results in the following sections.

Placing the reflexive pronoun *się* at Period 1h30

The first word order test administered at Period 1h30 contained two sentences in which learners were asked to place *się*, as shown below:

12) Context sentence: *Jak się nazywasz?*
                      Comment se (tu) appelles?
                      (How Refl [you] are called?)
Words to put in order: *się – Barbara – nazywam.*
                      se – Barbara – (je) appelle
                      (Refl – Barbara – [I] am called)

13) Context sentence: *Jak ona się nazywa?*
                      Comment elle se appelle?
                      (How she Refl is called?)
Words to put in order: *ona – Anka – się – nazywa.*
                      elle – Anka – se – appelle
                      (she – Anka – Refl – is called)

The results of this first test reveal a diversity of responses, although each learner placed *się* in the same position in the two sentences. As we saw with our learners' placement of the negator *nie* in the previous section, here too our learners seem to have formulated hypotheses about the placement of *się* that they generalise to all sentences in which *się* is present. Table 9.7 shows the input received at Period 1h30 and the learners' responses.

Table 9.7 A comparison between Refl-V and V-Refl structures in the input and learners' responses on the word order test at Period 1h30

Structures in input			Learners' responses (raw scores, n =8)		
Refl-V	*V-Refl*	*Other*	*Refl-V*	*V-Refl*	*Other*
51%	49%	0%	3	5	0

Three learners, Dalia, Gilles and Luc, responded in both cases with the order Refl-V (the order found in French and one of the orders in the input), whereas five responded with V-Refl (one of the two orders present in the input). It is important to point out here that the context sentences, both of which were questions, contained the Refl-V structure. For the three learners who opted for the order Refl-V, two interpretations are possible. Either the order present in the context sentences influenced the learners' sentence construction (i.e. they simply copied the order), or the learners relied on the order of their L1, in which the reflexive pronoun precedes the verb.

The more interesting question is why five of our learners opted for the order that is not in their L1 when the input affirms that both orders are possible in Polish. Firstly, the learners may have perceived the difference in word order between the declarative and interrogative sentences and therefore understood that the appropriate position for *się* in a declarative sentence is post-verbal. This would imply a particularly strong, and highly unlikely, discerning of the input, if, after only 1h30 of input, learners were able to disentangle the occurrences of Refl-V and V-Refl in declarative versus interrogative sentences to such an extent that they were able to disregard their L1 word order in their placement of the reflexive pronoun. As the frequency of the two orders, Refl-V and V-Refl, was approximately equal in the input, we searched for another explanation for this post-verbal preference. We propose the interpretation that the learners in fact relied on SVO word order to correctly place the reflexive pronoun. As we mentioned in our analysis of French and Polish reflexive pronouns in Chapter 3, the French reflexive pronoun functions as direct object or indirect object. The order V-Refl or V-patient or V-object, regardless of the terminology used, is 'logical' for a V-O language. In other words, a learner whose L1 shows the order V-O would expect pronouns to occupy the same position as a noun phrase, even though French reflexive verbs prove an exception to the rule. It follows that learners may rely on certain cues of their L1 (the order of basic constituent word order in this case) even if a specific structure in their L1 fails to reflect this cue. In sum, we have observed that the majority of our learners, after 1h30 of exposure to Polish, did not place the reflexive pronoun in the position that a simple transfer of the equivalent structure in their L1 would predict. It appears that learners may have concluded that the order V-Refl formally corresponds to VO and thus to the formal organisation of semantic role relations in French.

Placing the reflexive pronoun *się* at Period 3h30

Table 9.8 shows the position of *się* in the input during Period 3h30, compared to that of Period 1h30. We observe that at Period 3h30 the order V-Refl took over as the more frequent of the two. This means then that the input and the learners' L1 did not share the same positioning of the reflexive pronoun, therefore placing the input structure and the L1 structure in competition with each other. The question now is: faced with these two orders, will the learners choose the one that is more frequent in the input or the one that is found in their L1?

Table 9.8 The position of the reflexive pronoun *się* (Refl) in the input at Periods 1h30 and 3h30

Period	*Refl-V*	*V-Refl*	*Other*
1h30	37 (51%)	35 (49%)	0
3h30	23 (31%)	50 (68%)	1 (1%)

Two sentences from the Period 1h30 word order test were used again in the test at Period 3h30:

14) Context sentence: *Jak się nazywasz?*
       Comment se (tu) appelles?
       (How Refl [you] are called?)
 Words to put in order: *się – Barbara – nazywam.*
       se – Barbara – (je) appelle
       (Refl – Barbara – [I] am called)

15) Context sentence: *Jak ona się nazywa?*
       Comment elle se appelle?
       (How she Refl is called?)

Words to put in order: *ona – Anka – się – nazywa.*
                    elle – Anka – se – appelle
                    (she – Anka – Refl – is called)
A third sentence was introduced for the first time at Period 3h30:

16) Context sentence: *Jacek jest w restauracji i*
                    Jacques est au restaurant et
                    (James is at restaurant and)
Words to put in order: *napije – piwa – się.*
                    (il) boira – bière – se
                    ([he] will drink – beer – Refl)

This time only five of the eight learners responded in the same way for all three sentences, suggesting that they may have processed the verbs *się nazywać* and *się napić* differently. We will look at this point in more detail below. Table 9.9 shows the percentage of each order in the input, as well as the learners' responses as raw scores.

Table 9.9 A comparison between Refl-V and V-Refl structures in the input and learners' responses on word order tests at Periods 1h30 and 3h30

Period	Structures in input-cumulative			Learners' responses (raw scores, n =8)			
	Refl-V	*V-Refl*	*Other*	*Refl-V*	*V-Refl*	*Refl-V and V-Refl*	*Other*
1h30	51%	49%	0%	3	5	0	0
3h30	41%	58%	1%	0	5	1	2

As shown in Table 9.9, a simple explanation of surface level transfer of the reflexive pronoun in pre-verbal position appears to no longer be an option. The tendency for V-Refl at Period 1h30 is confirmed at Period 3h30. At the same time, it is at Period 3h30 that we witness a confusion on the part of the learner as to where in fact one should place *się*. Of the five learners who responded with V-Refl, four of them (Sabine, Emma, Julie and Sandra) had responded as such during the test at Period 1h30. It appears then that these learners formulated the 'post-verbal' hypothesis after only 1h30 of input and maintained it through the subsequent 2 hours of input. Gilles, on the other hand, responded with the order Refl-V at Period 1h30 and reformulated his hypothesis in favour of V-Refl at Period 3h30. Although at Period 1h30 Dalia was in the group who originally formulated the post-verbal hypothesis, she was apparently not convinced by this hypothesis and responded at Period 3h30 in what appears to be a random manner with three ungrammatical orders: she used Refl-V[6] (response with a form of *nazywać*) in one sentence and the order Refl-O-V (a form of *napić*) and S-Refl-C-V (a form of *nazywać*) in the remaining two. Luc, who responded with Refl-V at Period 1h30, appeared less than content with his hypothesis and responded at Period 3h30 with the order Refl-V[7] (*napić*) in one sentence and the order V-C-Refl (ungrammatical in Polish) in the other two (*nazywać*). Nadine, who opted for V-Refl at Period 1h30 responded with V-Refl again in two sentences at Period 3h30 (*nazywać*), but with Refl-V[8] for the third (*napić*). The translation test administered subsequently to the word order test confirmed that all the learners understood the individual components of the sentences, with the exception of *się*, which was often not translated into French. It is only in Nadine's response that we observe a possible effect of the lexical item *nazywać* vs. *napić* on her choice of word order. With the seven remaining learners, there appears to be no difference in their ability to place *się* before or after a grammatical variant of *nazywać* versus *napić*.

In summary, the results fail to confirm the alternation hypothesis in that learners did not opt for the position of the reflexive pronoun found in their L1. As mentioned in our analyses of the data collected at Period 1h30, it is possible that basic constituent word order played a role in our learners' placement of the reflexive pronoun in Polish. Defying the specific feature in their L1, they were more influenced by the fundamental SVO word order, in which Refl can be seen as normally occupying the position of the object, following the verb.

The placement of the reflexive pronoun *się* at Period 7h00

The input provided to learners between Periods 3h30 and 7h00 contained a considerably larger proportion of V-Refl sentences than Refl-V ones, as can be seen in Table 9.10.

Table 9.10 The position of the reflexive pronoun *się* (Refl) in the input at Periods 1h30, 3h30 and 7h00

Period	Refl-V	V-Refl	Other
1h30	37 (51%)	35 (49%)	0
3h30	23 (31%)	50 (68%)	1 (1%)
7h00	22 (21%)	80 (77%)	2 (2%)

The Period 7h00 word order test contained the same sentences as the Period 3h30 test, with no new sentences containing *się* being introduced. As shown in Table 9.11, we analysed the placement of the reflexive pronoun *się* at three periods (1h30, 3h30 and 7h00) and as a function of the Polish input received.

Table 9.11 A comparison between Refl-V and V-Refl structures in the input and learners' responses on word order tests at Periods 1h30, 3h30 and 7h00

Period	Structures in input-cumulative			Learners' responses (raw scores, n =8)			
	Refl-V	*V-Refl*	*Other*	*Refl-V*	*V-Refl*	*Refl-V and V-Refl*	*Other*
1h30	51%	49%	0%	3	5	0	0
3h30	41%	58%	1%	0	5	1	2
7h00	33%	66%	1%	0	7	0	1

Results presented in Table 9.11 reveal that at Period 7h00, seven learners responded regularly with V-Refl in the three sentences. Only Luc responded with different orders for each sentence, one with V-Refl (note that this was his first attempt at using this order – the verb is a form of *nazywać*), one with Refl-V (also with *nazywać*) and a third ungrammatical order, V-O-Refl (*napić*). Again, the lexical items *nazywać* and *napić* seem to have had no effect on the learners' choice of word order.

In sum, after 7h00 of exposure to Polish, seven learners out of eight placed *się* in post-verbal position in all three sentences that contained *się*. Two interpretations are possible. On one hand, we could argue that these results do not confirm the alternation hypothesis, according to which, faced with two alternatives in the input, learners will opt for the alternative that exists in their L1. Rather, it appears that frequency of the item in the input (V-Refl being more frequent than Refl-V) proves cumulatively to be a stronger cue than the L1 (Refl belongs in front of the verb). The input effect reinforces the tendency mentioned earlier that our learners relied on the basic constituent word order V-O of their L1, a strong cue that even the exception in French concerning the position of the reflexive pronoun did not override. According to this latter interpretation, we are in the presence of two distinct types of L1 transfer, and if this is the case, further investigation is needed in order to distinguish between them.

Verbal Morphology

As pointed out in Chapter 3, the fairly weak morphological system in French differs significantly from the complex system of Polish. We expect, therefore, that French learners of Polish, especially those in the early stages of L2 acquisition, will have problems linked to Polish morphology, specifically in identifying Polish morphological markers. Our principal question in this section is: to what extent are learners able to perceive morphological errors in a Polish written text after limited exposure to Polish? In terms of the Polish input that learners received, forms that were introduced in the oral input were generally included in handouts distributed at the end of an activity or a class session summarising the content of the lesson. Forms that were introduced spontaneously in class without prior preparation were generally noted on the blackboard by the Polish instructor. All forms were presented within a context (picture descriptions, dialogues, etc.), and no grammatical lists, such as endings for cases or verb conjugations, were provided. As mentioned in Chapter 4, learners were asked not to consult such lists during the experimental portion of the Polish course. To investigate our research question, we collected data by means of grammaticality judgement tests administered at Periods 1h30, 3h30 and 7h00, tests that were used as well to test our learners' preferences for basic constituent word order in their TL. Each test consisted of a short text, ensuring a certain level of context. Table 9.12 shows the results of the series of grammaticality judgement tests in terms of verbal morphology.

Two interesting points revealed in Table 9.12 concern the group as a whole. Firstly, in 100% of the cases where learners indicated noticing errors in verbal morphology, they corrected them with the appropriate morphological forms. Secondly, a repeated measures ANOVA of the results presented in Table 9.12 showed that $F(2,14) = 4.93$; $p < 0.05$. This confirms an effect of hours of instruction (the first 7 hours) on our learners' ability to find and correct errors of verbal morphology in Polish.

In terms of individual performance, Table 9.12 displays a wide range. Five of our learners – Emma, Gilles, Nadine, Sabine and Sandra – showed signs of a sensitivity to verbal morphology already at Period 1h30. They all found and corrected at least one error in the text. At Periods 3h30 and 7h00, Emma, Nadine and Sandra found and corrected all of the errors. Luc and Julie, on the other hand, had trouble in the first two periods, but seemed to be sensitised to verbal morphology as of Period 7h00. At all periods, Sabine found some but not all errors, Gilles found and corrected more errors in the first two periods than he did in the third, and throughout the duration of the experimental period, Dalia found and corrected none of the incorrect morphological forms.

The results on verbal morphology inform us in two important areas. Firstly, as demonstrated in Chapter 6, individual differences must be taken into account in models of SLA. Research has generally attributed differences in learner performance to two variables: L1 (problem of transfer) or input (different exposure to the TL, either in terms of quantity or in terms of the nature of the input). In our case, eight learners shared the same L1 and were exposed to the same TL input. L1 and TL input were therefore constants in this study, not variables. Given this fact, how can we explain why our eight learners responded so differently to

Table 9.12 Percentage of verbal morphology errors corrected during grammaticality judgement tests at Periods 1h30, 3h30 and 7h00

Learners	*Errors corrected*	*Maximum possible*	*% corrected*
Period 1h30			
Dalia	0	3	0
Emma	1	3	33
Gilles	2	3	67
Julie	0	3	0
Luc	0	3	0
Nadine	1	3	33
Sabine	1	3	33
Sandra	2	3	67
Total	7	24	**29**
Period 3h30			
Dalia	0	3	0
Emma	3	3	100
Gilles	2	3	67
Julie	0	3	0
Luc	0	3	0
Nadine	3	3	100
Sabine	1	3	33
Sandra	3	3	100
Total	12	24	**50**
Period 7h00			
Dalia	0	2	0
Emma	2	2	100
Gilles	1	2	50
Julie	2	2	100

Table 9.12 (*Continued*)			
Learners	*Errors corrected*	*Maximum possible*	*% corrected*
Luc	2	2	100
Nadine	2	2	100
Sabine	1	2	50
Sandra	2	2	100
Total	12	16	**75**

the task of finding and correcting errors of verbal morphology? Clearly interlearner variation needs further investigation. Secondly, the results presented in this section indicate that learners are sensitive to grammatical information very early on in the L2 acquisition process. We have demonstrated that this information can be accessed for written perception after only 1h30 of exposure to the TL, that is through a controlled, highly metalinguistic written grammaticality judgement test. In addition to replicating these findings with a larger participant pool, we need to identify ways to access information about sensitivity to verbal morphology in real-time oral perception. This is a challenge for the future.

Discussion

The results presented in this chapter suggest that language transfer alone, be it transfer from the L1 or from another L2, cannot explain the performance of our learners in their analysis of certain grammatical features of Polish. The results show that learners begin to process certain grammatical structures of a novel TL *before* they are able to generate such structures in the given TL. In other words, the starting point of non-native grammatical knowledge occurs well before learners produce their first inflected verb forms. Many researchers have alluded to this possibility, but few have identified suitable methodological means to investigate it.

Let us return for a moment to basic constituent word order. We observed a strong preference for SVO in spite of the presence of other orders in the input. This said, after 7h00 of exposure to the TL, we see the first signs of a possible recognition on the part of some learners that an order other than SVO may be appropriate in certain contexts.

In Chapter 5 we presented analyses of data collected from French informants at first exposure to Polish which revealed a sensitivity to nominal morphology already in the first stages of L2 acquisition. The results presented in this chapter in which learners were asked to identify and correct ungrammatical forms reveal a sensitivity to verbal morphology as well. However, this sensitivity to the formal features of the TL depends to a large extent on the individual learner. Some are clearly more sensitive than others at different periods.

The hypotheses elaborated by our learners concerning the placement of the Polish negator *nie* varied at Period 1h30. After 1h30 of exposure to Polish and with limited occurrences of *nie* in the input, our learners formulated four distinct hypotheses as to the appropriate position for *nie* in a Polish sentence. The majority (7 out of 8 learners) had reformulated these hypotheses by Period 3h30, placing the negator correctly at Periods 3h30 and 7h00. It is worth emphasising the fact that very little input (only 3h30) was sufficient for learners to discover the appropriate hypothesis for the position of *nie* or, in generativist terms, to reset parameters. Regardless of one's research framework or terminology, our learners' development as concerns this feature was quick. As mentioned earlier, this does not imply that they will always be able to properly place *nie* or apply the rule in all cases, nor that they have eternally 'learned' the rule. The results do, however, show that our learners first 'learned' the Polish rule for *nie* at some point between Period 0h00 and Period 3h30. Future research would ideally take two more steps: 1) retest this phenomenon and pinpoint more carefully at what point learners understand the rule and under what conditions they are able to apply it; 2) follow the development of this phenomenon in learners as they pass through the various phases of L2 acquisition.

Analysis of learners' placement of the reflexive pronoun *się* allowed us to test the alternation hypothesis (Jansen *et al.*, 1981), which was borne out in our examination of basic constituent word order. Our investigation of the placement of *się*, however, did not fully corroborate this hypothesis. Faced with two alternatives, both of which appear in the input (in this case the placement of Polish *się* in either pre- or post-verbal position) but only one of which is found in the L1 (the French reflexive pronoun appears in pre-verbal position), the majority of our learners opted for the position not found in French, that of post-verbal position already at Period 1h30 when both positions were equally frequent in the input. By Period 7h00, all but one learner placed *się* in post-verbal position. Our explanation of these results is two-fold: the post-verbal position was more frequent in the input as of Period 3h30; and the learners may have relied on L1 canonical word order to place the relative pronoun as such pronouns normally occupy the object position, that is, the position following the verb.

From the point of view of grammatical analysis, our findings fail to confirm a full transfer of the L1. Results from the word order test reveal a strong preference for SVO, which is not surprising considering that SVO order is not only the dominant order in French, but also the preponderant order in the Polish input. Analyses on placing the Polish negator *nie*, however, do not reveal a simple reliance on L1, nor do the results on placing the reflexive pronoun *się*. Learners' hypotheses differ to a significant extent, but their analyses of the input clearly lead their interlanguage systems to gradually converge with TL forms.

Conclusion

The results in this chapter suggest that the paths learners follow in their linguistic discovery vary significantly from learner to learner at the initial stages of L2 acquisition. There are similarities, however, in how their new TL skills develop. Our results shed light on a number of combined factors implied in their development: how and to what extent learners use their L1 and other L2 knowledge, make use of the TL input, *and* manage to formulate and reformulate hypotheses about the TL. We will return to these points in our final discussion in the following chapter.

Notes

1. We do not distinguish between the allomorphs *wer/ur/u(r)*.
2. See also Véronique (2005: 119) for an overview of Negation in Moroccan Arabic. He concludes as well that negation in Moroccan Arabic '. . . is mainly expressed by *ma* in pre-verbal position'.
3. Cf. the relevant part of the third section of Chapter 3 for a detailed discussion of negation in French.
4. The instructor's 'Yes' was a confirmation to the student that she had understood the question. The response to the question, however, was incorrect, hence the use of the negator in the statement.
5. The instructor repeated the ungrammatical form spoken by the learner, *Portugalką* 'Portuguese' (feminine), but *Tom* obviously requires the masculine form.
6. Dalia's response *'się nazywam Barbara'* 'Refl (I) call Barbara' is ungrammatical because the pronoun *się* cannot occupy the sentence initial position (cf. 'Reflexive verbs' in the third section of Chapter 3 for details about this phenomenon).
7. See note 6. Luc responded *'się napije piwa'* (ungrammatical in Polish).
8. See note 6. Nadine responded *'się napije piwa'* (ungrammatical in Polish).

Chapter 10
Concluding Remarks

Our study of initial processing of foreign language input began with an overview of how various theories, models and frameworks of second language acquisition attempt to explain a learner's processing of target language input, and how the terms 'input' and 'intake' are characterised and defined. In addition, we looked at what these diverse perspectives have to say about the initial stages of L2 acquisition and found that few say much about it. In Chapter 2 we examined the few studies that have investigated L2 acquisition upon first exposure to the L2 and argued the need for further studies of this kind. We then entered into the details of the current study, examining differences between the learners' NL (French) and TL (Polish) in Chapter 3, identifying potential 'difficulties' that could be predicted. We introduced and described the study's participants and data collection procedures in Chapter 4. Here the reader came to understand the nature of our learners/informants, that of French university students who share French as their NL, and who have learned *about* French during their many years of French schooling. The reader also came to understand the highly metalinguistic nature of the tasks that our participants were asked to perform. In sum, we emphasised that the institutional education and academic level of our participants, as well as the highly metalinguistic nature of our tasks, needed to be taken into consideration when interpreting and discussing results. We also set out in this study to completely control the TL input provided to the learners. In Chapter 4, we described how this was done. We also attempted to identify the knowledge available to learners before exposure to the TL and the strategies used by the learners upon first exposure to the TL input. We responded to this objective in Chapter 5 with a characterisation of the state of an adult native French speaker when first exposed to Polish input. Results presented in Chapters 6–9 address our remaining two objectives: to analyse specific language activities (speech perception, speech comprehension, and grammatical analysis) relative to the input provided at this early stage of acquisition, and to identify what aspects of this input are taken in by the learner and to what extent this intake is subsequently used for further processing. In this final chapter, we briefly summarise our findings in terms of language task and language activity. This summary will be followed by a discussion of how the results and research methodology can be applied to future studies investigating the starting point of L2 acquisition.

Learners' Language Activities

Speech perception (sentence repetition test)

If we ever truly doubted the beneficial effect of language instruction on a learner's acquisition or learning of a foreign language, the results of the sentence repetition test alone prove us wrong. Global input (defined as hours of instruction) clearly had an effect on the learners' ability to perceive elements of the TL and to correctly reproduce them, as attested by the gradual increase in correct repetitions over the 8-hour instruction period. We also found that certain factors that render items in the input more salient give precision to the role played by global input. For example, we found that transparency and phonemic distance relative to our learners' L1 had an effect on their ability to correctly reproduce Polish words. Words categorised as 'very transparent' were better repeated than those classified as 'opaque'. Polish words that were phonetically closer to French words were better repeated than those classified as phonetically more distant. It follows that the capacity to reproduce a word in an unknown language implies the possibility of resorting to semantic and phonological phenomena of the L1 and/or other L2s. In other words, these results suggest an influence of prior linguistic knowledge on the processing of a novel TL. This said, our participants repeated more words in utterance initial and final positions than words in middle position, corroborating cross-linguistic research findings in L1 acquisition and later stages of L2 acquisition that initial and final positions are more salient than middle position (cf. Klein, 1986; Slobin, 1985; VanPatten, 2000). Results of these studies taken together lead us to conclude that one factor appearing to affect saliency, and therefore perception, is the position of the word or linguistic item in the speech stream. Another is stress. Our informants repeated stressed Polish words better than unstressed words in spite of the fact that their L1 (French) does not have fixed lexical stress.[1] Our results suggest that these two factors, sentence position and stress, are unrelated to L1 transfer, providing support for the hypothesis that general cognitive perceptual factors, not necessarily directly related to the L1 organisation, play an important role in a learner's capacity to perceive and reproduce words in an unknown language. Finally, the frequency of a word in the input showed no significant effect on correct repetitions in the first 8 hours of exposure (an effect was found after 8 hours, but not before), suggesting that, in Slobin's (1985) terms, L2 learners are not immediately able to take note of 'sameness' (in the sense of 'I've seen this before') and increase the 'frequency count'. In other words, it takes a certain amount of exposure before frequency alone has an effect on a learner's ability to correctly repeat the lexical components of a sentence in a novel target language.

Comprehension (oral and written word and sentence translation tests)

The results of the comprehension tests also reveal that first exposure informants and learners used previous linguistic knowledge to perform both oral and written tasks. With regard to the *word* translation tests, we found that informants made use of all pertinent linguistic knowledge to accomplish the task in Polish. In both oral and written conditions, they used this knowledge to translate not only lexical information of a Polish word into French, but also grammatical information. Paying attention to word endings in Polish, some informants (with no prompting) formulated hypotheses about the Polish inflexional systems for gender, number and person. They also made use of their knowledge of other languages to determine the word class of given Polish words. In sum, our results provide evidence that our learners' L1 *and* L2 systems were activated and made available for the processing of a novel TL. The results also attest to the important work that learners do at the grammatical level, suggesting that there may well be grammar acquisition in the 'silent period' that precedes first productions, as White (1996) predicts. This implies that the starting point of non-native grammatical knowledge occurs well before learners produce their first inflected verb, and that Schwartz and Sprouse (1996) have not yet explored the true 'initial state' of the L2 learner.

This brings us to the issue of third language acquisition. Although our data do not allow us to go as far as to specify the degree to which various factors, such as competency, typology and recency, determine 'transfer' to the L3, we have observed tendencies. It appears that upon first exposure to the new language, it is not the level of mastery of the available L2s that determines whether or not elements of a specific L2 would be activated and 'used' to accomplish the task at hand. We presented evidence in Chapter 5 that learners used knowledge of their L2s even when their proficiency level in the given L2 was quite low. To investigate the factors involved in L3 acquisition in more depth, precise tasks with limited variables are needed. In an attempt to control for linguistic knowledge, for example, a study might select informants based solely on their L1 and their L2s (with similar L2 proficiency levels), in essence creating a group of learners with similar linguistic profiles, as in the case studies of Gilles and Luc presented in Chapter 6. Tasks can then be designed with not only the NL and TL in mind, but also the L2s. Our results show that the degree of activation of any given language during a translation task depends on the feature being treated, the language activity in which the individual is engaged, and the combination of languages in question. We believe that this is an individual process, following Kellerman's (1983) thesis of psychotypology. For instance, in our study, several informants translated the Polish word *mówię* '(I) speak' with the French 'film' or 'cinéma', activating the English word 'movie' to arrive at a translation, whereas other informants, even those with a strong level of English, provided no translation. Some informants translated *kolega* 'colleague' (sg, m) with a feminine form, likely due to the presence of the affix *-a*, which could be interpreted as denoting a feminine noun in Spanish and Italian, L2s known by some of our informants. The typology factor seems irrelevant here in that the Polish language is *not* typologically close to Spanish or Italian in any traditional sense of the word.

The oral sentence translation tests, as with the sentence repetitions, allowed us to observe the effect of various factors on participants' ability to process (translate) Polish sentences. The oral sentence translation tests revealed the important role transparency played in comprehension, but revealed as well that its influence was variable with respect to the position of the word in a sentence. Words categorised as 'very transparent' in the oral sentence translation test were better translated when they were found in initial and final position regardless of the syntactic structure of the sentence. In terms of the role that basic constituent word order played in speech comprehension, learners generally understood the elements of an OVS-type sentence to the same degree as those of an SVO-type sentence, at least when the sentence comprised an animate subject and an inanimate object as predicted by the Competition Model (cf. Bates & MacWhinney, 1981, 1987). Future studies of the interaction between transparency and word order should envisage presenting naïve subjects with sentences composed of basic constituents that appear in various orders and in which *all* items are transparent. Results could then be compared with those of another subject group who are presented with the same word orders as the previous group, but in which *no* items are transparent. Such tests could be designed for different combinations of factors, effectively limiting the number of variables involved in each testing condition.

Taken as a whole, the results of the perception and comprehension tasks reveal that it is possible to identify knowledge sources that help a true beginner associate a *signifié* with a TL *signifiant*. For instance, the fact that lexical transparency was a factor in the word and sentence translation tests *and* in the sentence repetition test implies that transparency helps for form-meaning associations (reflected in correct *translations*) and, because of this, also helps in segmenting the speech stream (reflected in correct *repetitions*).

Grammatical analysis (word order tests, grammaticality judgement tests, and oral and written word translation tests)

With regard to grammatical analysis, data collected from the written word order and grammaticality judgement tests revealed a clear preference on the part of our learners for SVO word order (i.e. their L1 normative word order) throughout the 8-hour experimental period in spite of the fact that the Polish input comprised not only SVO utterances, but other orders as well. These findings provide support for the alternation hypothesis (Jansen *et al.*, 1981), which predicts that learners will select the order of the L1 if confronted with two possible orders in the TL (one of which is attested in their L1).We used the word order and grammaticality judgement tests as well to observe our learners' placement of the negative particle *nie* in Polish after 1h30 of exposure. Learners' responses varied greatly. Certain learners placed the negative particle in pre-verbal position, others in post-verbal position. The former might be explained by the pragmatic principle 'place the scope particle before that which it has scope over' (cf. Giuliano, 2004), the latter by L1 activation or reliance. Some learners placed the negative particle in initial or final sentence position. These results clearly suggest that a hypothesis claiming full L1 transfer at the first stages of L2 acquisition is untenable as it fails to explain the entirety of these phenomena. We then analysed the possibility of other L2 transfer. We found that transfer from an L2 to an L3 indeed provides a possible explanation in certain cases, but that this type of transfer does not constitute the sole influential factor either. In summary, our results suggest that several factors intervened in the placement of the negator in Polish: the L1, other L2s and general principles of information structure.

The placement of the Polish reflexive pronoun *się* was also studied using these tests. We found that individual learners were generally consistent in their placement of *się* during any given testing period, placing *się* in the same position in all obligatory contexts. This suggests that each learner based all contexts on one single hypothesis about the placement of *się*. Between Periods 1h30, 3h30 and 7h00, we observed their evolution with respect to this phenomenon, suggesting that their hypotheses were operative, as we had predicted them to be (cf. Giacobbe, 1992a). A between-learner analysis revealed differences in the way each learner processed and formulated hypotheses about the placement of *się* and the path that each learner took towards acquiring the new structure. This is made evident as well in results reported in Chapter 6 in which we compared the acquisition of two learners, Gilles and Luc. At the onset of our study, Gilles and Luc arrived with no knowledge of Polish or another Slavic language, they were exposed to the same Polish input, and they shared the same L1 (French) and L2 (English). They nevertheless performed quite differently, not only on tasks requiring the placement of *się*, but on other tasks as well. These differences cannot, therefore, be explained by differences in TL proficiency level (they were both at Level 0), their L1, other L2s, or prior input received. They are likely due to differences in learner styles, as suggested by Perdue and Klein (1992),

Meisel *et al.* (1981) and Lambert (1994b). For this reason, research needs to continue its characterisation of learner profiles and to incorporate these profiles into models of SLA. Both inter- and intralearner variation should be considered.

By means of the grammaticality judgement tests, we also collected data on our learners' ability to find and correct errors of verbal morphology in a Polish written text. Results showed that our learners got better at finding and correcting errors of morphology: 29% of the errors were found and corrected at Period 1h30, 50% at Period 3h30 and 75% at Period 7h00. Again, the effect of instruction, even as little as 8 hours, is obvious. We found interlearner variation here as well. Our learners did not necessarily find and correct the *same* errors, nor did they evolve in their ability to perceive these errors at the same rate (cf. Chapter 6 for an analysis of Gilles' and Luc's data). One learner, for example, never found an error.

To conclude this section, we invite the reader to reflect on two points in particular, the first being the usage of the term 'transfer' in SLA literature. The more we know about how learners work on their input, the more we are inclined to say that the 'transfer' metaphor is unsuitable for this process. It is not so much a 'transfer' of one knowledge base to another, but rather an 'activation' of a particular knowledge source that is pertinent and potentially useful for the task at hand. Some of this 'activation' may be language specific, i.e. activation of certain forms in a learner's given languages (as suggested by the continuum of lexical and morphological transparency proposed in Chapter 5); however, some of this 'activation' may have as its source a non-language-specific property, as our results of the effect of word position and stress on language perception suggest.

This leads us to our second point, that of 'psychotypology'. Kellerman (1983) defines 'psychotypology' as the learner's perceived distance between the L1 and L2. We have attempted here to provide more precision to this definition. Our results suggest that prior linguistic knowledge and metalinguistic strategies make up learners' psychotypologies, and that their ability to consult this linguistic knowledge in order to formulate operative hypotheses about the new language, and to test and reformulate these hypotheses, is cognitive activity that depends on this psychotypology. Psychotypology is therefore individual – no two learners share the same psychotypology, just as no two speakers speak any given language in exactly the same way. If this is the case, we might conclude that there is no common 'initial state' or starting point for L2 acquisition. A random group of adult learners will obviously come to a new TL with drastically diverse prior knowledge, experience and levels of metalinguistic awareness. While we have emphasised the need for learner variability to be considered in models of SLA, we have, at the same time, identified general tendencies in our participants, such as paying attention to transparency, stress, and initial and final positions, indicating that some of what learners do at first exposure can be predicted. Further research at this early stage of L2 acquisition is needed to confirm whether or not the tendencies observed constitute universals.

Towards a Characterisation of 'Intake'

In this section, we return to hypotheses concerning the characterisation and role of 'intake' presented in Chapter 1. According to VanPatten (1996), intake denotes data that are held in working memory and are available for further processing. VanPatten and Sanz (1995) assume that intake, which is essential to learning, is the result of input that is perceived and 'processed', that is, the input that is 'comprehended'. It is thanks to this intake that grammatical information can be rendered available for the developing system. Carroll (2001), on the other hand, views intake as a mental representation of the physical stimuli (input). In contrast to proponents of the comprehensible input hypothesis, she concludes that, '... the view that intake is comprehended speech is mistaken and has arisen from an uncritical examination of the implications of Krashen's (1985) claims to this effect' (Carroll, 2001: 9).

Within the interactionist approach, Matthey (1996) makes a distinction between 'prise' in tokens of 'données – prises' (occurrences of giving and taking) and 'saisie' (intake), emphasising that not every 'prise' constitutes a 'saisie' and that not every 'saisie' will be manifested as a 'prise'. In other words, the learner may be able to repeat a word in the target language, but this does not mean that the word has necessarily been 'taken in'. She proposes, however, that certain 'prises' mark some sort of process of cognitive intake.

What is needed at this point is complementary tests using the same stimuli by means of which perception is tested in one and comprehension in the other. Take, for example, the sentence repetitions presented in Chapter 7. Participants were asked to listen to Polish sentences and repeat them. This test was designed to discover more about perception than comprehension. If we modified the task, however, and asked another group of participants to listen and *translate* the sentences, we would find out more about comprehension than perception.[2] Such data would indeed provide useful information about the relation between perception and comprehension. To take this a step further, future studies should include collecting data by means of perception, comprehension and production tasks while maintaining the TL lexical items that appear in each task constant. Such a methodology would provide at least partial responses to the following questions: under what conditions can learners understand what they perceive, and under what conditions can they produce what they perceive and/or comprehend? It is worth pointing out here that the terms 'perceive', 'comprehend' and 'produce' must be carefully defined in this type of approach.

Following the example of Slobin (1985) and Peters (1985), we assume that saliency facilitates perception and allows for extraction. We showed in Chapter 7 that certain operating principles proposed by Slobin for L1 acquisition can be applied to L2 acquisition as well. Our results validate the fact that saliency of an item facilitates perception, but can we go as far as to say that this perception constitutes intake? We may wish to say that perception constitutes one *level* of intake. What then is needed for the next level to transpire? We may need to distinguish between several *levels* or *types* of intake. It is possible, for example, to store a word in long-term memory without understanding it. Noizet (1980: 128) points out that listeners are able to perceive non-words that, by definition, they do not understand. As Zwitserlood *et al.* (2000) found as well, learners upon first exposure to their TL can recognise that a TL item is a word even if they do not understand it. One can also understand a TL form without being able to (re)produce it. And one can (re)produce a TL form without comprehending it, and so forth. Hence, we propose a typology of intake as follows:

(0) *No* intake when the item is *not* perceived, comprehended or (re)produced.
    Intake of various types:
(1) The item is perceived, but it is neither comprehended nor (re)produced.
(2) The item is perceived and (re)produced, but not comprehended.
(3) The item is perceived and comprehended, but not (re)produced.
(4) The item is perceived, comprehended, and (re)produced.

The category '(re)produced' will eventually need to be divided into three subgroups: repetition, spontaneous use and productive mastery of all form-function mappings. When this is done, Levelt's (1989) speech production model and de Bot's (1992) bilingual production model can be applied.

Taking one step at a time, however, the first question is how to go about testing these intake types. How can we know if an item has (or has not) been perceived? Types 0 and 1 may be a mission for neurolinguists; however, once again, 'perception' must be carefully defined, in this case with regard to brain activity. Type 2 intake could be tested in simultaneous repetition/comprehension tasks, such as the sentence repetition and sentence comprehension tests reported in this book. Separate first exposure groups listen to sentences in the TL. One group is asked to *repeat,* and the other is asked to *translate.* If learners are able to reproduce the TL word, we know they have perceived it. If in a subsequent task, they are unable to show comprehension of the given word, then we have a case of type 2 intake (the item is perceived and (re)produced, but not comprehended). Type 3 could be tested by means of a picture-matching task whereby the learners are asked both to repeat and select an image. If a learner selects the correct image, but is unable to repeat the word, we can assume a case of type 3 intake (the item is perceived and comprehended, but not (re)produced). Type 4 (the item is perceived, comprehended, and (re)produced) can only be tested by means of a combination of tasks (perception, comprehension, and (re)production) in which the same items appear in each task. Such tasks may be designed to investigate perception, comprehension and (re)production of phonetic, phonological, lexical, morphosyntactic, semantic and/or pragmatic information. We predict that results of such tests will confirm that a clear distinction needs to be made between 'intake' at the *perceptual* level, at the *comprehended* level, and at the *(re)production* level, the latter being 'intake' that is converted for (re)production. This does not imply that intake is required for production *per se*, but it is required for *meaningful* production in an L2. It is also important to mention here that attentional factors *must* be taken into account when studying 'intake'.

The above typology of intake serves in some sense as a response to questions raised in the introduction to this book about the nature of 'input processing', defined as what learners 'do' with the TL input they receive. This somewhat vague definition of 'processing' was used because 'processing' itself was under investigation in this book. Following analysis of our data, we conclude that 'processing' is indeed an umbrella term that encompasses a variety of operations. In order to describe what learners do, we need to break down their processing into precise categories: processing of oral versus written input, processing for perception (segmenting the speech stream) and processing for comprehension (mapping form to meaning or meaning to form). As mentioned above, the specific category of processing that takes place at any given time will depend to a large extent on the type of task and language activity required of the learner.

The Need for First Exposure Studies

Let us return now to Corder's (1967: 165) insightful quote introduced at the beginning of Chapter 1. He states that '... we may reasonably suppose that it is the learner who controls this input, or more properly his intake'. His shift from 'input' ('what is *available* for going in') to 'intake' ('what goes in') is clearly intentional, acknowledging the fact that learners do *not* control their input (unless of course they alone decide what radio station to listen to, what book to read, etc. – they are then controlling it to a certain extent), but that they probably *do* control their intake. Our study provides evidence for this supposition. Whether this control is conscious or unconscious is as yet unclear, although evidence for both types is suggested in studies on implicit and explicit knowledge and learning. In order to observe 'intake', we need to tease apart 'input' and 'intake'. Input can be measured and controlled. Intake, on the other hand, is more problematic, which is why controlling and measuring input seems a more logical place to start. The most obvious way to *completely* control the TL input is to control it from the very beginning, that is from the moment a learner is first exposed to the input. This is precisely what we did in this study.

Let us now return to several second language acquisition research frameworks. If, for example, the connectionists want to know more about what learners do with the input they receive, they clearly need to distinguish between 'input' and 'intake' as well. They need to be particularly clear about what 'input' they feed into their networks, and they need to know what knowledge they can attribute to a learner. As we have seen in this book, that knowledge comes in many forms: knowledge of one's L1, knowledge of various aspects of one's L2s (for as many L2s as the learner knows), implicit and explicit knowledge, and encyclopaedic knowledge. Connectionists also need to know what cognitive factors, such as principles of extraction and scope properties, affect language processing and acquisition. The Competition Model has provided considerable human data for the testing of connectionist hypotheses. This book has made suggestions as to how first exposure studies can use the Competition Model framework to further inform us about the processes involved in sentence interpretation.

We are convinced that the act of disentangling linguistic 'input' from what the learner 'takes in' is extremely important for interactionist studies as well. Their focus is generally the negotiation of input, but yet again, a similar question is raised: At what point does this negotiation process result in 'intake'? Only through complete control of the input and of the negotiation of that input will interactionists be able to know when that magic 'intake' moment occurs. This can be said as well for those working in the focus-on-form approach. At what point does the expected consequence of input enhancement – 'noticing' – occur, and at what point is the 'noticed' item or feature taken in? Controlling the enhancement in and of itself is insufficient because too much else is going on with exposure to large quantities of other uncontrolled input. The only way to really answer this question is to completely control the input, control the enhancement itself, record the noticing and then observe what the learner *does* with that which is noticed.

We have observed that cognitive processes independent of the L1 play a vital role in the learners' ability to accomplish a task in the unknown language, as claimed by Slobin (1985) and Peters (1985) for L1 acquisition and VanPatten (2000) and Robinson (2001) for L2 acquisition. As Giacobbe (1992b: 247) puts it, the L1 is the 'principal driving force', but it does not reflect the total initial system from which development begins. 'The learner's activity...is the result of a complex system of transformations which is part of the adult's cognitive propensity for acquiring an L2' (Giacobbe, 1992b: 249). Our data corroborate his hypothesis.

The act of disentangling 'input' from 'intake' in order to better understand the relationship between L2 acquisition and speech processing is what much of Carroll's recent work is all about. As noted in Carroll (2002: 227), other approaches have yet to acknowledge, let alone explain, certain fundamentals about L2 language development, such as '... hearing the speech stream initially as continuous noise and not as sequences of "words"', or '... being able to detect a phonetic feature in a discrimination task but not being able to "hear" it when processing words in sentences...', (she provides numerous examples), and what this all means from a developmental perspective. Results presented in Chapters 5 and 7 revealed that individuals exposed to a language for the first time are able to extract quite a bit of information from the input, and that this extraction is aided by certain factors (transparency, word stress, etc.). At the same time, we observed the stage in which our participants heard 'just noise' and were unable to make sense of what they heard. Our focus in Chapter 5 was on 'recognised' words. The majority of words, however, were *not* recognised. We assume they were *not* recognised because they lacked the elements that allowed for 'recognised' words to be recognised (transparency, word stress, etc.). Future research is needed to further identify factors that lead naïve learners to 'perceive' and/or 'comprehend' elements of the speech stream. This can be extended as well to factors that lead such learners to 'comprehend' elements of written text in an unknown language, be it in alphabets with which they are familiar or those with which they are not.

Conclusion

In the course of this study, we identified certain knowledge that is available to the adult learner upon first contact with a new target language. We observed how learners make use of their prior linguistic knowledge, as well as extralinguistic knowledge and cognitive capacities independent of the specificities of any given languages, to perceive and make sense of their new TL input.

We were able to characterise the input provided to the learners by means of a complete control of the input and a transcription using the CHILDES programs, calculating the frequency of specific words and forms in the input with a view to comparing the input with the performance of our learners on given tasks. This control of the input allowed us to analyse our learners' performance relative to hours of exposure to the TL and to the frequency of specific items in the input. We were, therefore, able to observe the role played by the TL input itself, L1 knowledge and L2 knowledge in the learners' processing of the TL input. We analysed various language activities – speech perception, comprehension and grammatical analysis – relative to the controlled input, examining how learners worked on the input they received. Finally, we proposed a typology of 'intake' which suggests how we might better investigate what aspects of this input are taken in by the learner, and to what extent this intake is subsequently used for further processing.

We conclude by emphasising the need for further studies in which the TL input is controlled and measured from the moment of first exposure. We must pursue the search for adequate methodologies from all perspectives of second language acquisition research with a view to characterising the starting point of adult L2 acquisition. In this way we will finally come to understand how a non-native language is born and be in a position to describe the first hours of its acquisition. So far, we have managed to analyse some of the determining factors which must serve as ... input (!) for a comprehensive theory of initial language processing by the adult learner.

Notes

1. Some of our learners' L2s show lexical stress. Although we investigated the influence of our learners' L2 systems on their processing of Polish input, we did not control for this when analysing the effect of lexical stress.
2. We conducted this test on a group of first exposure informants; however, problems with data collection and interpretation led us to exclude the data from reported results.

Appendix 1

Word Translation Test (Oral and Written Period 0h00)

1. jeden
2. jest
3. lekcja
4. francji
5. amerykańskim
6. wam
7. pochodzę
8. pracuje
9. francuski
10. jestem
11. polką
12. paryżu
13. koleżanka
14. się
15. hiszpański
16. mieszkam
17. włosku
18. lubię
19. nazywam
20. zaprezentuje
21. angielski
22. zaczne
23. nie
24. polski
25. amerykanką
26. z
27. wykładowcą
28. ale
29. pracuję
30. w
31. paryż
32. włoski
33. mówi
34. lubi
35. więc
36. i
37. hiszpańsku
38. temat
39. dobrze
40. prezentacja
41. mnie
42. ode
43. koleżankę
44. ja
45. angielsku
46. teraz
47. zna
48. mieszka
49. uniwersytecie
50. stańow zjednoczonych
51. osiem
52. ona
53. po
54. polsku
55. na
56. francusku
57. język
58. znaczy
59. to
60. pochodzi
61. moja
62. lekcji
63. we
64. mówię
65. znam
66. nazywa
67. ze
68. nauczyciel

69. zupę
70. studentem
71. moją
72. warszawie
73. informatykę
74. marek
75. lekarz
76. piwa
77. krakowie
78. włoszech
79. brat
80. mojego
81. lody
82. kolegę
83. również
84. anna
85. książke
86. studiuje
87. piotra
88. go
89. jacka
90. nauczyciela
91. marii
92. film
93. kolega
94. opowiada

95. hiszpanem
96. świetnie
97. anka
98. zje
99. ją
100. znają
101. napije
102. papierosa
103. marka
104. juan
105. mieszkają
106. lekarza
107. włoską
108. bardzo
109. mama
110. znają
111. chętnie
112. kolegi
113. piotr
114. pali
115. jackowi
116. ewa
117. do
118. mój
119. kelner

Appendix 2

Sentence Repetition Test (Periods 0h00, 4h00, 8h00)

1) Piotr, mieszka w Krakowie, i studiuje informatykę.
2) Anna jest Włoszką, i mieszka we Włoszech.
3) Nauczyciel zna Marka, i mój brat zna go również.
4) Piotra mama, Marka zna również. (*Not analysed*)
5) Piotra mama, wykładowcą jest na uniwersytecie.
6) Ewa zje lody. (*Not analysed*)
7) Jestem w Warszawie, i znam ją bardzo dobrze.
8) Zupe Marek zje chętnie.
9) Marek, zna mojego kolegę, i mojego kolegę, zna również mój brat.
10) Anka i Marek, nie mieszkają w Krakowie, ale znają go dobrze.
11) Juan jest Hiszpanem, i mówi świetnie po polsku.
12) Lekarz, nie zna mojego kolegi.
13) Piwa napije się Piotr.
14) Lekarza, zna mój kolega.
15) Książke mojego kolegi, zna Piotr bardzo dobrze.
16) Podchodzi kelner do Jacka.
17) Mojego nauczyciela zna moja mama.
18) Marek pali papierosa. (*Not analysed*)
19) Piotr, Marii, i Jackowi, opowiada film.
20) Marek jest studentem, i mieszka w Krakowie.

Appendix 3

Oral Sentence Translation Test Period 1h30

(1) Po polsku mówi ona dobrze.
(2) Ona pochodzi z Francji.
(3) Nie lubi Ewa Krakowa.
(4) W Krakowie pracuje Jacek.
(5) Ona się nazywa Anna.
(6) Inżynierem jest on w fabryce.
(7) Ines nie zna dobrze języka polskiego.
(8) Nazywa się on Marek.

Oral Sentence Translation Test Period 3h30

(1) Nie lubi Ewa Krakowa.
(2) Nazywa się on Marek.
(3) Anna lubi lody.
(4) Po polsku mówi ona dobrze.
(5) Zupę zje Jacek.
(6) Ewa napije się herbaty.
(7) Nie chce Anna piwa ale herbatę.
(8) Ja również zjem deser.
(9) Kartę przynosi kelnerka.
(10) Lody lubi Anna.

Oral Sentence Translation Test Period 7h00

(1) Ona nazywa się Ewa.
(2) Charlot chce wrócić do więzienia.
(3) Marek lubi zupę.
(4) Charlot nie placi w restauracji.
(5) Jacek zna restaurację.
(6) Oni są na obiedzie u Jacka.
(7) Ona się nazywa Ewa.
(8) Restaurację zna Jacek.
(9) Zupę lubi Marek.
(10) Ja równiez napiję się piwa.

Appendix 4

Word Order Test Period 1h30

A)   1 : Maria pracuje na uniwersytecie.
      2 : ona – wykładowcą - jest

B)   1 : Anna po angielsku mówi dobrze.
      2 : lubi - angielski - ona - język

C)   1 : Marek jest Amerykaninem.
      2 : pochodzi - Stanów Zjednoczonych – on - ze

D)   1 : Tomek mieszka w Paryżu.
      2 : nie - on – lubi - Paryża

E)   1 : Jak się nazywasz ?
      2 : się – Barbara - nazywam

F)   1 : Angelika jest sekretarką
      2 : pracuje – nie – ona – na - uniwersytecie

G)   1 : Jim jest Anglikiem.
      2 : zna – polskiego – on - języka - nie

H)   1 : Hans jest Niemcem.
      2 : w – mieszka – on - Berlinie

I)   1 : Język rosyjski Monika zna dobrze, ale
      2 : nie – rosyjskiego - lubi

J)   1 : Jak ona się nazywa ?
      2 : ona – Anka – się - nazywa

Word Order Test Period 3h30

A)   1 : Maria pracuje na uniwersytecie.
      2 : ona – wykładowcą - jest

B) 1 : Zupę pomidorową zje Ewa, i gulasz.
    2 : również - Jacek – gulasz - zje

C) 1: Jacek jest w restauracji i
    2 : napije – piwa - się

D) 1 : Tomek mieszka w Paryżu.
    2 : nie – on – lubi - Paryża

E) 1 : Jak się nazywasz ?
    2 : się – Barbara - nazywam

F) 1 : Angelika jest sekretarką
    2 : pracuje – nie – ona – na - uniwersytecie

G) 1 : Ewa zje lody. Ponieważ lubi desery.
    2 : Jacek - lubi – nie - deserów

H) 1 : Ewa jest w restauracji.
    2 : chce – herbatę - ona

I) 1 : Marek nie lubi zupy pomidorowej.
    2 : Anna – lubi – również - nie - zupy pomidorowej

J) 1 : Jak ona się nazywa ?
    2 : ona – Anka – się – nazywa

Word Order Test Period 7h00

A) 1 : Maria pracuje na uniwersytecie.
    2 : ona – wykładowcą - jest

B) 1 : Zupę pomidorową zje Ewa, i gulasz.
    2 : również - Jacek – gulasz - zje

C) 1: Jacek jest w restauracji i
    2 : napije – piwa - się

D) 1 : Jak ona się nazywa ?
    2 : ona – Anka – się - nazywa

E) 1 : Jak się nazywasz ?
    2 : się – Barbara - nazywam

F)   1 : Angelika jest sekretarką
      2 : pracuje – nie – ona – na - uniwersytecie

G)   1 : Ewa zje lody. Ponieważ lubi desery.
      2 : Jacek – lubi – nie - deserów

H)   1 : Ewa jest w restauracji.
      2 : chce – herbatę - ona

I)   1 : Marek nie lubi zupy pomidorowej.
      2 : Anna – lubi - również – nie - zupy pomidorowej

J)   1 : Charlot idzie do restaurancji.
      2 : obiad – pije – je – nie - i - płaci

K)   1 : Jaki ma Marek charakter ?
      2 : wesoły – i – jest - sympatyczny - bardzo

L)   1 : Tomek mieszka w Paryżu.
      2 : nie – on – lubi - Paryża

M)   1 : Charlot nie płaci w restauracji.
      2 : policja – i - zabiera – Charlot – przyjeżdża - do więzienia

Appendix 5

Grammaticality Judgement Test (and Translation Test) Period 1h30

Rebekah prezentuje koleżankę :
To moja koleżanka. Nazywa się ona Mary. Jest Amerykanką i pochodzisz ze Stanów Zjednoczonych. Mieszkam ona w Chicago. Architektką jest i znasz dobrze język hiszpański, ale nie zna języka niemieckiego.

Grammaticality Judgement Test (and Translation Test) Period 3h30

Piotr jest w restauracji. Piwa napije się on i zjem kotlet schabowy. On również chcą zieloną sałatę, ale nie chce ciasta. Piotr lubię nie deserów.

Grammaticality Judgement Test (and Translation Test) Period 7h00

To jest moja koleżanka. Nazywa się ona Ewa. Pochodzi z Krakowa i Kraków zna ona dobrze. Wesoła jest i sympatyczna. Ma okulary i jest blondynką. Mieszka w Paryżu i po francusku mówi bardzo dobrze. Pracuje ona w biurze, jest sekretarką. Ewa zna Paryż bardzo dobrze ale nie lubi Paryża. Chce ona wrócić do Krakowa.

References

Allwood, J. (1993) Feedback in second language acquisition. In C. Perdue (ed.) *Adult Language Acquisition: Cross-linguistic Perspectives* (Vol. II, pp. 196–235). Cambridge: Cambridge University Press.

Bardel, C. (2006) La connaissance d'une langue étrangère romane favorise-t-elle l'acquisition d'une autre langue romane? Influences translinguistiques dans la syntaxe en L3. *Acquisition et Interaction en Langue Étrangère* 24, 149–180.

Bardel, C. and Lindqvist, C. (2005) The role of proficiency and typology in lexical cross-linguistic influence: A study of a multilingual learner of Italian L3. Unpublished manuscript, Department of French and Italian, University of Stockholm.

Bardovi-Harlig, K. (2000) *Tense and Aspect in Second Language Acquisition: Form, Meaning, and Use.* Oxford: Blackwell.

Bardovi-Harlig, K. (2004) The emergence of grammaticalized future expression in longitudinal production data. In B. VanPatten, J. Williams, S. Rott and M. Overstreet (eds) *Form-Meaning Connections in Second Language Acquisition* (pp. 115–137). Mahwah, NJ: Lawrence Erlbaum Associates.

Bates, E. and MacWhinney, B. (1981) Second language acquisition from a functionalist perspective: Pragmatic, semantic and perceptual strategies. In H. Winitz (ed.) *Native Language and Foreign Language Acquisition* (pp. 190-214). New York: New York Academy of Sciences.

Bates, E. and MacWhinney, B. (1987) Competition, variation, and language learning. In B. MacWhinney (ed.) *Mechanisms of Language Acquisition* (pp. 157–193). Hillsdale, NJ: Lawrence Erlbaum Associates.

Benmamoun, E. (1997) Licensing of negative polarity items in Moroccan Arabic. *Natural Language and Linguistic Theory* 15 (2), 263–287.

Bernini, G. (1995) Au début de l'apprentissage de l'italien: L'énoncé dans une variété prébasique. *Acquisition et Interaction en Langue Étrangère* 5, 15–45.

Bernini, G. (2000) Negative items and negation strategies in nonnative Italian. *Studies in Second Language Acquisition* 22 (3), 399–440.

Best, C. and Strange, W. (1992) Effects of phonological and phonetic factors on cross-language perception of approximates. *Journal of Phonetics* 20, 305–330.

Bialystok, E. and Swain, M. (1978) Methodological approaches to research in second language learning. *McGill Journal of Education* 8, 137–44.

Bielec, D. (1998) *Polish: An Essential Grammar.* London: Routledge.

Bley-Vroman, R. (1990) The logical problem of foreign language learning. *Linguistic Analysis* 20, 3–49.

Bosque, I. (1980) *Sobre la Negacion.* Madrid: Catedra.

Bremer, K., Roberts, C., Vasseur, M.-T., Simonot, M. and Broeder, P. (1996) *Achieving Understanding: Discourse in Intercultural Encounters.* London: Longman.

Brooks, P.J., Braine, M.D.S., Catalano, L., Brody, R.E. and Sudhalter, V. (1993). Acquisition of gender-like noun subclasses in an artificial language: The contribution of phonological markers to learning. *Journal of Memory and Language* 32, 76–95.

Brown, S. (1999) *The Syntax of Negation in Russian: A Minimalist Approach.* Stanford: Center for the Study of Language and Information.

Cammarota, M.-A. and Giacobbe, J. (1986) L'acquisition du lexique en français par des adultes hispanophones. *Langages* 84, 65–78.

Carroll, S. (1995) The hidden danger in computer modelling: Remarks on Sokolik and Smith's connectionist learning model of French gender. *Second Language Research* 11 (3), 193–205.

Carroll, S. (1997) Le point de départ: La notion d'input dans une théorie de l'acquisition d'une langue seconde. *CAlap: Processus d'Acquisition en Dialogue* 15, 33–51.

Carroll, S. (1999) Putting 'input' in its proper place. *Second Language Research* 15 (4), 337–388.

Carroll, S. (2001) *Input and Evidence: The Raw Material of Second Language Acquisition.* Amsterdam: John Benjamins.

Carroll, S. (2002) Induction in a modular learner. *Second Language Research* 18 (3), 224–249.

Carroll, S. (2004) Commentary: Some general and specific comments on input processing and processing instruction. In B. VanPatten (ed.) *Processing Instruction: Theory, Research, and Commentary* (pp. 293–309). Mahwah, NJ: Lawrence Erlbaum Associates.

Carroll, S. (2006) Conceptualising listening comprehension from an L2 acquisition perspective. Plenary paper presented at the *Second Annual Conference of the British Association of Applied Linguistics,* Southampton, UK.

Carroll, S. and Swain, M. (1993) Explicit and implicit negative feedback: An empirical study of the learning of linguistic generalizations. *Studies in Second Language Acquisition* 15, 357–386.

Caubet, D. (1996) La négation en arabe maghrébin. In S. Chaker and D. Caubet (eds) *La Négation en Berbére et en Arabe Maghrébin* (pp. 79–97). Paris: L'Harmattan.

Cenoz, J. (1997) L'acquisition de la troisime langue: bilinguisme et plurilinguisme au pays basque. *Acquisition et Interaction en Langue Etrangère* 10, 159–175.

Cenoz, J. (2001) The effect of linguistic distance, L2 status and age on cross-linguistic influence in third language acquisition. In J. Cenoz, B. Hufeisen and U. Jessner (eds) *Cross-linguistic Influence in Third Language Acquisition: Psycholinguistic Perspectives* (pp. 8–20). Clevedon: Multilingual Matters.

Cenoz, J., Hufeisen, B. and Jessner, U. (eds) (2001) *Cross-linguistic Influence in Third Language Acquisition: Psycholinguistic Perspectives.* Clevedon: Multilingual Matters.

Chaker, S. (1996) Quelques remarques préliminaires sur la négation en berbère. In S. Chaker and D. Caubet (eds) *La Négation en Berbére et en Arabe Maghrébin* (pp. 9–22). Paris: L'Harmattan.

Chomsky, N. (1959) Review of *Verbal Behavior* by B.F. Skinner. *Language* 35 (1), 26–58.

Chomsky, N. (1965) *Aspects of the Theory of Syntax.* Cambridge, MA: MIT Press.

Chomsky, N. (1981) Principles and parameters in syntactic theory. In N. Hornstein and D. Lightfoot (eds) *Explanations in Linguistics: The Logical Problem of Language Acquisition* (pp. 32–75). London: Longman.

Chomsky, N. (1995) *The Minimalist Program.* Cambridge, MA: MIT Press.

Clahsen, H., Meisel, J. and Pienemann, M. (1983) *Deutsch als Zweitsprache: Der Spracherwerb ausländischer Arbeiter.* Tübingen: Narr.

Cohen, A. and Dörnyei, Z. (2002) Focus on the language learner: Motivation, styles, and strategies. In N. Schmitt (ed.) *An Introduction to Applied Linguistics* (pp. 170–190). London: Arnold.

Corder, S.P. (1967) The significance of learner's errors. *International Review of Applied Linguistics* 5 (4), 161–170.

Cummins, R. and Schwarz, G. (1992) Connexionnisme, computation et cognition. In D. Andler (ed.) *Introduction aux Sciences Cognitives* (pp. 374–394). Paris: Gallimard.

Dalewska-Greń, H. (2002) *Języki Słowiańskie*. Warszawa: Wydawnictwo Naukowe PWN.

De Bot, K. (1992) A bilingual production model: Levelt's 'speaking' model adapted. *Applied Linguistics* 13, 1–24.

de Graaff, R. (1997) The eXperanto experiment: Effects of explicit instruction on second language acquisition. *Studies in Second Language Acquisition* 19 (2), 249–276.

de Hérédia, C. (1986) Intercompréhension et malentendus: étude d'interactions entre étrangers et autochtones. *Langue Française* 71, 48–69.

DeKeyser, R. (1997) Beyond explicit rule learning: Automatizing second language morphosyntax. *Studies in Second Language Acquisition* 19 (2), 195–221.

Dewaele, J.M. (2001) Activation or inhibition? The interaction of L1, L2 and L3 on the language mode continuum. In J. Cenoz, B. Hufeisen and U. Jessner (eds) *Cross-linguistic Influence in Third Language Acquisition: Psycholinguistic Perspectives* (pp. 69–89). Clevedon: Multilingual Matters.

Dietrich, R and Grommes, P. (1998) 'nicht'. Reflexe seiner Bedeutung und Syntax im Zweitspracherwerb. In H. Wegener (ed.) *Eine zweite Sprache lernen. Empirische Untersuchungen zum Zweitspracherwerb* (pp. 173–202). Tübingen: Narr.

Dijkstra, T., Grainger, J. and Van Heuven, W. (1999) Recognition of cognates and interlingual homographs: The neglected role of phonology. *Journal of Memory and Language* 41, 496–518.

Dimroth, C., Gullberg, M., Indefrey, P. and Roberts, L. (2006) The effects of exposure to an unknown L2+. Annual Report, Max-Planck Institute for Psycholinguistics, Nijmegen.

Dimroth, C. and Starren, M. (eds) (2003) *Information Structure and the Dynamics of Language Acquisition*. Amsterdam: John Benjamins.

Dommergues, J.-Y. and Segui, J. (1989) List structure, monotony, and levels of processing. *Journal of Psycholinguistic Research* 18 (3), 245–253.

Dörnyei, Z. and Skehan, P. (2003) Individual differences in second language learning. In C. Doughty and M. Long (eds) *The Handbook of Second Language Acquisition* (pp. 589-630). Malden, MA: Blackwell.

Doughty, C. (1991) Does second language instruction make a difference: Evidence from empirical study of SL relativisation. *Studies in Second Language Acquisition* 13, 431–469.

Doughty, C. (2003) Instructed SLA: Constraints, compensation, and enhancement. In C. Doughty and M. Long (eds) *The Handbook of Second Language Acquisition* (pp. 256–310). Malden, MA: Blackwell.

Doughty, C. and Williams, J. (eds) (1998) *Focus on Form in Classroom Second Language Acquisition*. Cambridge: Cambridge University Press.

Dreyfus, H.L. (1992) La porte philosophique du connexionnisme. In D. Andler (ed.) *Introduction aux Sciences Cognitives* (pp. 353–373). Paris: Folio Gallimard.

Ecke, P. (2001) Lexical retrieval in a third language: Evidence from errors and tip-of-the-tongue states. In J. Cenoz, B. Hufeisen and U. Jessner (eds)

Cross-linguistic Influence in Third Language Acquisition: Psycholinguistic Perspectives (pp. 90–114). Clevedon: Multilingual Matters.

Ellis, N. (ed.) (1994) *Implicit and Explicit Learning of Languages*. London: Academic Press.

Ellis, N. (2002) Frequency effects in language processing: A review with implications for theories of implicit and explicit language acquisition. *Studies in Second Language Acquisition* 24 (2), 143–188.

Ellis, R. (1994) *The Study of Second Language Acquisition*. Oxford: Oxford University Press.

Ellis, R. (2001) *Form-focused Instruction and Second Language Learning*. Malden, MA: Blackwell.

Epstein, S., Flynn, S. and Martohardjono, G. (1998) The strong continuity hypothesis: Evidence concerning functional categories in adult L2 acquisition. In S. Flynn, G. Martohardjono and W. O'Neil (eds) *The Generative Study of Second Language Acquisition* (pp. 61–78). Mahwah, NJ: Lawrence Erlbaum Associates.

Eubank, L. (1994) Optionality and the initial state in L2 development. In T. Hoekstra and B. Schwartz (eds) *Language Acquisition Studies in Generative Grammar* (pp. 369–388). Amsterdam: John Benjamins.

Færch, C. and Kasper, G. (1986) The role of comprehension in second-language learning. *Applied Linguistics* 7 (3), 257–274.

Flege, J.E. (1995) Second-language speech learning: Theory, findings, and problems. In W. Strange (ed.) *Speech Perception and Linguistic Experience: Theoretical and Methodological Issues*. Timonium, MD: York Press.

Flynn, S., Foley, C. and Vinnitskaya, I. (2004) The Cumulative-Enhancement Model for language acquisition: Comparing adults' and childrens' patterns of development in first, second and third language acquisition of relative clauses. *The International Journal of Multilingualism* 1 (1), 3–16.

Fouser, R. (2001) Too close for comfort? Sociolinguistic transfer from Japanese into Korean as an L ≥ 3. In J. Cenoz, B. Hufeisen and U. Jessner (eds) *Cross-linguistic Influence in Third Language Acquisition: Psycholinguistic Perspectives* (pp. 149-169). Clevedon: Multilingual Matters.

Frauenfelder, U. and Porquier, R. (1980) Le problème des tâches dans l'étude de la langue de l'apprenant. *Langages* 57, 61–71.

Gaatone, D. (1971) *Etude Descriptive du Système de la Négation en Français Contemporain*. Genève: Librairie Droz.

Gaonac'h, D. (ed.) (1990) *Acquisition et Utilisation d'une Langue Étrangère: L'Approche Cognitive*. Paris: Hachette.

Gaonac'h, D. (1991) *Théories d'Apprentissage et Acquisition d'une Langue Étrangère*. Paris: Éditions Didier.

Gass, S. (1997) *Input, Interaction, and the Second Language Learner*. Mahwah, NJ: Lawrence Erlbaum Associates.

Gattegno, C. (1976) *The Common Sense of Teaching Foreign Languages*. New York, NY: Educational Solutions.

Giacalone-Ramat, A. (1992) Sur quelques manifestations de la grammaticalisation dans l'acquisition de l'italien comme deuxième langue. *Acquisition et Interaction en Langue Étrangère* 1, 143–170.

Giacobbe, J. (1992a) *Acquisition d'une Langue Étrangère: Cognition et Interaction*. Paris: CNRS Éditions.

Giacobbe, J. (1992b) A cognitive view of the role of L1 in the L2 acquisition process. *Second Language Research* 8 (3), 232–250.

Giacobbe, J. and Lucas, M. (1980) Quelques hypothèses sur le rapport langue maternelle-systèmes intermédiares à propos d'une étude sur l'acquisition des verbes *ser* et *estar* par des adultes francophones. *Encrages* Automne (numéro spécial), 25–36.

Giacomi, A. and de Hérédia, C. (1986) Réussites et échecs dans la communication linguistique entre locuteurs francophones et locuteurs immigrés. *Langages* 84, 9–24.

Giuliano, P. (2004) *La Négation dans l'Acquisition d'une Langue Étrangère. Un Débat Conclu?* Bern: Peter Lang.

Gniadek, S. (1979) *Grammaire Contrastive Franco-Polonaise*. Warszawa: Panstwowe Wydawnictwo Naukowe.

Goldschneider, J. and DeKeyser, R. (2001) Explaining the 'natural order of L2 morpheme acquisition' in English: A meta-analysis of multiple determinants. *Language Learning* 51, 1–50.

Gómez, R. (2006) Dynamically guided learning. In Y. Munakata and M. Johnson (eds) *Processes of Change in Brain and Cognitive Development* (pp. 87–110). Oxford: Oxford University Press.

Grainger, J. and Jacobs, A. (1998) On localist connectionism and psychological science. In J. Grainger and A. Jacobs (eds) *Localist Connectionist Approaches to Human Cognition* (pp. 1-38). Mahwah, NJ: Lawrence Erlbaum Associates.

Green, D.W. (1986) Control, activation and resource: A framework and a model for the control of speech in bilinguals. *Brain and Language* 27, 210–223.

Grevisse, M. (1993) *Le Bon Usage* (13th edn). Paris: Éditions Duculot.

Gullberg, M. (1998) *Gesture as a Communication Strategy in Second Language Discourse. A Study of Learners of French and Swedish*. Lund: Lund University Press.

Gullberg, M. (2006) Handling discourse: Gestures, reference tracking, and communication strategies in early L2. *Language Learning* 56 (1), 155–196.

Hall, C. (2002) The automatic cognate form assumption: Evidence for the parasitic model of vocabulary development. *International Review of Applied Linguistics* 40, 69–87.

Hammarberg, B. (2006) Activation de L1 et L2 lors de la production orale en L3. Étude comparative de deux cas. *Acquisition et Interaction en Langue Étrangère* 24, 45–74.

Harrington, M. (1987) Processing transfer: Language-specific strategies as a source of interlanguage variation. *Applied Psycholinguistics* 8, 351–378.

Harris, M. (1987) French. In B. Comrie (ed.) *The World's Major Languages* (pp. 210–235). London: Croom Helm.

Hatch, E. (1983) Simplified input and second language acquisition. In R.W. Andersen (ed.) *Pidginization and Creolization as Language Acquisition* (pp. 64-88). Rowley, MA: Newbury House.

Havranek, F. and Cesnik, H. (2001) Factors affecting the success of corrective feedback. *EUROSLA Yearbook* 1, 99–122.

Heidelberger Forschungsprojekt 'Pidgin-Deutsch' (HPD) (1979) *Studien zum Spracherwerb ausländischer Arbeiter* (Research Report V), Germanistisches Seminar der Universitt Heidelberg.

Heilenman, L.K. and McDonald, J.L. (1993) Processing strategies in L2 learners of French: The role of transfer. *Language Learning* 43 (4), 507–557.

Henderson, A.I. and Nelms, S. (1980) Relative salience of intonation fall and pause as cues to the perceptual segmentation of speech in an unfamiliar language. *Journal of Psycholinguistic Research* 9 (2), 147–159.

Hendriks, H. and Prodeau, M. (1999) Isn't Dutch a Mixture of English and German?: On the influence of a second language on the acquisition of a third one. Paper presented at *The Ninth Annual European Second Language Association Conference*, Lund.

Hintzman, D.L. (1988) Judgements of frequency and recognition memory in a multiple-trace memory model. *Psychological Review* 95, 528–551.

Hudson Kam, C. and Newport, E. (2005). Regularizing unpredictable variation: The roles of adult and child learners in language formation and change. *Language Learning and Development* 1 (2), 151–195.

Hulstijn, J. (2002) Towards a unified account of the representation, processing and acquisition of second language knowledge. *Second Language Research* 18 (3), 193–223.

Hulstijn, J. (2005) Theoretical and empirical issues in the study of implicit and explicit second-language learning: Introduction. *Studies in Second Language Acquisition* 27 (2), 129–140.

Huot, D. and Schmidt, R. (1996) Conscience et activité métalinguistique: Quelques points de rencontre. *Acquisition et Interaction en Langue Étrangère* 8, 89–128.

Hyltenstam, K. (1977) Implicational patterns in interlanguage syntax variation. *Language Learning* 27 (2), 383–411.

Jackendoff, R.S. (1990) *Semantic Structures*. Cambridge, MA: MIT Press.

Jakobson, R. (1963) *Essais de Linguistique Générale*. Traduction de Nicolas Ruwet. Paris: Les Éditions de Minuit.

Jansen, B., Lalleman, J. and Muysken, P. (1981) The alternation hypothesis: Acquisition of Dutch word order by Turkish and Moroccan foreign workers. *Language Learning* 31, 315–336.

Jespersen, O. (1917) *Negation in English and Other Languages*. Copenhagen: A.F. Host.

Kail, M. (1990) Le traitment des données de langage: la prise d'indices et leur utilisation. In D. Gaonac'h (ed.) *Acquisition et Utilisation d'une Langue Étrangère: L'Approche Cognitive* (pp. 70–79). Paris: Hachette.

Kail, M. (2000) Acquisition syntaxique et diversité linguistique. In M. Kail and M. Fayol (eds) *L'Acquisition du Langage: Le Langage en Développement, Au Delà de Trois Ans* (Vol. 2, pp. 9–44). Paris: Presses Universitaires de France.

Karolak, S. (1995) Aspect: Les interférences virtuelles polono-franaises. In Z. Cygal-Krupa (ed.) *Les Contacts Linguistiques Franco-Polonais* (pp. 65–84). Lille: Presses Universitaires de Lille.

Kellerman, E. (1979) Transfer and non-transfer: Where are we now? *Studies in Second Language Acquisition* 2, 37-57.

Kellerman, E. (1980) Œil pour œil. *Encrages* Automne (numéro spécial), 54–63.

Kellerman, E. (1983) Now you see it, now you don't. In S. Gass and L. Selinker (eds) *Language Transfer in Language Learning* (pp. 112–134). Rowley: Newbury House.

Kilborn, K. and Ito, T. (1989) Sentence processing strategies in adult bilinguals. In B. MacWhinney and E. Bates (eds) *The Cross-linguistic Study of Sentence Processing* (pp. 257–291). Cambridge: Cambridge University Press.

Klein, E. (1995) Second versus third language acquisition: Is there a difference? *Language Learning* 45 (3), 419–465.

Klein, W. (1986) *Second Language Acquisition*. Cambridge: Cambridge University Press.

Klein, W. and Perdue, C. (1992) *Utterance Structure: Developing Grammars Again*. Philadelphia: John Benjamins.

Koffka, K. (1935) *Principles of Gestalt Psychology.* New York: Harcourt Brace.

Krashen, S. (1978) Individual variation in the use of the monitor. In W. Ritchie (ed.) *Second Language Acquisition Research.* New York: Academic Press.

Krashen, S. (1985) *The Input Hypothesis: Issues and Implications.* London: Longman.

Labocha, J. (1996) *Gramatyka Polska: Skladnia.* Krakowie: Editions Ksiegarnia Akademicka.

Lacheret-Dujour, A. and Beaugendre, F. (2002) *La Prosodie du Français.* Paris: CNRS Éditions.

Lado, R. (1957) *Linguistics Across Cultures: Applied Linguistics for Language Teachers.* Ann Arbor: University of Michigan.

Lalleman, J. (1999) The Alternation Hypothesis revisited: Early L2 intuitions about the direction of gapping in Dutch. *Acquisition et Interaction en Langue Étrangère* 2 (Special Issue), 157–172.

Lambert, M. (1990) Approche cognitive et didactique des langues: Des processus aux exercices. Round Table. In D. Gaonac'h (ed.) *Acquisition et Utilisation d'une Langue Étrangère: L'Approche Cognitive* (pp. 182–191). Paris: Hachette.

Lambert, M. (1994a) *La Variabilité Interindividuelle dans l'Acquisition d'une Seconde Langue.* Thèse d'habilitation, Université Paris VIII.

Lambert, M. (1994b) Les profiles d'apprenants comme mode de description et d'explication à la variabilité des apprentissages en langue étrangère. *Acquisition et Interaction en Langue Étrangère* 4, 81–107.

Lambert, M. and Voutsinas, N. (2001) La compréhension en langue étrangère. Paper presented at the *Ninth Annual Conference of the European Second Language Association*, Lund.

Laufer, B. (1993-94) Appropriation du vocabulaire: mots faciles, mots difficiles, mots impossibles. *Acquisition et Interaction en Langue Étrangère* 3, 97–113.

Leow, R. (1993) To simplify or not to simplify: A look at intake. *Studies in Second Language Acquisition* 15, 333–355.

Leung, Y-K. (2005) L2 vs. L3 initial state: A comparative study of the acquisition of French DPs by Vietnamese monolinguals and Cantonese-English bilinguals. *Bilingualism: Language and Cognition* 8 (1), 39–61.

Levelt, W.J.M. (1989) *Speaking: From Intention to Articulation.* Cambridge, MA: MIT Press.

Long, M. (1983) Native speaker/nonnative speaker conversation and the negotiation of comprehensible input. *Applied Linguistics* 4, 126–141.

Lozanov, G. (1978) *Outlines of Suggestology and Suggestopedy.* London: Gordon and Breach.

MacWhinney, B. (2000) *The CHILDES Project: Tools for Analyzing Talk, Vol. II: The Database* (3rd edn). Mahwah, NJ: Lawrence Erlbaum Associates.

MacWhinney, B. and Snow, C. (1985) The Child Language Data Exchange System. *Journal of Child Language* 12, 271–296.

Marslen-Wilson, W.D. (1987) Functional parallelism in spoken word-recognition. *Cognition* 25 (1-2), 71–102.

Marslen-Wilson, W.D. and Tyler, L.K. (1980) The temporal structure of spoken language understanding. *Cognition* 8, 1–71.

Matthews, C. (1999) Connectionism and French gender attribution: Sokolik and Smith re-visited. *Second Language Research* 15 (4), 412–427.

Matthey, M. (1996) *Apprentissage d'une Langue et Interaction Verbale.* Bern: Peter Lang.

Meisel, J. (1977) Linguistic simplification: A study of immigrant workers' speech and foreigner talk. In S.P. Corder and E. Roulet (eds) *The Notions of*

Simplification, Interlanguages and Pidgins and Their Relation to Second Language Pedagogy (pp. 88–113). Geneva: Droz.

Meisel, J. (1997) The acquisition of the syntax of negation in French and German: Contrasting first and second language development. *Second Language Research* 13 (3), 227–263.

Meisel, J., Clahsen, H. and Pienemann, M. (1981) On determining developmental stages in natural second language acquisition. *Studies in Second Language Acquisition* 3 (2), 109–135.

Merikle, P.M., Smilek, D. and Eastwood, J.D. (2001) Perception without awareness: Perspectives from cognitive psychology. *Cognition* 79 (1-2), 115–134.

Miao, X. (1981) Word order and semantic strategies in Chinese sentence comprehension. *International Journal of Psycholinguistics* 8, 109–122.

Mintz, T. (2002) Category induction from distributional cues in an artificial language. *Memory and Cognition* 30 (5), 678–686.

Miodunka, W. and Wróbel, J. (1986) *Polska Po Polsku* (Vol. II). Warszawa: Wydawnictwo Interpress.

Muñoz, C. (2006) Influence translinguistique et changement de code dans la production orale d'une L4. *Acquisition et Interaction en Langue Étrangère* 24, 75–99.

Nayak, N., Hansen, N., Krueger, N. and McLaughlin, B. (1990) Language-learning strategies in monolingual and multilingual adults. *Language Learning* 40 (2), 221–244.

Noizet, G. (1980) *De la Perception à la Compréhension du Langage*. Paris: Presses Universitaires de France.

Odlin, T. (1989) *Language Transfer: Cross-linguistic Influence in Language Learning*. Cambridge: Cambridge University Press.

Odlin, T. (2003) Cross-linguistic influence. In C. Doughty and M. Long (eds) *The Handbook of Second Language Acquisition* (pp. 436–486). Malden, MA: Blackwell.

Oxford, R. (2001) Language learning styles and strategies. In M. Celce-Murcia (ed.) *Teaching English as a Second or Foreign Language* (3rd edn) (pp. 359–366). Boston: Heinle & Heinle/Thompson International.

Paryski, M. (1938) *A Practical Polish Grammar*. Toledo: Paryski Publishing Company.

Pekarek Doehler, S. (2000) Approches interactionnistes de l'acquisition des langues étrangères: Concepts, recherches, perspectives. *Acquisition et Interaction en Langue Étrangère* 12, 3–26.

Perdue, C. (ed.) (1993) *Adult Language Acquisition: Cross-linguistic Perspectives* (Vol. I and II). Cambridge: Cambridge University Press.

Perdue, C. (1995) *Former des Énoncés: L'Acquisition du Français et de l'Anglais par des Adultes*. Paris: CNRS Éditions.

Perdue, C. (1996) Pre-basic varieties. The first stages of second language acquisition. *Toegepaste Taalwetenschap in Artikelen* 55, 135–150.

Perdue, C. and Klein, W. (1992) Why does the production of some learners not grammaticalize? *Studies in Second Language Acquisition* 14 (3), 259–272.

Peters, A. (1985) Language segmentation: Operating principles for the perception and analysis of language. In D. Slobin (ed.) *The Crosslinguistic Study of Language Acquisition* (Vol. II, pp. 1029-1067). Hillsdale, NJ: Lawrence Erlbaum Associates.

Pica, T. (1991) Input as a theoretical and research construct: From Corder's original definition to current views. *International Review of Applied Linguistics* 29 (3), 185–196.

Pienemann, M. (1998) *Language Processing and Second Language Development: Processability Theory.* Amsterdam: John Benjamins.

Pienemann, M. and Håkansson, G. (1999) A unified approach toward the development of Swedish as L2: A Processability account. *Studies in Second Language Acquisition* 21, 383–420.

Pienemann, M., Johnston, M. and Brindley, G. (1988) Constructing an acquisition-based procedure for second language assessment. *Studies in Second Language Acquisition* 10, 217–243.

Pinker, S. (1979) Formal models of language learning. *Cognition* 7, 217–283.

Pinker, S. (1994) *The Language Instinct.* London: Penguin.

Pinker, S. and Prince, A. (1988) On language and connectionism: Analysis of a parallel distributed processing model of language acquisition. In S. Pinker and J. Mehler (eds) *Connections and Symbols.* Cambridge, MA: MIT Press.

Pléh, C. (1990) Word order and morphophonological factors in the development of sentence understanding in Hungarian. *Linguistics* 28 (6), 1449–1470.

Pogonowski, I.C. (1997) *Unabridged Polish-English Dictionary* (Vol. I, II, III). New York: Hippocrene Books.

Pollock, J.-Y. (1989) Verb movement, universal grammar and the structure of IP. *Linguistic Inquiry* 20 (3), 365–424.

Pujol-Berché, M. (1993) Interaction bilingue et acquisition simultanée de deux langues. *Acquisition et Interaction en Langue Étrangère* 2, 109–142.

Py, B. (1989) L'acquisition vue dans la perspective de l'interaction. *DRLAV* 41, 83–100.

Rast, R. (1998) *Le Traitement de l'Input dans l'Acquisition du Polonais par des Apprenants Francophones.* Mémoire de DEA, Université Paris VIII.

Rast, R. (1999) The first hours of second language acquisition. *Acquisition et Interaction en Langue Étrangère* 2 (Special Issue), 73–88.

Rast, R. (2003) *Le Tout Début de l'Acquisition: Le Traitement Initial d'une Langue Non Maternelle par l'Apprenant Adulte* (Vols. I and II). Doctoral dissertation, Université Paris VIII.

Rast, R. (2006) Le premier contact avec une nouvelle langue étrangère: Comment s'acquitter d'une tâche de compréhension? *Acquisition et Interaction en Langue Étrangère* 24, 119–147.

Rast, R. and Dommergues, J.-Y. (2003) Towards a characterisation of saliency on first exposure to a second language. *EUROSLA Yearbook* 3, 131–156.

Reber, A.S. (1967) Implicit learning of artificial grammars. *Journal of Verbal Learning and Verbal Behavior* 6, 855–863.

Ringbom, H. (1987) *The Role of the First Language in Foreign Language Learning.* Clevedon: Multilingual Matters.

Ringbom, H. (2001) Lexical transfer in L3 production. In J. Cenoz, B. Hufeisen and U. Jessner (eds) *Cross-linguistic Influence in Third Language Acquisition: Psycholinguistic Perspectives* (pp. 59–68). Clevedon: Multilingual Matters.

Roberts, L. (2007) Investigating real-time sentence processing in the second language. *Stem-, Spraak- en Taalpathologie* 15 (1), 115-127.

Robinson, P. (2001) Individual differences, cognitive abilities, aptitude complexes and learning conditions in second language acquisition. *Second Language Research* 17 (4), 368–392.

Rowlett, P. (1993) On the syntactic derivation of negative sentence adverbials. *Journal of French Language Studies* 3, 39–69.

Rule, S. and Marsden, E. (2006) The acquisition of functional categories in early French second language grammars: The use of finite and non-finite verbs in negative contexts. *Second Language Research* 22 (2), 188–218.

Rumelhart, D. and McClelland, J. (eds) (1986) *Parallel Distributed Processing: Explorations in the Microstructure of Cognition, Vol. 1 Foundations*. Cambridge, MA: Bradford MIT Press.

Saffran, J.R. (2002) Constraints on statistical learning. *Journal of Memory and Language* 47, 172–196.

Safont Jordà, M.P. (2005) *Third Language Learners: Pragmatic Production and Awareness*. Clevedon: Multilingual Matters.

Schachter, J. (1988) Second language acquisition and its relationship to Universal Grammar. *Applied Linguistics* 9, 219–235.

Schinke-Llano, L. (1993) On the value of a Vygotskian framework for SLA theory and research. *Language Learning* 43 (1), 121–129.

Schmidt, R. (1994) Implicit learning and the cognitive unconscious: Of artificial grammars and SLA. In N. Ellis (ed.) *Implicit and Explicit Learning of Languages* (pp. 165–209). London: Academic Press.

Schulpen, B., Dijkstra, T., Schriefers, H.J. and Hasper, M. (2003) Recognition of interlingual homophones in bilingual auditory word recognition. *Journal of Experimental Psychology: Human Perception and Performance* 29, 1155–1178.

Schwartz, B. and Eubank, L. (1996) What is the 'L2 initial state'? *Second Language Research* 12 (1), 1–5.

Schwartz, B. and Sprouse, R. (1994) Word order and nominative case in nonnative language acquisition: A longitudinal study of L1 Turkish German interlanguage. In T. Hoekstra and B. Schwartz (eds) *Language Acquisition Studies in Generative Grammar* (pp. 317–368). Amsterdam: John Benjamins.

Schwartz, B. and Sprouse, R. (1996) L2 cognitive states and the Full Transfer/Full Access model. *Second Language Research* 12 (1), 40–72.

Selinker, L. (1992) *Rediscovering Interlanguage*. London: Longman.

Sharwood Smith, M. (1986) Comprehension versus acquisition: Two ways of processing input. *Applied Linguistics* 7 (3), 239–256.

Sharwood Smith, M. (1993) Input enhancement in instructed SLA: Theoretical bases. *Studies in Second Language Acquisition* 15, 165–180.

Sharwood Smith, M. (1996) The Garden of Eden and beyond: On second language processing. *CLCS Occasional Paper* 44, 1–20.

Sharwood Smith, M. and Kellerman, E. (1986) Crosslinguistic influence in second language acquisition: An introduction. In. E. Kellerman and M. Sharwood-Smith (eds) *Crosslinguistic Influence in Second Language Acquisition* (pp. 1–9). New York: Pergamon.

Silberstein, D. (2001) Facteurs interlingues et spécifiques dans l'acquisition non-guidée de la négation en anglais L2. *Acquisition et Interaction en Langue Étrangère* 14, 25–58.

Singleton, D. (1993-94) Introduction: Le rôle de la forme et du sens dans le lexique mental en L2. *Acquisition et Interaction en Langue Étrangère* 3, 3–27.

Singleton, D. (1999) *Exploring the Second Language Mental Lexicon*. Cambridge: Cambridge University Press.

Singleton, D. (2003) Le facteur de l'âge dans l'acquisition d'une L2: Remarques préliminaires. *Acquisition et Interaction en Langue Étrangère* 18, 3–15.

Singleton, D. and Little, D. (1984) A first encounter with Dutch: Perceived language distance and language transfer as factors in comprehension. In L. Mac Mathúna and D. Singleton. *Language Across Cultures: Proceedings of a Symposium*, St. Patrick's College, Drumcondra, Dublin. IRAAL.

Singleton, D. and Ó Laoire, M. (2006) Psychotypologie et facteur L2 dans l'influence translexicale: Une analyse de l'influence de l'anglais et de l'irlandais sur le français L3 de l'apprenant. *Acquisition et Interaction en Langue Étrangère* 24, 101–117.

Singleton, D. and Ryan, L. (2004) *Language Acquisition: The Age Factor* (2nd edn). Clevedon: Multilingual Matters.

Skinner, B.F. (1957) *Verbal Behavior*. New York: Appleton-Century-Crofts.

Slobin, D. (1985) Crosslinguistic evidence for the language-making capacity. In D. Slobin (ed.) *The Crosslinguistic Study of Language Acquisition* (Vol. II, pp. 1157–1256). Hillsdale, NJ: Lawrence Erlbaum Associates.

Smoczyńska, M. (1985) The acquisition of Polish. In D. Slobin (ed.) *The Crosslinguistic Study of Language Acquisition* (Vol. I, pp. 595–686). Hillsdale, NJ: Lawrence Erlbaum Associates.

Sokolik, M. and Smith, M. (1992) Assignment of gender to French nouns in primary and secondary language: A connectionist model. *Second Language Research* 8 (1), 39–58.

Starren, M. (2001) *The Second Time: The Acquisition of Temporality in Dutch and French as a Second Language*. Utrecht: LOT.

Stone, G. (1987) Polish. In B. Comrie (ed.) *The World's Major Languages* (pp. 348–366). London: Croom Helm.

Taraban, R., McDonald, J. and MacWhinney, B. (1989) Category learning in a connectionist model: Learning to decline the German definite article. In R. Corrigan, F. Eckman and M. Nooman (eds) *Linguistic Categorization*. Amsterdam: John Benjamins.

Trévise, A. (1986) Is it transferable, topicalization? In E. Kellerman and M. Sharwood Smith (eds) *Crosslinguistic Influence in Second Language Acquisition* (pp. 186–206). New York: Pergamon.

Trévisiol, P. (2003) *Problèmes de Référence dans la Construction du Discours par des Apprenants Japonophones du Français L3*. Doctoral dissertation, Université Paris VIII.

Trévisiol, P. (2006) Influence translinguistique et alternance codique en français L3. Rôles des L1 et L2 dans la production orale d'apprenants japonais. *Acquisition et Interaction en Langue Étrangère* 24, 13–43.

Trévisiol, P. and Rast, R. (2006) Présentation. *Acquisition et Interaction en Langue Étrangère* 24, 3–11.

Trueswell, J.C. (1996) The role of lexical frequency in syntactic ambiguity resolution. *Journal of Memory and Language* 35, 566–585.

Vainikka, A. and Young-Scholten, M. (1994) Direct access to X'-theory: Evidence from Korean and Turkish adults learning German. In T. Hoekstra and B. Schwartz (eds) *Language Acquisition Studies in Generative Grammar* (pp. 265–316). Amsterdam: John Benjamins.

Vainikka, A. and Young-Scholten, M. (1998) The initial state in the L2 acquisition of phrase structure. In S. Flynn, G. Martohardjono and W. O'Neil (eds) *The Generative Study of Second Language Acquisition* (pp. 17–34). Mahwah, NJ: Lawrence Erlbaum Associates.

VanPatten, B. (1996) *Input Processing and Grammar Instruction: Theory and Research*. Norwood, NJ: Ablex.

VanPatten, B. (1999) Processing instruction as form-meaning connections: Issues in theory and research. In J. Lee and A. Valdman (eds) *Form and Meaning: Multiple Perspectives* (pp. 43–68). Boston: Heinle & Heinle.

VanPatten, B. (2000) Thirty years of input. In B. Swierzbin, F. Morris, M. Anderson, C. Klee and E. Tarone (eds) *Social and Cognitive Factors in Second Language Acquisition: Selected Proceedings of the 1999 Second Language Research Forum* (pp. 287–311). Somerville: Cascadilla Press.

VanPatten, B. (ed.) (2004) *Processing Instruction: Theory, Research, and Commentary.* Mahwah, NJ: Lawrence Erlbaum Associates.

VanPatten, B. and Cadierno, T. (1993) Explicit instruction and input processing. *Studies in Second Language Acquisition* 15, 225–243.

VanPatten, B. and Oikkenon, S. (1996) Explanation versus structured input in processing instruction. *Studies in Second Language Acquisition* 18, 495–510.

VanPatten, B. and Sanz, C. (1995) From input to output: Processing instruction and communicative tasks. In F. Eckman, D. Highland and P.W. Lee (eds) *Second Language Acquisition Theory and Pedagogy* (pp. 169–185). Mahwah, NJ: Lawrence Erlbaum Associates.

Véronique, D. (2005) Syntactic and semantic issues in the acquisition of negation in French. In J.-M. Dewaele (ed.) *Focus on French as a Foreign Language* (pp. 114–134). Clevedon: Multilingual Matters.

Vion, R. and Mittner, M. (1986) Activité de reprise et gestion des interactions en communication exolingue. *Langages* 84, 25–42.

von Stutterheim, C. and Klein, W. (1989) Referential movement in descriptive and narrative discourse. In R. Dietrich and C. Graumann (eds) *Language Processing in Social Context* (pp. 39–76). Amsterdam: North-Holland.

Vygotsky, L.S. (1962) *Thought and Language.* Cambridge, MA: MIT Press.

Weist, R. (1990) Neutralization and the concept of subject in child Polish. *Linguistics* 28 (6), 1331–1349.

Wexler, K. and Culicover, P. (1980) *Formal Principles of Language Acquisition.* Cambridge, MA: MIT Press.

White, L. (1989) *Universal Grammar and Second Language Acquisition.* Amsterdam: John Benjamins.

White, L. (1996) The tale of the ugly duckling (or the coming of age of second language acquisition research). In A. Stringfellow, D. Cahana-Amitay, E. Hughes and A. Zukowski (eds) *Proceedings of the Boston University Conference on Language Development* (pp. 1–17). Somerville, MA: Cascadilla Press.

White, L. (2003) *Second Language Acquisition and Universal Grammar.* Cambridge: Cambridge University Press.

Williams, S. and Hammarberg, B. (1998) Language switches in L3 production: Implications for a polyglot speaking model. *Applied Linguistics* 19, 295–333.

Winter, B. and Reber, A.S. (1994) Implicit learning and the acquisition of natural languages. In N. Ellis (ed.) *Implicit and Explicit Learning of Languages* (pp. 115–145). London: Academic Press.

Wong, W. and Simard, D. (2000) La saisie, cette grande oubliée! *Acquisition et Interaction en Langue Étrangère* 14, 59–86.

Yang, L. and Givón, T. (1997) Benefits and drawbacks of controlled laboratory studies of second language acquisition: The Keck second language learning project. *Studies in Second Language Acquisition* 19 (2), 173–193.

Zanuttini, R. (1997) *Negation and Clausal Structure: A Comparative Study of Romance Languages.* Oxford: Oxford University Press.

Zaremba, C. (2001) *Vingt Leçons de Polonais.* Aix-en-Provence: Université de Provence.

Zwitserlood, P. (1989) The locus of the effects of sentential-semantic context in spoken-word processing. *Cognition* 32 (1), 25–64.

Zwitserlood, P., Klein, W., Liang, J., Perdue, C. and Kellerman, E. (2000) The first minutes of foreign-language exposure. Unpublished manuscript, Max-Planck Institute for Psycholinguistics, Nijmegen.

Index

Allwood, J. 16-17
Alternation Hypothesis 22, 40, 64, 115, 123, 127, 193, 198, 214, 219-220, 224, 230
attention 18-20, 25-26, 35, 74, 79, 103, 132, 140, 143-144, 147-148, 161-162, 228, 232, 234
Autonomous Induction Theory 23-24

Bardel, C. 32
Bardovi-Harlig, K. 36, 119
Basic Variety 28, 35, 80, 206
Bates, E. 11, 64, 71, 78, 118, 173, 189, 229
Beaugendre, F. 51
Benmamoun, E. 203-204
Bernini, G. 80, 205-206
Best, C. 165
Bialystok, E. 81
Bielec, D. 51, 63
Bilingual Production Model 25-26, 233
Bley-Vroman, R. 21
Bosque, I. 204
Braine, M.D.S. 37
Bremer, K. 16, 78, 125, 130, 146
Brindley, G. 26
Brody, R.E. 37
Broeder, P. 16, 78, 125, 130, 146
Brooks, P.J. 37
Brown, S. 204

Cadierno, T. 20
Cammarota, M-A. 35-36
Carroll, S. xv, 4, 9-10, 16-17, 23-24, 36, 78-79, 232, 236
Catalano, L. 37
Caubet, D. 203-204
Cenoz, J. 32-33, 106
Cesnik, H. 16-17
Chaker, S. 203
CHILDES 8, 28, 69, 73-74, 149, 236
Chomsky, N. 3, 20
Clahsen, H. 26, 35, 206, 231
Cohen, A. 141
Competition Model 5, 11, 20, 28, 58, 64, 71, 78, 118, 173, 189, 229, 235
comprehensible input 17-19, 145, 232
connectionism / connectionist 5-11, 33, 235
Corder, S.P. 3, 19, 234
cross-linguistic influence (see 'transfer')
Culicover, P. 28
Cummins, R. 7

Dalewska-Greń 49
De Bot, K. 25-26, 233
de Graaff, R. 40-41
de Hérédia, C. 16
DeKeyser, R. 40-42, 149
Dewaele, J.-M. 32-33
Dietrich, R. 206
Dijkstra, T. 84, 106
Dimroth, C. 32, 34, 38, 205
Dommergues, J.-Y. 146, 164
Dörnyei, Z. 141
Doughty, C. 18, 20, 24
Dreyfus, H.L. 7

Eastwood, J. D. 34
Ecke, P. 104
Ellis, N. 29, 33-34, 149
Ellis, R. 18, 20, 24
enhanced input 18-19, 162, 235
Epstein, S. 21
Eubank, L. 21-22, 104, 205
European Science Foundation project in SLA (ESF) 16, 28, 35, 80
exposure to input (measured in time) 29, 35, 38-43, 71, 74, 76, 81, 146, 150-151, 162, 164, 167,186, 196-198, 202-203, 214, 221, 224, 227, 230, 235-237

Færch, C. 78
first exposure xiii-xiv, xvi, 21, 28-29, 36-43, 47, 56, 63, 66, 68-69, 76, 81, 83, 99, 102-107, 124, 143-144, 147, 154, 163, 192, 223, 226-237
Flege, J.E. 165
Flynn, S. 21, 32
Foley, C. 32
Fouser, R. 32
Frauenfelder, U. 28, 77, 80
frequency (in the input) 8, 23, 35, 38, 42, 58, 70, 73, 76, 113-118, 121, 123, 127, 129-131, 135-137, 140-141, 146, 149, 155-165, 167-181, 188-190, 192-193, 202, 206-207, 209, 212, 216-217, 220, 224, 227, 236-237
Full Transfer / Full Access Hypothesis (FT/FA) 21-22, 40, 80, 104, 193, 205, 209, 228

Gaatone, D. 55, 205
Gaonac'h, D. 78-79, 143, 166

258

Gass, S. 21
Gattegno, C. xiv
Giacalone-Ramat, A. 105
Giacobbe, J. 29-31, 35-36, 106, 142, 230, 236
Giacomi, A. 16
Giuliano, P. 55, 80, 206, 230
Givón, T. 40-42
Gniadek, S. 50, 52, 60-61
Goldschneider, J. 149
Gómez, R. 37
Grainger, J. 6, 84, 106
Green, D.W. 25
Grevisse, M. 52, 56
Grommes, P. 206
Gullberg, M. 32, 34, 38

Håkansson, G. 56
Hall, C. 103, 105
Hammarberg, B. 32-33
Hansen, N. 33
Harrington, M. 13
Harris, M. 51, 55
Hasper, M. 84, 106
Hatch, E. 3, 18
Havranek, F. 16-17
Heidelberger Forschungsprojekt
    'Pidgin-Deutsch' (HPD) 39, 144, 166
Heilenman, L.K. 11, 13
Henderson, A.I. 37
Hendriks, H. 39
Hintzman, D.L. 149
Hudson Kam, C. 37
Hufeisen, B. 32
Hulstijn, J. 29, 33-34
Huot, D. 34
Hyltenstam, K. 56, 206

implicit subject 53-54, 57, 64, 73, 75, 111,
    114, 125, 135, 196
Indefrey, P. 32, 34, 38
information structure 31, 53, 56, 80, 204-206,
    210-211, 214, 217, 230
initial state (L2) 21-22, 27, 36, 80, 104, 228,
    231
initial state (L3) 107
input processing xii-xv, 3-4, 7-8, 14-16,
    18-21, 23-24, 26-27, 29-35, 42, 68-69, 74,
    78-79, 81, 96, 103, 106, 108, 139-140, 142,
    145, 148, 163, 173, 190, 192, 196, 215, 226,
    232, 234-237
intake xiv-xvi, 3-6, 8, 15-20, 23-24, 27, 34, 42,
    47, 128, 139, 190, 221, 226, 232-237
interactionist 5, 14-18, 26, 28, 78, 196, 232,
    235
Ito, T. 12-13

Jackendoff, R.S. 23
Jacobs, A. 6
Jakobson, R. 83, 97, 105

Jansen, B. 64, 115, 123, 127, 193, 198, 214,
    224, 230
Jespersen, O. 55
Jessner, U. 32
Johnston, M. 26

Kail, M. 11, 173
Karolak, S. 61
Kasper, G. 78
Kellerman, E. 31-32, 34-35, 38, 102, 105, 143,
    205, 228, 231, 233
Kilborn, K. 12-13
Klein, E. 33
Klein, W. 28, 34-35, 38, 53, 78, 80, 105,
    143-144, 166-167, 190, 205, 227, 230, 233
Koffka, K. 143
Krashen, S. 18, 28, 145, 232
Krueger, N. 33

Labocha, J. 51
Lacheret-Dujour, A. 51
Lado, R. 30
Lalleman, J. 22, 40, 64, 115, 123, 127, 193,
    198, 214, 224, 230
Lambert, M. 78-79, 190, 231
Laufer, B. 104
learner strategies xiii-xiv, 12-14, 20, 38, 56,
    58, 64, 70, 75, 78-80, 83, 85, 102-106, 117,
    122, 128, 132, 137, 141-2, 145-146,
    166-167, 176, 196, 205, 210-213, 226, 231
learner style 16, 35-36, 133, 142, 190, 230-231
learner variability (inter- and intra-) 29,
    35-36, 43, 133-134, 139-142, 174-175, 190,
    201, 221, 223-225, 230-231
learner working hypotheses xiii, 30, 33,
    35-36, 63, 70, 78, 97, 100-101, 103-106,
    111, 115, 126-127, 130, 136-137, 140-142,
    208, 212-214, 218-219, 223-225, 228,
    230-231
Leow, R. 18
Leung, Y.-K. 32, 107
Levelt, W.J.M. 24-26, 79, 233
Liang, J. 34, 38, 143, 233
Lindqvist, C. 32
Little, D. 37
Long, M. 18
Lozanov, G. xiv
Lucas, M. 30

MacWhinney, B. 6-9, 11, 28, 64, 69, 71, 73,
    78, 118, 149, 173, 189, 229
Marsden, E. 65, 205
Marslen-Wilson, W.D. 84, 89
Martohardjono, G. 21
Matthews, C. 9
Matthey, M. 15, 78, 232
McClelland, J. 6, 8
McDonald, J.L. 6-9, 11, 13, 28
McLaughlin, B. 33

Meisel, J. 18, 26, 35, 56, 206, 231
Merikle, P.M. 34
Miao, X. 12
Mintz, T. 37
Miodunka, W. 58
Mittner, M. 14
Muñoz, C. 32
Muysken, P. 64, 115, 123, 127, 193, 198, 214, 224, 230

Nayak, N. 33
negation 54-56, 64-65, 111, 115, 120, 123, 126, 130-131, 135, 140-141, 172, 192, 194, 203-214, 216, 224-225, 230
Nelms, S. 37
Newport, E. 37
Noizet, G. 233
nominal morphology 13-14, 52, 58-60, 63-64, 71-73, 85-86, 99-106, 122, 166, 188, 223, 229

Odlin, T. 13, 32
Oikkenon, S. 20
Ó Laoire, M. 32
On-line Input Processing 19-20, 145, 148
Oxford, R. 141

Paryski, M. 49
Pekarek Doehler, S. 14-15
Perdue, C. 16, 28, 30, 34-35, 38, 80, 104-105, 143, 145, 205, 230, 233
Peters, A. 144, 146, 161-162, 233, 235
phonemic distance 35, 47-50, 63, 76, 117, 147, 152-153, 158-162, 164-165, 227
Pica, T. 14
Pienemann, M. 19, 26-28, 35, 56, 206, 231
Pinker, S. xiii, 6, 28
Pléh, C. 188
Pogonowski, I.C. 50
Pollock, J-Y. 65, 205
Porquier, R. 28, 77, 80
position (of word in sentence/utterance) 20, 26, 35, 39, 42-43, 52, 57, 76, 117, 122, 131, 146, 148-150, 154-155, 157-161, 163-164, 185, 190, 196, 208-210, 213, 227, 229-232
pre-basic variety 80, 206
Prince, A. 6
prior system 29-31, 39-40, 81, 84, 104, 205, 227, 231, 236
Processability Theory 26-27
Prodeau, M. 39
psychotypology 31-32, 35, 102, 105, 204-205, 211, 228, 231
Pujol-Berché, M. 15
Py, B. 14-15

Rast, R. xiii, 32, 38, 66, 106, 164, 193, 206, 214
Reber, A.S. 33-34, 37
reflexive pronoun 56-58, 64-65, 71-72, 110-112, 115-116, 120-121, 123, 127,

131-132, 135-137, 140-141, 192, 194, 214-220, 224-225, 230
Ringbom, H. 32
Roberts, C. 16, 78, 125, 130, 146
Roberts, L. 32, 34, 38, 78
Robinson, P. 141, 236
Rowlett, P. 65, 205
Rule, S. 65, 205
Rumelhart, D. 6, 8
Ryan, L. xiv

Saffran, J.R. 37
Safont Jordà, M.P. 32
saliency 18, 35, 39, 41, 54, 122, 139, 144-146, 148-149, 162-164, 173, 227, 233
Sanz, C. 232
Schachter, J. 21
Schinke-Llano, L. 15
Schmidt, R. 34, 42
Schriefers, H.J. 84, 106
Schulpen, B. 84, 106
Schwartz, B. 21-22, 40, 80, 104, 193, 205, 209, 228
Schwarz, G. 7
Segui, J. 146
Selinker, L. 31
sentence length 167-170, 172, 174, 177-180, 188-191
sentence repetitions 14-17, 39, 41-43, 74-77, 117-118, 121-122, 133-134, 138-139, 141, 143-165, 167, 169, 186, 189, 227, 229, 232-234
Sharwood Smith, M. 18, 31
signifiant 64, 78, 83, 97, 101, 229
signifié 64, 83, 95, 97, 101, 229
Silbernstein, D. 206
Simard, D. 4, 23
Simonot, M. 16, 78, 125, 130, 146
Singleton, D. xiv, 32, 37, 85, 87, 104
Skehan, P. 141
Skinner, B.F. 3
Slobin, D. 20, 143-149, 155, 161, 163, 227, 233, 235
Smilek, D. 34
Smith, M. 8-10
Smoczyńska, M. 54, 58
Snow, C. 28
Sokolik, M. 8-10
Speech Production Model 24-26, 79, 233
Sprouse, R. 21-22, 40, 80, 104, 193, 205, 209, 228
Starren, M. 119, 205
Stone, G. 53, 62
Strange, W. 165
Sudhalter, V. 37
Swain, M. 24, 81

Taraban, R. 6-9, 28
third language acquisition (L3) xiv, 32-33,

37-38, 40, 43, 68, 81, 84-85, 95, 97, 104,
106, 205, 209-210, 228, 230
transfer 11-14, 27, 30-33, 39-40, 43, 58, 63-65,
75, 84-86, 102-107, 123, 174, 193, 204-205,
209-211, 214, 218, 220-228, 230-231
translation 41, 74-77, 81, 83-107, 109-110,
112-114, 116, 118-122, 124-135, 139,
147-148, 162, 166-192, 196, 201-202, 212,
215, 219, 228-229, 232-233
transparency 35, 39, 42-43, 76-77, 87-105,
117, 146-148, 150, 153-154, 161-164,
167-181, 188-189, 227, 229, 231-232, 236
Trévise, A. 52, 69
Trévisiol, P. 32-33
Trueswell, J.C. 149
Tyler, L.K 84

Universal Grammar (UG) 3, 20-21

Vainikka, A. 21-22, 36
Van Heuven, W. 84, 106
VanPatten, B. xv, 4, 18-20, 24, 34, 145,
148-149, 163, 227, 232, 236
Vasseur, M.-T. 16, 78, 125, 130, 146
verbal morphology 41, 47, 53-54, 60-62, 64,
73, 112-113, 116, 121, 123, 127-128,
132-133, 135, 137-138, 140-141, 166, 173,
188, 192, 196, 220-223, 231
Véronique, D. 225
Vinnitskaya, I. 32

Vion, R. 14
von Stutterheim, C. 53
Voutsinas, N. 78-79
Vygotsky, L.S. 14-15, 27-28

Weist, R. 57
Wexler, K. 28
White, L. 21, 36, 228
Williams, J. 18, 20, 24
Williams, S. 32-33
Winter, B. 33
Wong, W. 4, 23
word length 23, 35, 76, 146, 150-152,
157-158, 161, 164, 191
word order 11-13, 21-22, 26-27, 39-41, 47,
51-52, 54-58, 63-64, 69-75, 77, 81, 108-142,
166-168, 170, 172-190, 192-225, 229-230
word stress 16, 20, 35, 47, 51, 56-57, 76,
146-147, 150, 152, 158, 161-162, 164, 227,
231-232, 236-237
Wróbel, J. 58

Yang, L. 40-42
Young-Scholten, M. 21-22, 36

Zanuttini, R. 55, 205
Zaremba, C. 58
Zweitspracherwerb italienischer und
spanischer Arbeiter (ZISA) 26-27
Zwitserlood, P. 34, 38, 79, 143, 233